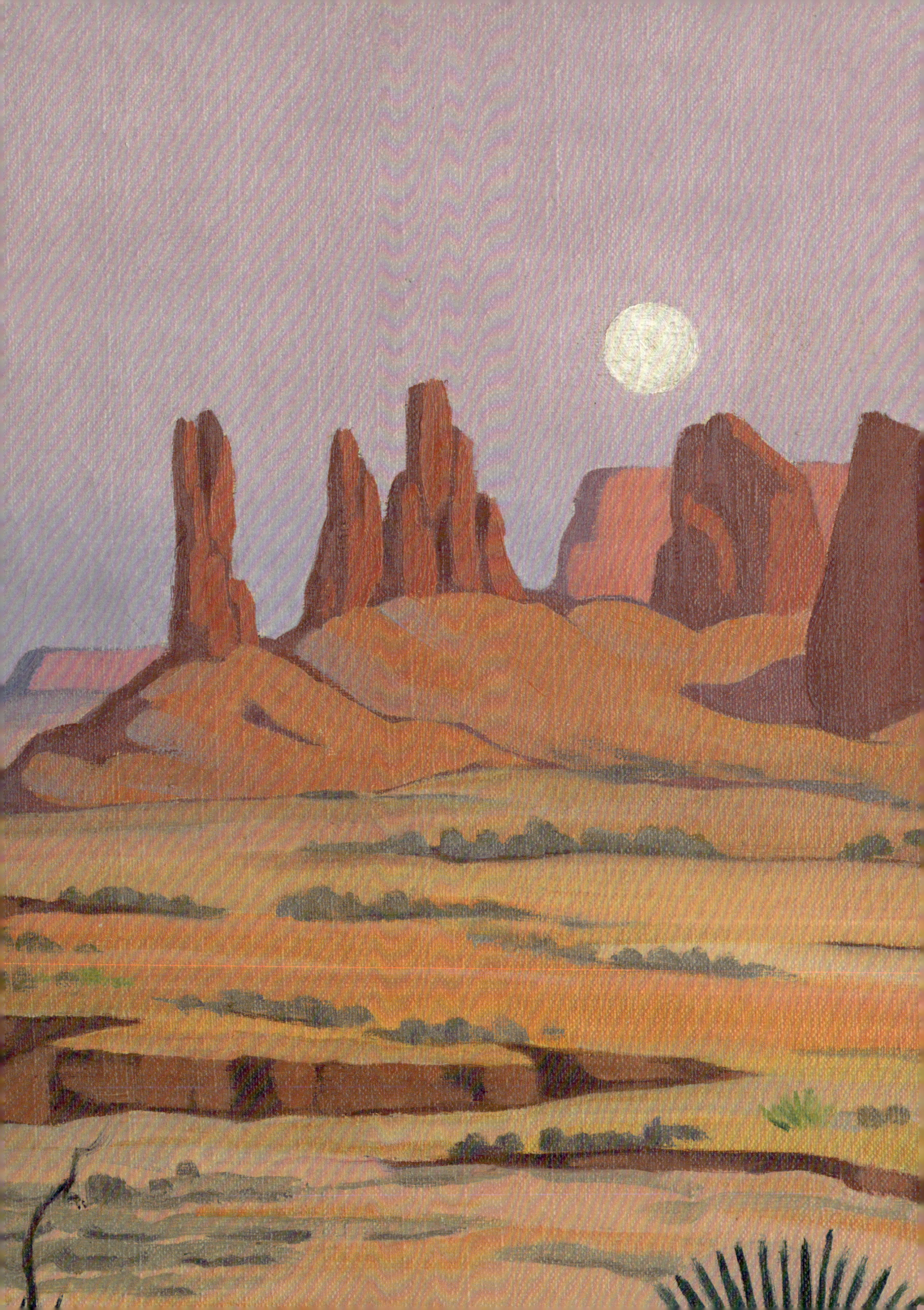

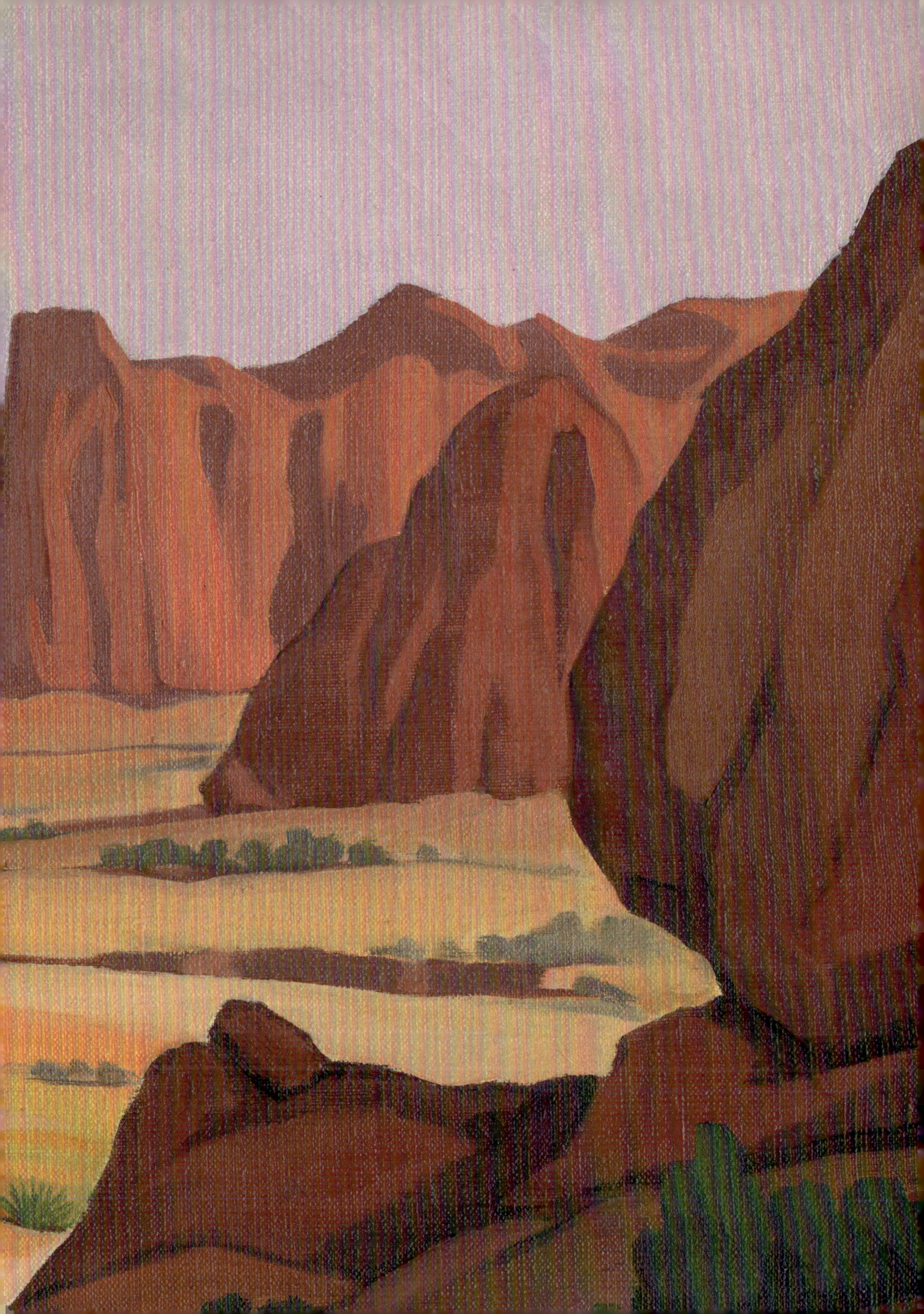

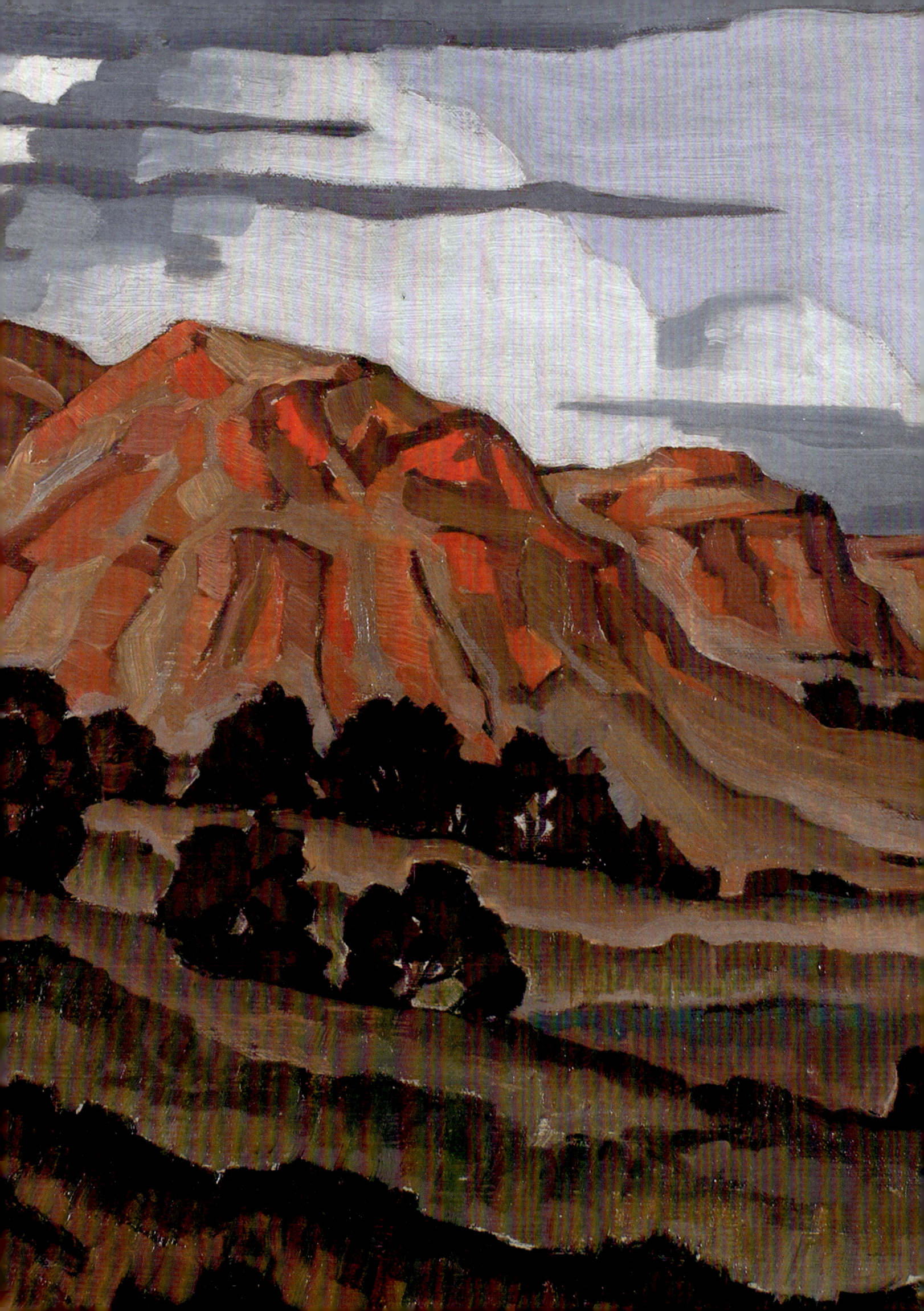

A World Unconquered:
The Art of Oscar Brousse Jacobson

FRED JONES JR. MUSEUM OF ART ❖ UNIVERSITY OF OKLAHOMA

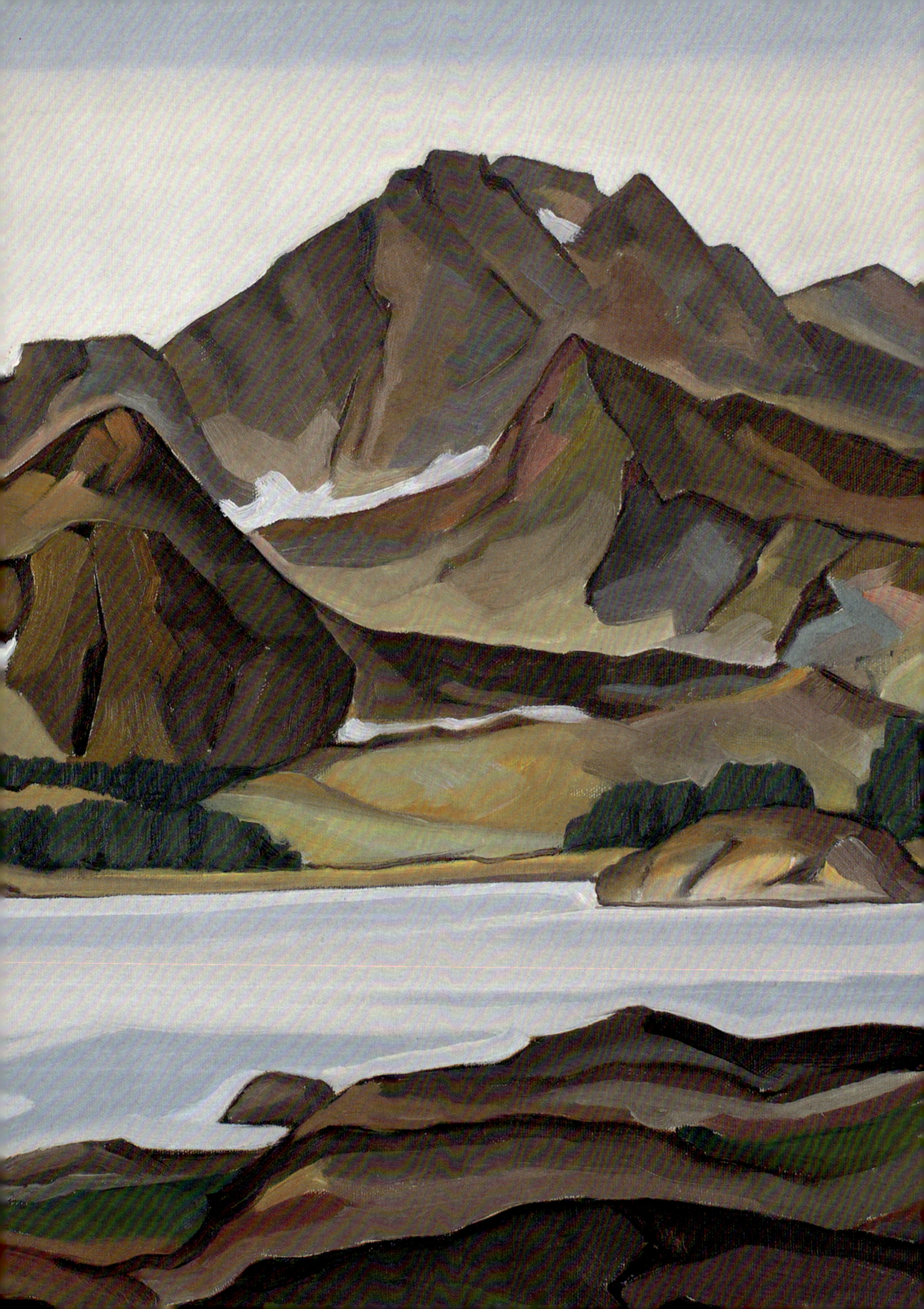

Contents

FRED JONES JR. MUSEUM OF ART ❖ UNIVERSITY OF OKLAHOMA

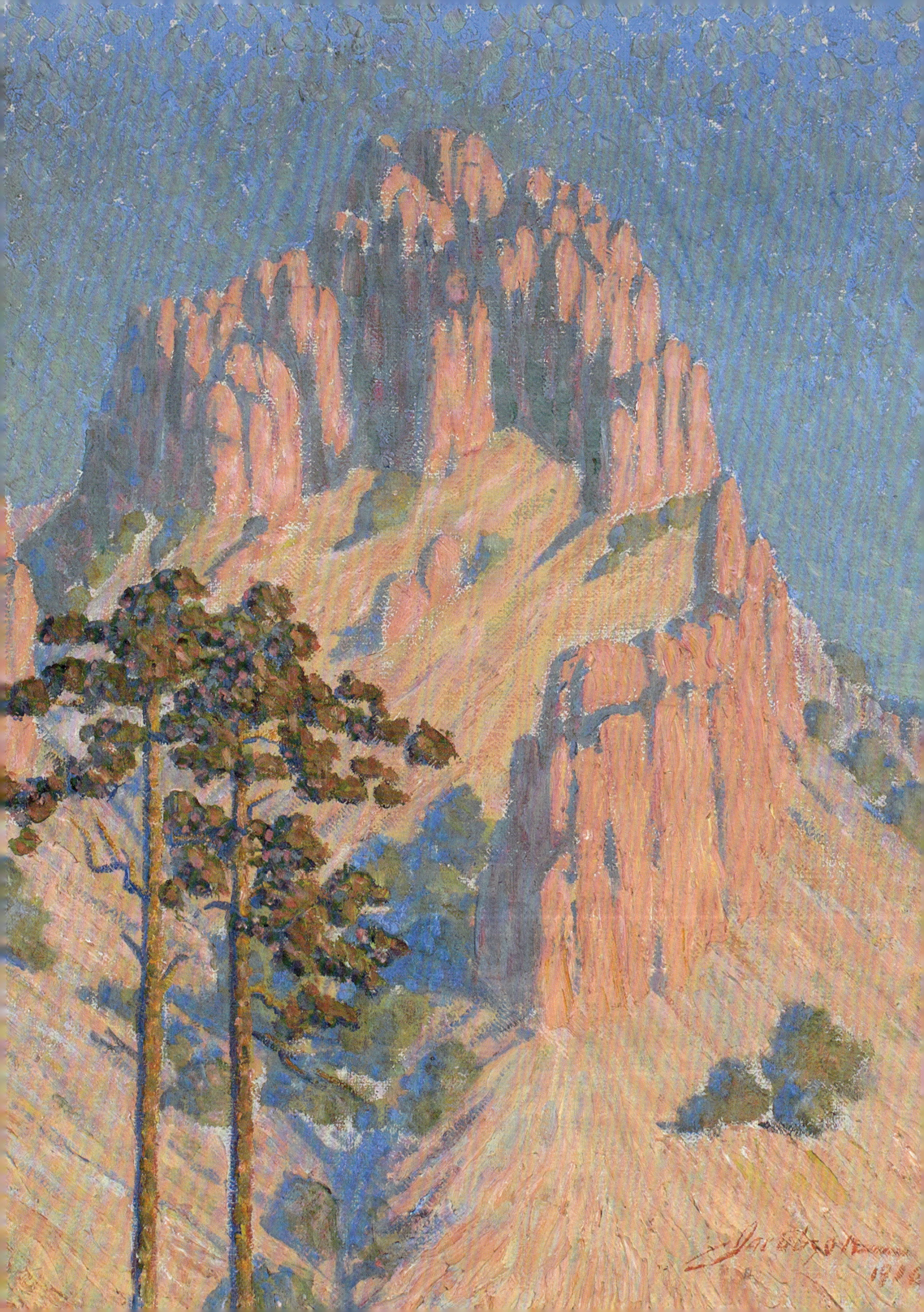

Acknowledgments

MARK ANDREW WHITE
Interim Director and
Eugene B. Adkins Senior Curator

A World Unconquered: The Art of Oscar Brousse Jacobson is an ambitious undertaking and an important milestone in the history of the Fred Jones Jr. Museum of Art. It commemorates the centennial of Jacobson's arrival at the University of Oklahoma in 1915, which would have a lasting impact on both the university and the state. As Director of the School of Art, he oversaw a tremendous expansion of the faculty and increased student enrollment. The prominence and success of the current School of Art and Art History is the result in part of the foundation Jacobson laid in the first decades of the twentieth century. His desire to create a museum on campus in the early 1920s, the first of its kind in Oklahoma, demanded a great deal of ambition and eventually resulted in the creation of the OU Museum of Art in 1936, following the gift of the Wentz-Matzene Collection. Jacobson served as director until his retirement from the university in 1952. In 1971, the museum was relocated to the Fred Jones Jr. Memorial Art Center after a generous contribution by the Fred Jones family in honor of their son, who died tragically in a plane crash. Without question, the FJJMA owes much of its current prominence to Jacobson's original vision.

Jacobson has been the subject of two previous retrospectives, in 1941 and 1961, the latter of which was organized by what was then the OU Museum of Art under Director Sam Olkinetzsky. The FJJMA mounted another exhibition in 1990–91, *Oscar Brousse Jacobson: Oklahoma Painter*, under Director and Chief Curator Thomas R. Toperzer and Assistant Director and Curator of Collections Edwin J. Deighton. *A World Unconquered* builds on the achievement of those previous exhibitions with the publication of this scholarly catalogue and an exhibition that examines Jacobson's career as a painter and as a figure

Detail, see Fig. 23, page 47

Oscar Jacobson

U.S., born Sweden, 1882–1966

Pink Mountain, 1916

of cultural significance, especially in his promotion of Native American, North African, and Asian art in both the state and the region. This exhibition also coincides with the 125th anniversary of the University of Oklahoma and helps to celebrate the significant history of the institution.

A project such as this would not have been possible without the invaluable support of numerous individuals. We would like to thank the Office of the President, and especially President David L. Boren and First Lady Molly Shi Boren, for their tremendous ongoing support of both the museum and this exhibition. This catalogue would not be possible without a generous grant from the Kirkpatrick Foundation. John E. and Eleanor Kirkpatrick were friends and supporters of Jacobson's career, and we are grateful to the Board of Trustees and the staff of the foundation for their support of this project. Finally, we would like to thank Ghislain d'Humières, Director of the Speed Art Museum and former Bill and Wylodean Saxon Director of the FJJMA, for his foresight in initiating this exhibition.

Both the catalogue and exhibition required considerable research, and we appreciate the time, effort, and insights of Tammi Hanawalt, Kaylin Martin, Melynda Seaton, and especially Chelsea Mitchell, who spent countless hours pouring through the Jacobson archives of the Western History Collection and the Research Center of the Oklahoma Historical Society. We also owe a debt to the Birger Sandzén Memorial Gallery, especially Director Ron Michael and Curator Cori Sherman North, for their assistance with Jacobson's early career and his relationship with Sandzén. And our special thanks to Anne Allbright and Dr. Janet Catherine Berlo for their excellent contributions to this volume.

We also owe a heartfelt thanks to the numerous collectors from across the country who assisted us in locating Jacobson's paintings. The exhibition is richer because of their help. Sally and Bruce van der Kamp, in particular, were generous with their time in showing me around Allenspark, Colorado.

The staff of the FJJMA has been vital to the success of this project, and I would like to thank the following for their contributions to both the exhibition and catalogue: Gail Kana Anderson, Deputy Director; Michael Bendure, Director of Communication; Tracy Bidwell, Chief Registrar; Selena Capraro, Associate Registrar; Brynnan Light-Lewis, Assistant Registrar; Brad Stevens, Chief Preparator and Exhibition Designer; Kristi Wyatt, Preparator and Associate Exhibition Designer; Michael Hatcher, Assistant Preparator; Susan Baley, Director of Education; and Becky Zurcher Trumble, Director of Administration and Finance.

It is with great pride that we present *A World Unconquered*, and we hope you will enjoy this tribute to Oscar Brousse Jacobson and his legacy.

Detail (right), see Fig. 6, page 15
Oscar Jacobson
U.S., born Sweden, 1882–1966
Untitled (Enchanted Mesa), 1915

Detail (pages 4–5), see Fig. 24, page 49
Oscar Jacobson
U.S., born Sweden, 1882–1966
Grand Canyon, ca. 1920

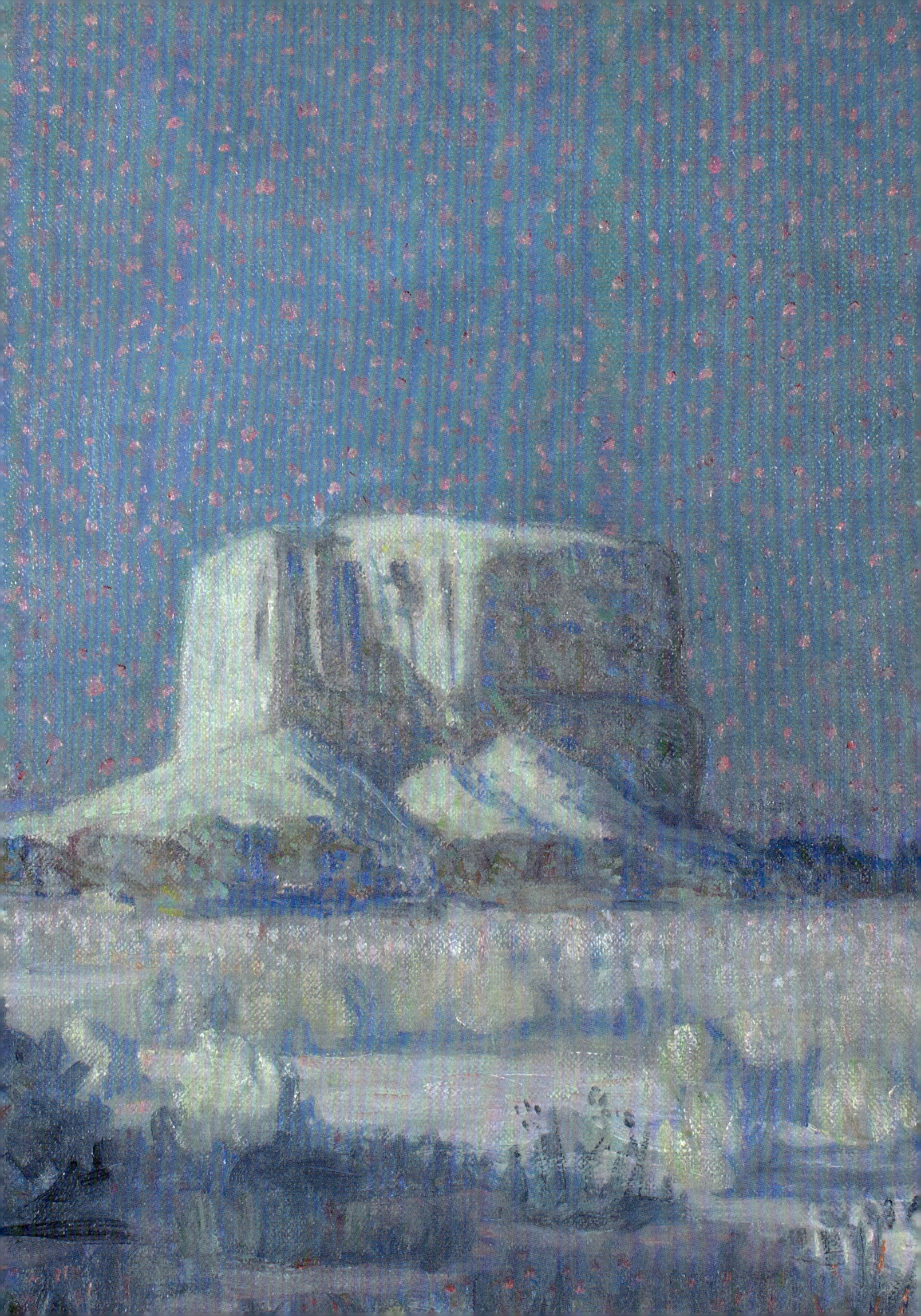

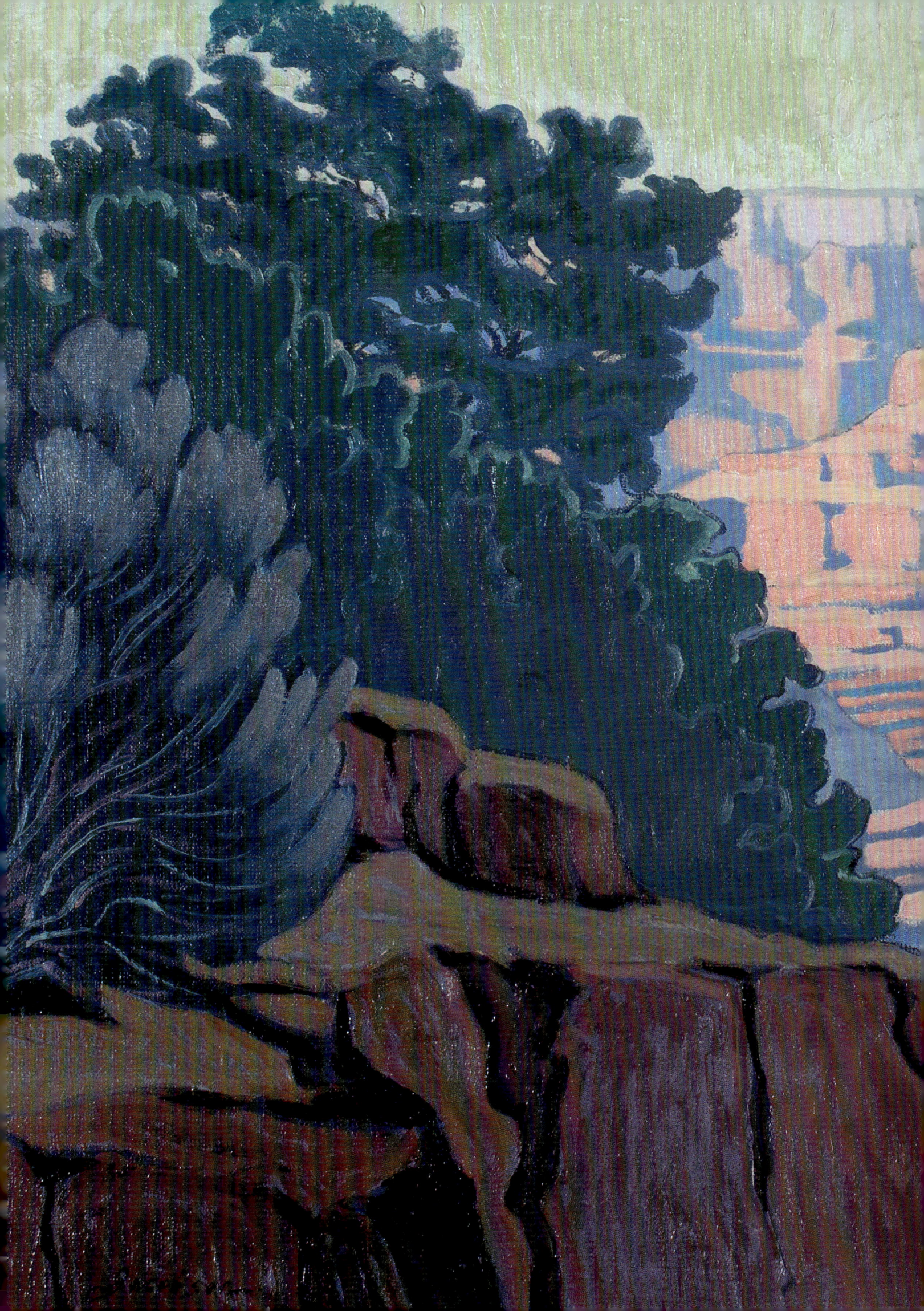

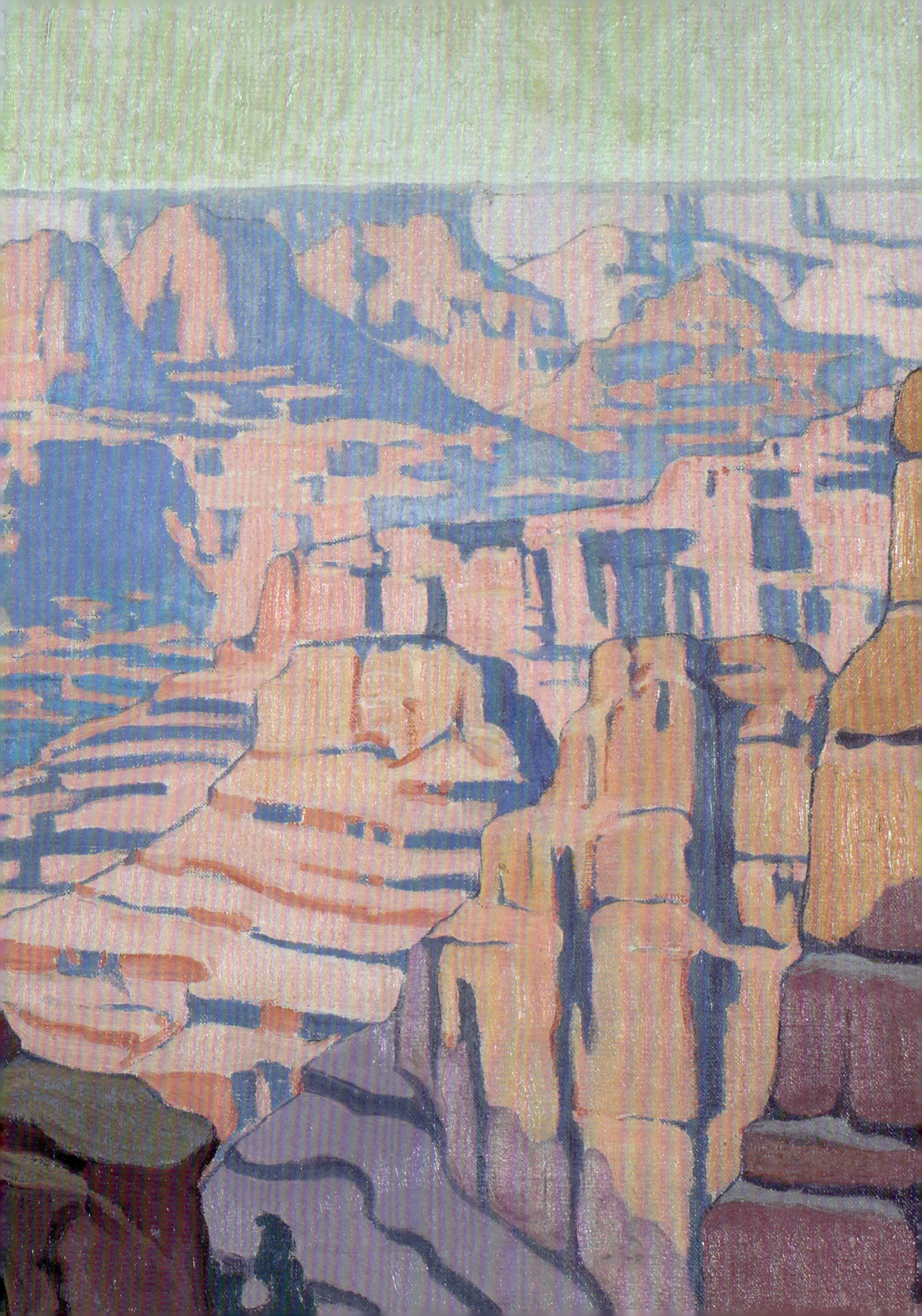

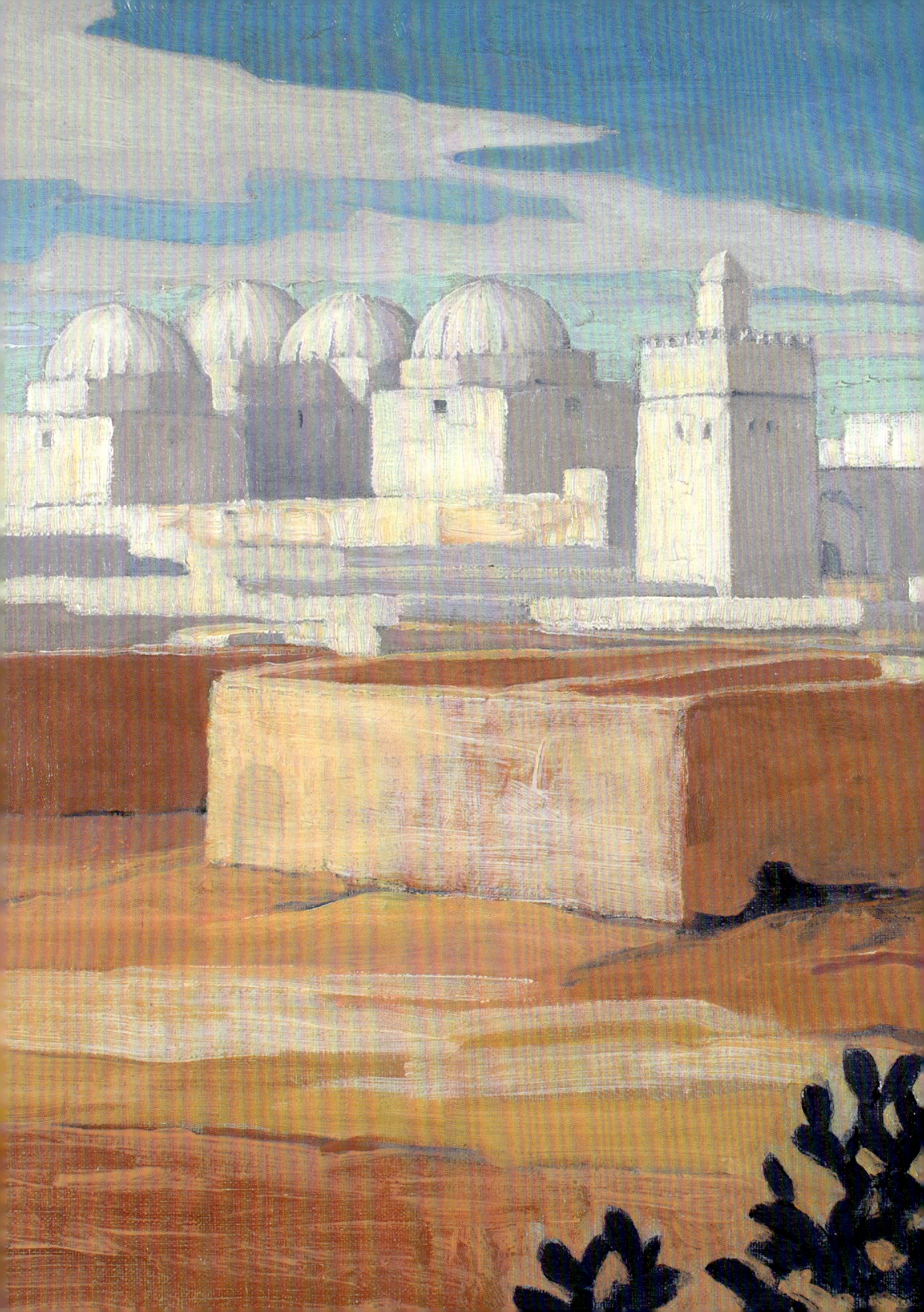

Oscar Brousse Jacobson, Culture Broker

Anne Allbright and Mark Andrew White

IN WHAT CAN ONLY BE DESCRIBED AS AN UNFORTUNATE HISTORICAL SLIGHT, Swedish born Oscar Brousse Jacobson (1882–1966) is too often identified solely for his work among the internationally acclaimed six Kiowa artists, who attended the University of Oklahoma. The Jacobson House, an American Indian arts and cultural center in Norman, Oklahoma, honors this legacy by continuing his efforts to promote Native art and awareness. But Jacobson had an extraordinarily multifaceted life, one that straddled various ethnic, cultural, and economic worlds.

One of Jacobson's most intriguing contributions to American society and culture was his role as a cultural broker. He not only encouraged Oklahomans, federal governmental officials, Southwest art patrons, and art circles to see that art from all cultures deserved attention and cultivation, but also convinced oilmen like Lew Wentz to invest in art collecting and urged people to support art of all kinds, including avant-garde styles like Cubism, Futurism, and Synchromism.[1] Jacobson believed a progressive society is one that invests in and supports art at the highest level, and the cumulative achievement of a nation is reflected and measured by its art.

Jacobson admired the artistic production of a range of cultures and ethnicities, including those of African Americans, North Africans, Muslims, Asians, Indians, and American Indians. Acting as director of the University of Oklahoma's School of Art, where he arrived in 1915, Jacobson used his position to educate students in the cultures of the world, as well as contemporary trends. During his own painting career, Jacobson explored styles such as Post-Impressionism and Fauvism. He publically encouraged a variety of art traditions and new movements at a time when modernism lacked support among the general public and critics, especially in the new state of Oklahoma. By his early thirties, Jacobson had become a sought-after lecturer, teacher, artist, and promoter of both American and international art.

Detail, see Fig. 11, page 21

Oscar Jacobson

U.S., born Sweden, 1882–1966

Kairouan, Tunis, Africa, 4th Holy City, Great Mosque, ca. 1925

At OU, he began to collect works of art for the university. Eventually, this led to the formation of OU's Museum of Art (now the Fred Jones Jr. Museum of Art). Jacobson favored Southwestern and Western artists, but he also understood the importance of buying the finest prints and original artwork representing the diversity of genres and eras of art history. He also used his writings, various connections in the art world, and position as director to bring art awareness to Oklahoma, and numerous sources point to Jacobson as the leading force behind the development of the visual arts in the state.

Born on May 16, 1882, on Västra Eknö, a small island community on the coast of Sweden, south of Stockholm, Jacobson spent his formative years surrounded by the sea.[2] As the son of Nils Petter Jacobson and Anne Lena Olofsdotter, the most prominent family in the village, young Oscar wanted for little. Life on the island presented an endless supply of pleasant and adventurous tasks for a boy possessed of unquenchable imagination. Jacobson found himself an active participant in the natural landscape.[3] Although the family lived on a small plot of land, they remained self-sufficient, for the most part. The community lacked a professional shoemaker, however, so every year a man arrived who made footwear. The children loved and looked forward to this annual event, and they always "plied him with questions about the big world outside."[4] Such interactions with foreign acquaintances helped spark Jacobson's growing imagination, whereas the lack of modernization on the island helped cultivate Jacobson's nostalgic views of a "simpler" time. In subsequent years, he resented aspects of modernity and looked back nostalgically on his childhood.

Throughout Jacobson's life, he liked to seek opportunities to push beyond expectations and limitations. Even as a young child, Jacobson often took risks that awed his older peers. According to his wife, Jeanne d'Ucel, Jacobson, at the age of three, jumped off his father's fishing boat without warning. Curious about the possibilities beneath the sea, young Jacobson plunged into the frigid Baltic even though he could not yet swim. And then, as a five year old, Jacobson, along with his slightly older brother Ernst, provided his family with another cause for alarm. Together, the two siblings stole a small boat and headed toward Russia for what they envisioned would be an exciting adventure. Luckily, they had only journeyed a mile or so away from shore when local fishermen spotted and retrieved them. These early experiences set the tone for Jacobson's life as he continued to seek adventure and test limits, both geographical and cultural.[5] They may have also provided the inspiration for one of his earliest extant paintings *At the Freezing Point (Vyd Fryspunkten)* (1901; fig. 1). The sea continued to fascinate Jacobson into his mature career, and he approached the subject in 1923

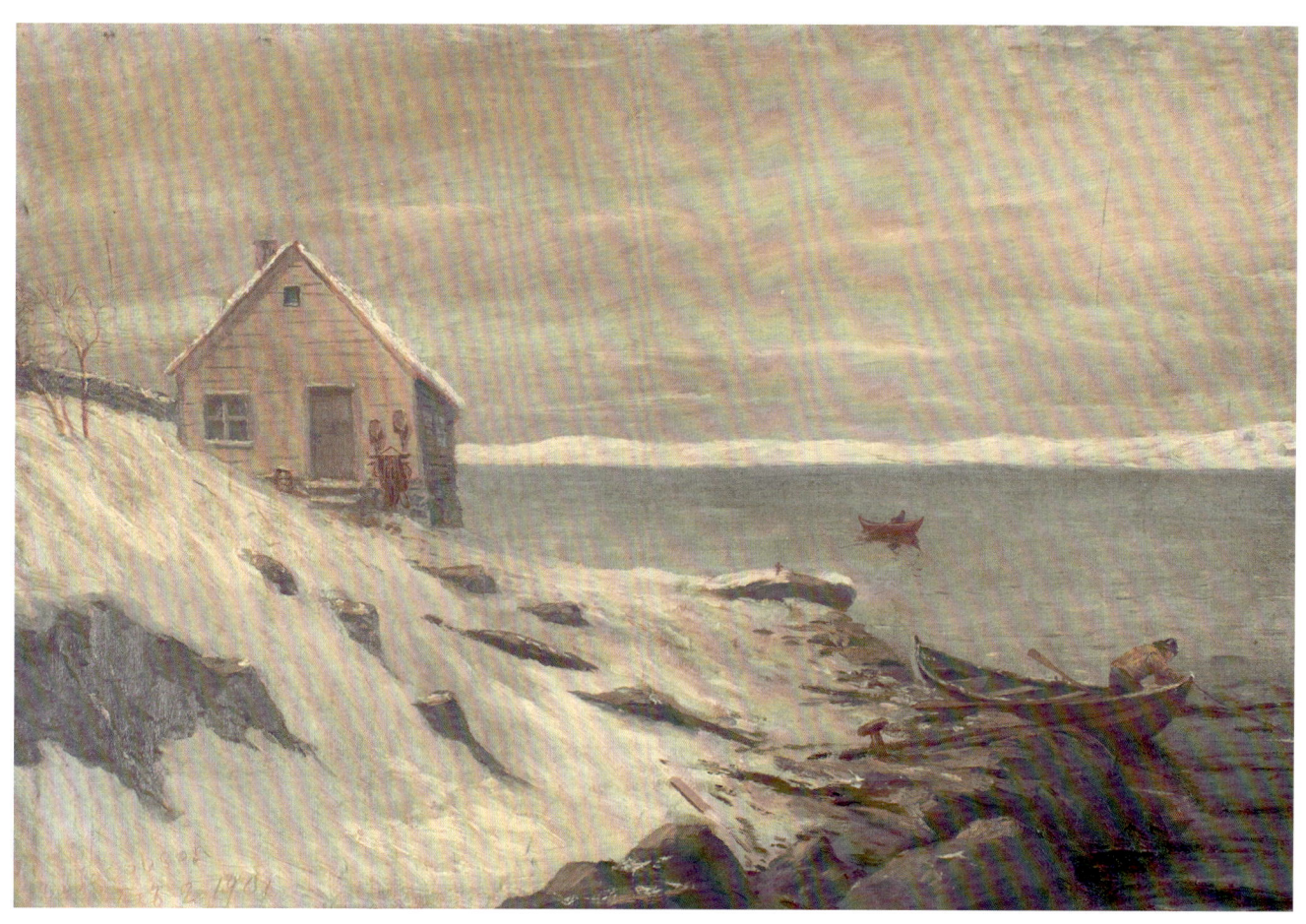

Fig. 1   Oscar Jacobson

U.S., born Sweden, 1882–1966

At the Freezing Point (Vyd Fryspunkten), 1901

Oil on canvas, 16³⁄₄ x 24³⁄₄ in.

Collection of Doctors Julia and Derek Irwin

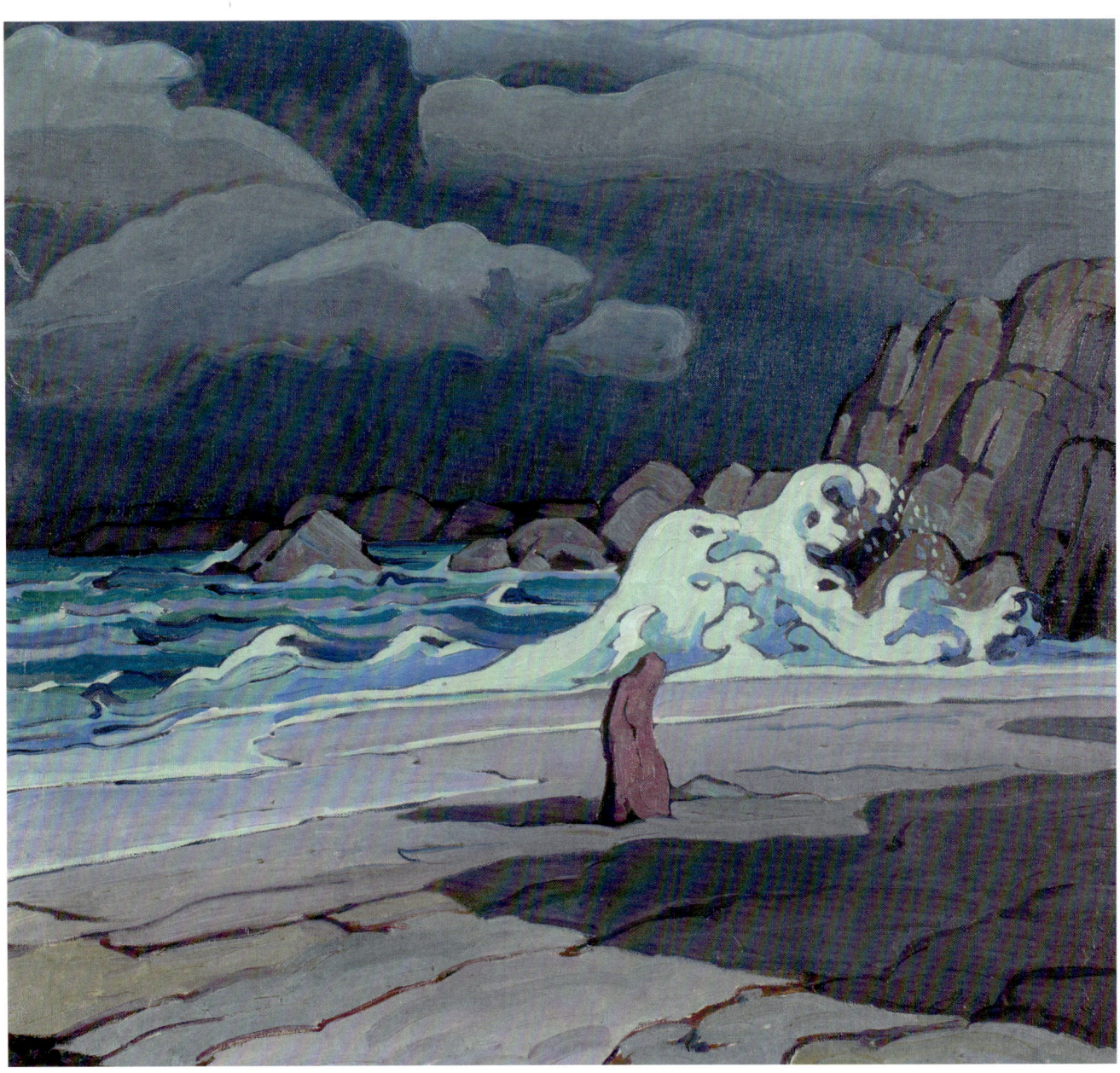

Fig. 2   Oscar Jacobson

U.S., born Sweden, 1882–1966

Elegy of the Sea (Coast of Sweden), 1923

Oil on canvas, 30 x 34 in.

University of Oklahoma, Elaine Bizzell Thompson Study Room.

University of Oklahoma Libraries

with some melancholy. *Elegy of the Sea (Coast of Sweden)* (fig. 2) likely depicts the frigid waters of the Baltic, with a lone figural rock bowed as if in lament.

In 1890, the Jacobsons decided to leave Sweden. Letters sent home by Oscar's oldest brother Karl spoke of the possibilities the United States offered immigrants. The family decided to pull up roots and move to the United States. At first, this decision devastated young Oscar. He was passionate about the coastal lifestyle, but his father believed that life on the island limited the large family's chances of staying together. Jacobson turned eight while traveling to the U.S., but he saw little to celebrate, as he resented and protested the move.[6] The Jacobsons arrived in Kansas on Memorial Day, 1890, and settled on a farm and ranch just outside the Swedish community of Lindsborg.

Soon after their arrival, his father gave him a horse, and Jacobson changed his outlook as he began to see the appeal of living in the West under vast open skies. He rode his horse and, with art supplies in hand, dreamed of Western adventures beyond Kansas. Working occasionally as a hired cattleman, he traveled to places that put him in contact with various Indian cultures of the Plains and the Southwest. These early explorations and experiences helped shape his interest in American Indians, the West, and painting. Unfortunately, archival records reveal few details of these early interactions with Native Americans. It is known, however, that Jacobson believed that the Indians he contacted sensed that he came as a friend. Intrigued by their art, he compared Puebloan pottery to the "archaic ware of Greece" and, according to d'Ucel, "He drank in the majestic beauty of the Indian dances" and studied their folklore, music, religious beliefs, and various customs. These cross-cultural interactions built the foundation for much of his life's pursuits.[7]

From his teenage years into early adulthood, Jacobson envisioned joining Theodore Roosevelt and his Rough Riders and wanted to project a Western Rough Rider persona.[8] He organized the boys of the neighborhood into a riding group, known locally as the Crazy Ridge Wild West Riders or Jakobson's Rough Riders. Twenty or so strong, they made quite a show for several years and performed at local fairs and events, receiving great publicity from the local newspapers. The newspaper promoted their appearance at the 1902 Fourth of July celebration along with Chief Ompolesogalah and his band of "picturesque Indian warriors."[9]

While cultivating his Western identity, Jacobson used his savings to attend Lindsborg's Bethany College. He enrolled in 1895 to pursue dual degrees in business and accounting, but also enrolled in drawing and painting classes with Birger Sandzén, a Swedish émigré with modernist training (fig. 3). Jacobson eventually changed his area of focus to art and, at the closing of the spring semester in 1903, he earned his Bachelor of Fine Arts, the only one awarded at the college that year.[10] Jacobson and Sandzén became lifelong friends and continued correspondence until Sandzén's death in 1954.

After graduation, Jacobson worked in the local post office, but the job failed to hold his interest. A critical juncture took place in his life in 1903 when he took a job in St. Louis at the upcoming 1904 World's Fair, or Louisiana Purchase Exposition. Jacobson viewed this as an ideal opportunity to study art on a large scale and interact with people from other cultures. With fifty dollars in hand, the twenty-one year old relocated.[11] For the first time, Jacobson saw art on a truly international scale and, as a result, he developed a deep-rooted appreciation for diverse traditions.[12] He worked as the Royal Commissioner of Sweden and oversaw Sweden's exhibition as the curator. The exposition understandably served as a breeding ground for cultural exchange among different ethnicities. Jacobson recalled it as a place for "liberal education." He became fascinated with all the different groups of people represented, such as American Indians and the "wild Igorots" from the Philippines, who he had the pleasure of joining for dinner.[13] Young and inquisitive, Jacobson relished these moments and others, such as working with a young Will Rogers in Wild West shows. As a showman, he delighted in the fact that his performances captivated the attendees, and he continued to cultivate a Western frontier image.[14]

After the World's Fair, Jacobson enrolled in graduate art courses at Yale in 1905. Feeling somewhat ostracized by the New Englanders, Jacobson roomed with three other young men who also hailed from west of the Mississippi (South Dakota, Colorado, and New Mexico). They paid homage to their Western lifestyles by decorating their room with memorabilia from both their homes and travels into Indian Territory, and they called their living quarters the Kawraw Kiotes den, most likely named after the Kaw tribe from Kansas. At Yale, Jacobson grew quite fond of others referring to him as "cowboy," though close acquaintances simply called him "Jake," his self-styled moniker from his Lindsborg days.[15]

Jacobson and his fellow Kawraw Kiotes staged Western-themed plays at Yale. *Sunset*, by Victor O. Freeburg, told the story of a student from Yale, who was originally a cowboy from Kansas and whose first love had been a Kaw Princess named Sunset. Jacobson played Sunset's father, a Chief named Mustango

Fig. 3 (facing page)
Oscar Jacobson
U.S., born Sweden, 1882–1966
Portrait of Birger Sandzén, 1902
Oil on canvas, 24 x 18 in.
Birger Sandzén Memorial Gallery, Lindsborg, Kansas

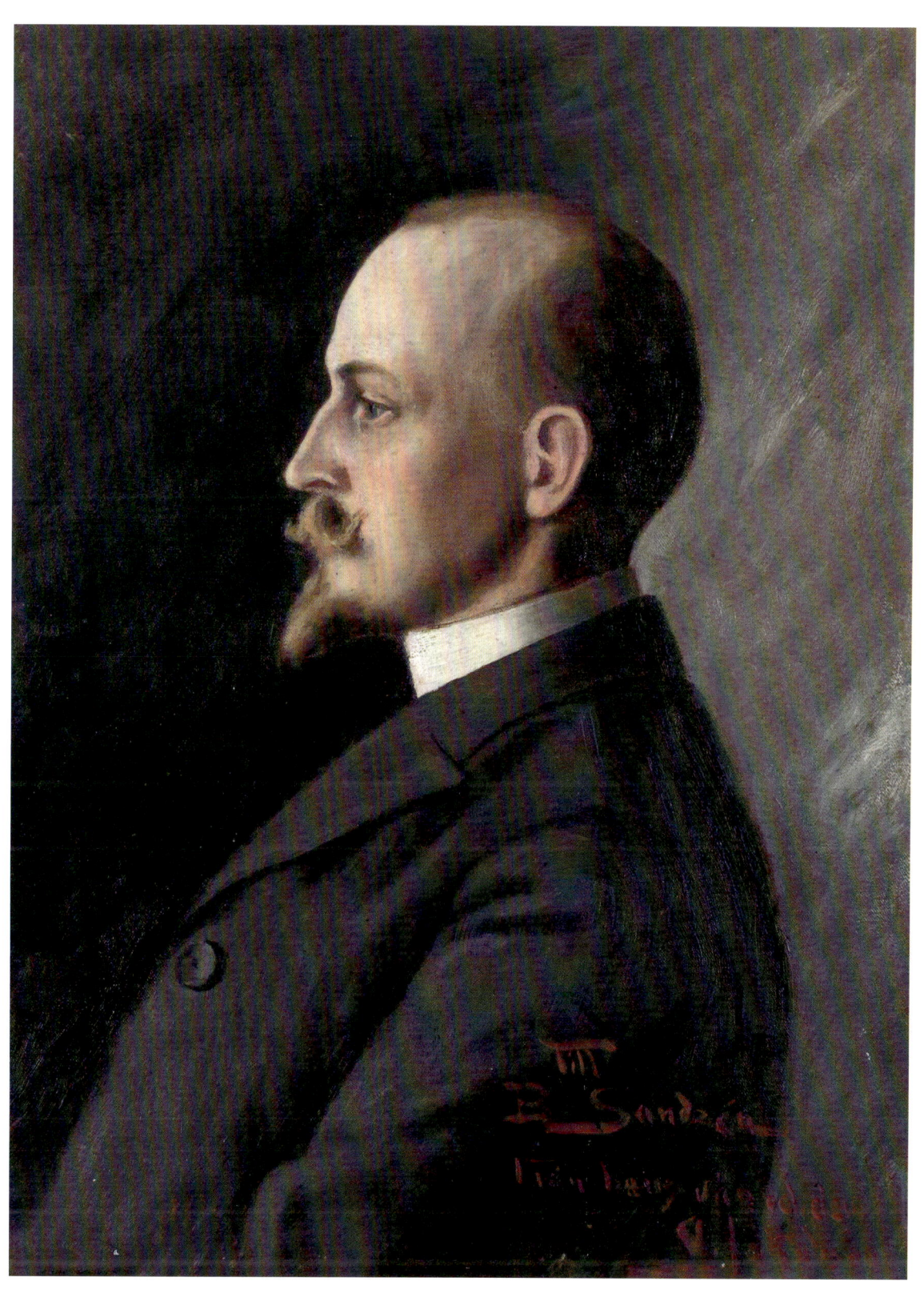

(fig. 4). This play received much acclaim, and they performed it often throughout 1907 and into 1908.[16] Jacobson darkened his skin with makeup and wore a full Indian headdress, reportedly collected from a reservation near Lindsborg.[17]

Prior to the award of his degree from Yale, which he eventually received in 1916, Jacobson accepted a position as chair of the newly formed art department at Minnesota College in 1908. His tenure there was short-lived, but he began lecturing for universities and civic organizations during this time and would continue the practice for much of his career. His topics ranged from "Impressionism in Art" to "Contemporary Artists of Sweden." He left his position in Minnesota in 1911 for the State College of Washington in Pullman (fig. 5), where he met and married in 1912 French immigrant Sophie Jeanne Brousse, who later went by the pen name Jeanne d'Ucel. Jacobson adopted Brousse as his middle name when the two applied for American citizenship that same year. Following his employment in Washington, Jacobson's art career started to take shape, and he became more prolific and experimental with his paintings. He had worked in an Impressionist style prior to this time, but now he adopted an expressive character similar to Vincent van Gogh. During a trip to western Europe in July 1914, Jacobson visited Paris to observe various museums and art exhibitions, including those that showcased Cubism and other modernist styles.[18] The Louvre presented thirty-two-year-old Jacobson with a wonderful opportunity to study an immense collocation of art ranging from classical to contemporary. This exposure did not result in a significant change to his style but did give him an appreciation for modernism that influenced his teaching career.

The State College of Washington proved a challenging tenure for Jacobson, and he had difficulty promoting the visual arts, as d'Ucel recalled: "The West, especially Washington State College because of its practical and technical character, looked upon art as a frill, something in the order of a lady's accomplishment. They couldn't conceive that a truly manly man might make it his career."[19] In 1915, Jacobson accepted a position at the University of Oklahoma, where he would spend the remainder of his career. An alum of Bethany College, Samuel Holmberg had begun the art program at OU in 1909 but, following his premature death in 1911, the program had been

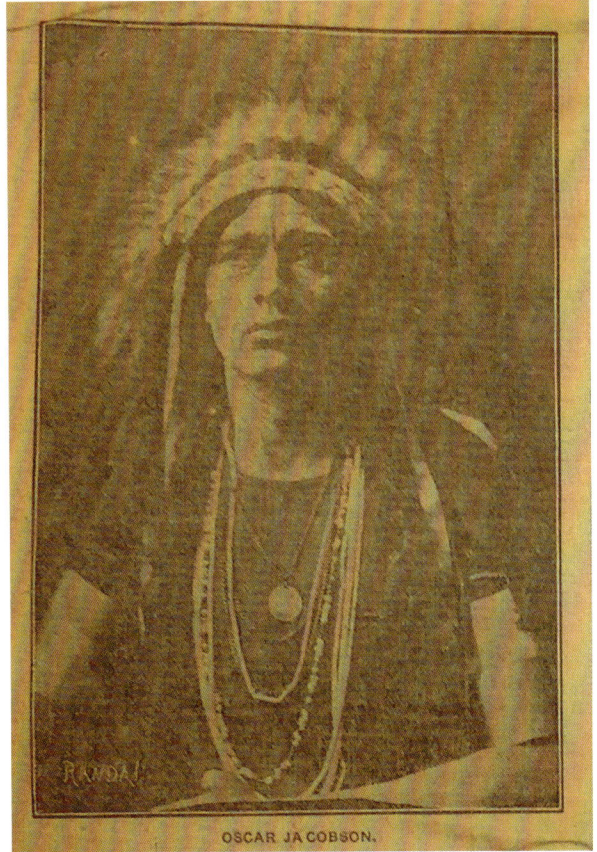

OSCAR JACOBSON.

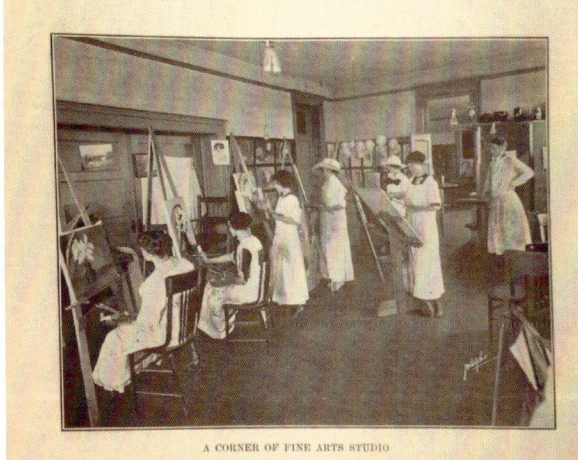

A CORNER OF FINE ARTS STUDIO

Fig. 4. Oscar Jacobson as "Mustango," from *New Haven Union*, December 22, 1907, in Oscar Brousse Jacobson and Jeanne d'Ucel scrapbooks, volume 1, "1902–1911"

Fig. 5. "A Corner of Fine Arts Studio" at the State College of Washington, Pullman, ca. 1911, in Oscar Brousse Jacobson and Jeanne d'Ucel scrapbooks, volume 2, "1911–1918"

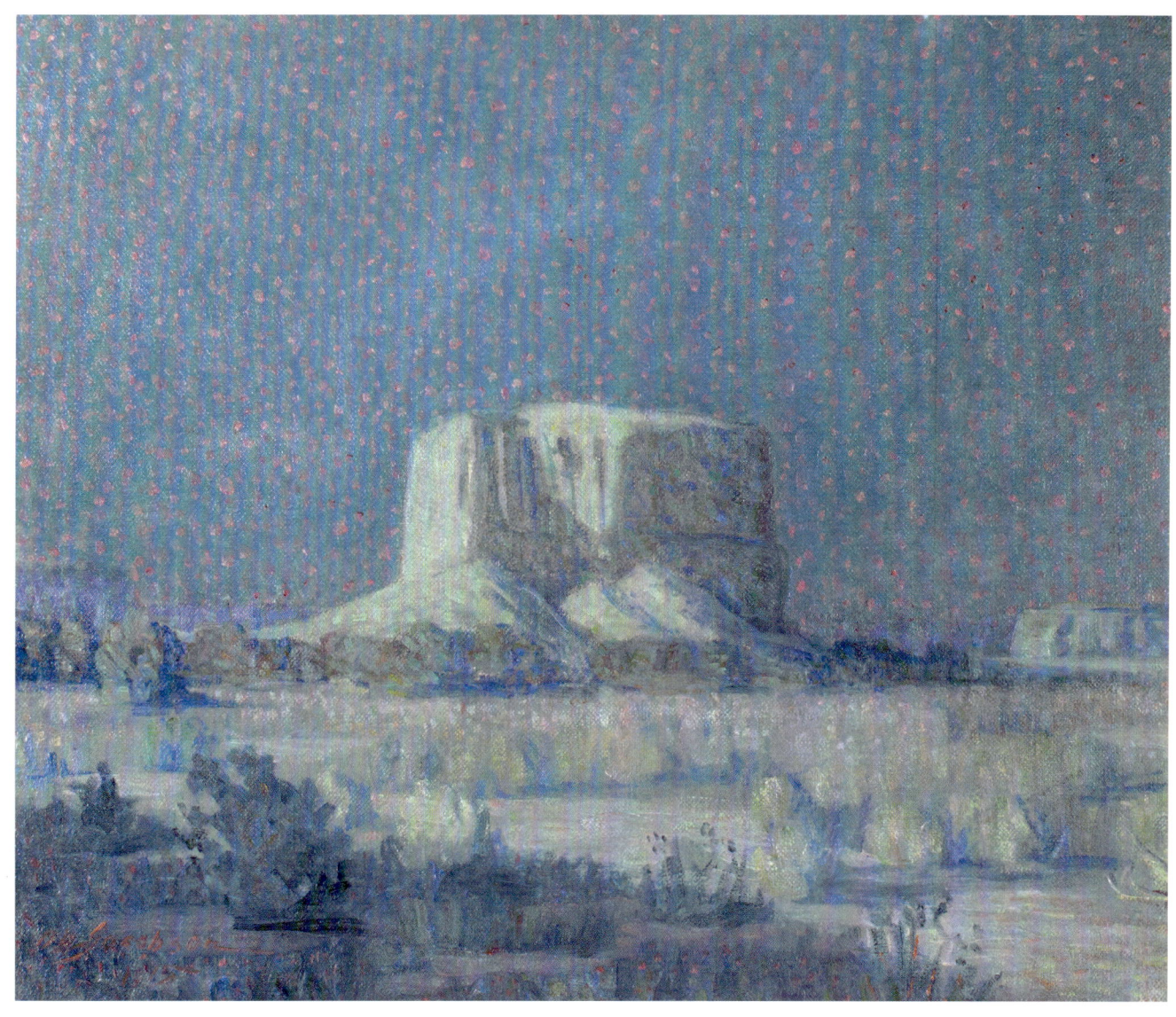

Fig. 6   Oscar Jacobson

U.S., born Sweden, 1882–1966

Untitled (Enchanted Mesa), 1915

Oil on canvas, 21^1$_{16}$ x 25^3$_{16}$ in.

Collection of Mary and Dick Clements

led by Patricio Gimeno. Jacobson replaced Gimeno, who was transferred to another department, and began to build the program.

In the summer prior to his first semester at OU, Jacobson and d'Ucel traveled the Southwest, including New Mexico, Arizona, and California. A visit to the New Mexico pavilion at the Panama-California Exposition in San Diego encouraged them to spend much of the summer in New Mexico. The Jacobsons visited many places of interest, including Laguna, and climbed Mesa Encantada (fig. 6), a difficult task that led Jeanne to reflect that she "grudgingly admired the indomitability of the Conquistadores who climbed, most of them to their death, up that impregnable redoubt."[20] The formation would command Jacobson's attention for another five years after, and he painted it at various times of day and using different techniques, similar in some respects to the varying images of Claude Monet's haystacks.

The Jacobsons also spent time in Santa Fe and probably Taos, where they became acquainted with many of the colony artists. In subsequent years, Jacobson exhibited with many of the New Mexicans, as well as Sandzén, in an exhibition variously titled *Artists of the Southwest* or the *Southwestern Art Exhibition*. He also hoped to bring a Taos Society of Artists exhibition to OU in 1917 and a similar show of works by Santa Fe artists to Norman the following year.[21] The Jacobsons counted Gerald Cassidy, Frank Applegate, B. J. O. Nordfeldt, and Jozef Bakos as their closest friends and colleagues among the Santa Fe art colony, and Jacobson purchased their work for his personal collection and for OU.[22]

Jacobson began his tenure at OU with a solo exhibition in October, a practice he continued until 1949 when he began hosting his exhibition at the family home. Also in 1915, he began working with the American Federation of Arts to bring exhibits to campus such as an *Exhibition of Paintings by American Masters*, which included Ernest Blumenschein, Childe Hassam, Robert Henri, and Bert Phillips, among others. He followed with an exhibition of embroidered Chinese tapestries in January 1916 and, in an attempt to give the Norman audience further experience with Asian art, he lectured on Ukiyo-e in 1917.[23] Jacobson also participated in the founding of the Association of Oklahoma Artists in March 1916, serving as its secretary. By 1917, his accomplishments earned him a promotion to associate professor.

The Jacobsons clearly felt at home in Norman within a very short time. They finished building their house in the Provençal vernacular style in 1918, and their family grew dramatically. Their first child, Yvonne Françoise Brousse Jacobson, was born in June 1917, followed by Oscar Andre Jacobson, Jr., in December 1919, and Yolanda Helene Brousse Jacobson in May 1921. Jacobson also increased the art department with the addition of full- and part-time faculty. Mollie Peterson had arrived the year before Jacobson in 1914 and continued to

Fig. 7 (facing page)
John Frank (U.S., 1905–1973)
Glazed Pot [Jacobson's brush jar] [detail], 1930
Ceramic, $7^3/_8$ x $8^1/_2$ in.
Collection of Sally van der Kamp

teach until 1921, and she was joined by Edith Mahier in 1917; James Brill and Estelle Manon each taught a year, Brill in 1918 and Manon in 1920; and Gwendolyn Meux began her tenure in 1921. Mahier, Meux, and Jacobson formed the core faculty until the mid-1920s and exhibited together in 1923 at the Delgado Museum of Art in New Orleans.

Jacobson's salad days at OU were not without controversy. At the Tenth Annual Convention of the American Federations of Arts, hosted by the Metropolitan Museum of Art, he gave the lecture "East and West," which was later published in the *American Magazine of Art* in 1920. The lecture was intended to provide a survey of cultural development in the young state of Oklahoma and imply that its rapid modernization had left little time for a flowering of the arts. The Associated Press then ran a story suggesting that Jacobson had connected a lack of cultural development to the oil boom. State newspapers quickly protested what they perceived as Jacobson's low valuation of Oklahoma culture. The *Daily Oklahoman* ran the most incendiary headline, "Crude Oil Means Crude Art; Professor Mourns Because Oklahoma Is Not Refined."[24] Retractions followed after the newspapers received copies of the speech, only to find no criticism of oil wealth or Oklahoma culture.

Jacobson's reputation received no lasting injury, but he was quick to demonstrate his worth in the years that followed. Under his direction, enrollment in the art school had increased from 23 to 255 students by 1920, and Jacobson announced in 1921 that he hoped to establish a museum on campus.[25] The faculty also continued to grow under his direction. Dorothy Kirk and Lawrence Williams joined the art department in 1924 and, following Williams's premature death in 1929, former student Leonard Good assumed his position. Joseph Taylor arrived to teach sculpture at OU in 1932. John Frank was hired to teach ceramics in 1927, but he left the school in 1935 to devote his career to his new business venture, Frankoma Pottery. Prior to his departure, Frank gave his former director a pot adorned with bison and bears, a nod to Jacobson's affection for the West (fig. 7). Roger Corsaw,

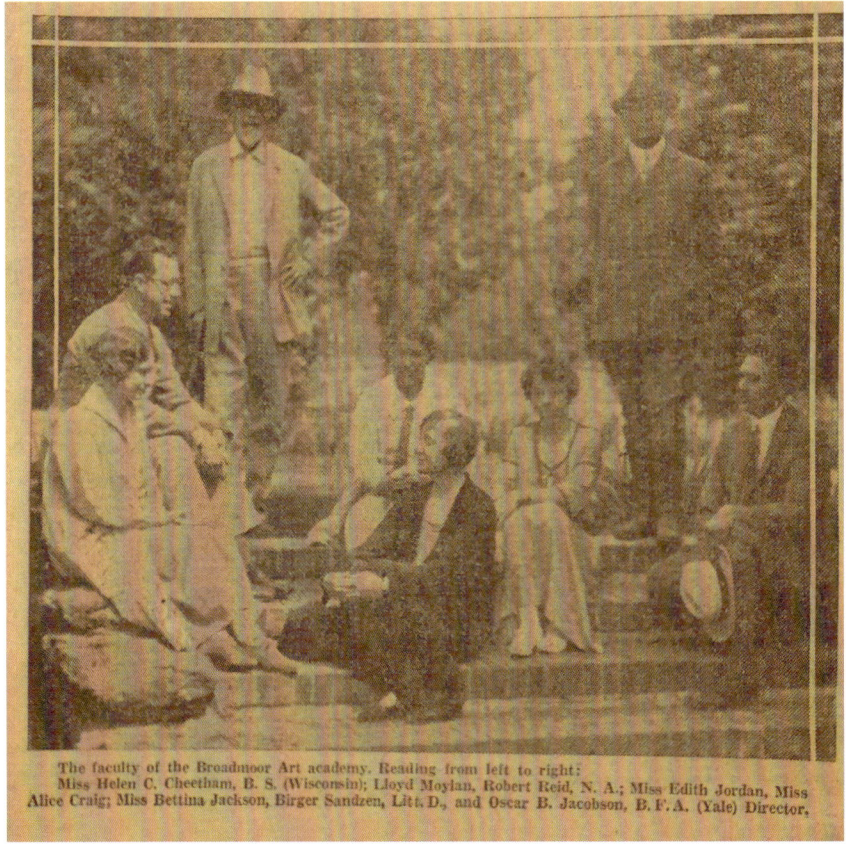

The faculty of the Broadmoor Art academy. Reading from left to right: Miss Helen C. Cheetham, B. S. (Wisconsin); Lloyd Moylan, Robert Reid, N. A.; Miss Edith Jordan, Miss Alice Craig; Miss Bettina Jackson, Birger Sandzen, Litt. D., and Oscar B. Jacobson, B. F. A. (Yale) Director,

Fig. 8. "Broadmoor Art Academy Faculty Attracts Record Crowd Students," *Colorado Springs Gazette-Telegraph*, July 1924, in Oscar Brousse Jacobson and Jeanne d'Ucel scrapbooks, volume 3, "1918–1926"

a former student of László Moholy-Nagy, began teaching ceramics in 1936, and William Harold Smith and John O'Neil started their lengthy tenure in 1936 and 1937, respectively.

Jacobson's ability to manage and develop a large program had been recognized as early as 1924. That year, he accepted an invitation to serve as director of the Broadmoor Art Academy in Colorado Springs and oversaw a distinguished faculty that included Sandzén and noted Impressionist Robert Reid (fig. 8). Colorado eventually commanded Jacobson's artistic attention in the 1930s, but he produced few paintings that summer. Returning to OU in the fall, he continued his efforts to expose the university community to world culture by exhibiting his personal collection of Asian art.[26]

Jacobson had earned his first sabbatical by 1925, and he took his family to western Europe and northern Africa with the ultimate intention of painting the Sahara Desert. After landing in Cherbourg, they stopped in Amiens and then Paris to see *L'Exposition internationale des arts décoratifs et industriels modernes*. They then went to Tours, where Jacobson passed his driving test, and drove south visiting numerous sites, including Loudun, Poitiers, Rocamadours, Montauban, Toulouse, the valley of the Aude River, Andorra, Carcassonne, and the Canal du Midi.[27] They proceeded to Nimes, Grenoble, and Jeanne's ancestral home of Chateau d'Ucel, where Jacobson sketched the chateau (1925, completed 1958; fig. 9).

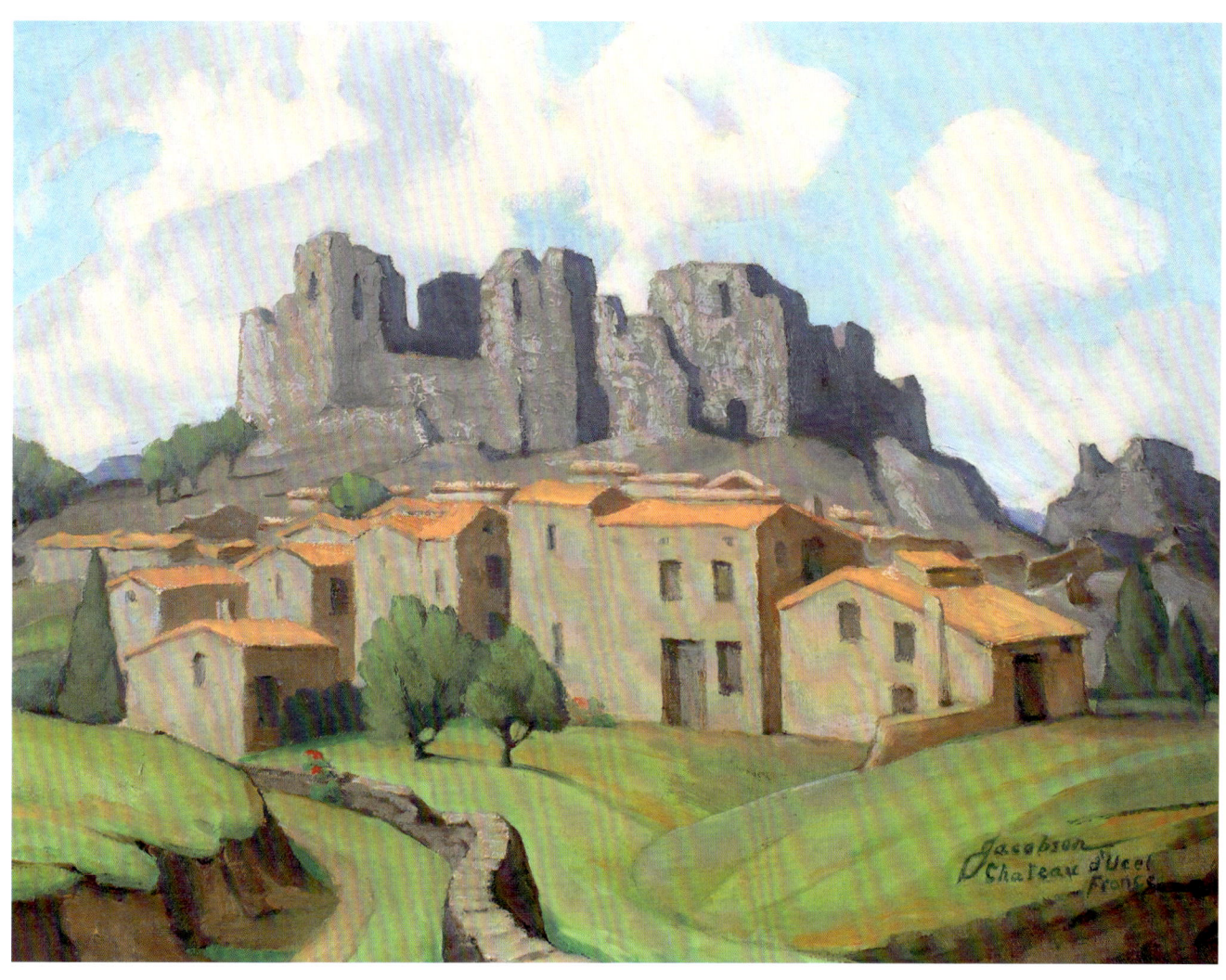

Fig. 9   Oscar Jacobson

U.S., born Sweden, 1882–1966

Chateau des Comtes d'Ucel, Southern France, 1925

(completed in 1958)

Oil on canvas 18 x 24 in.

Collection of Peter and Grace Harris

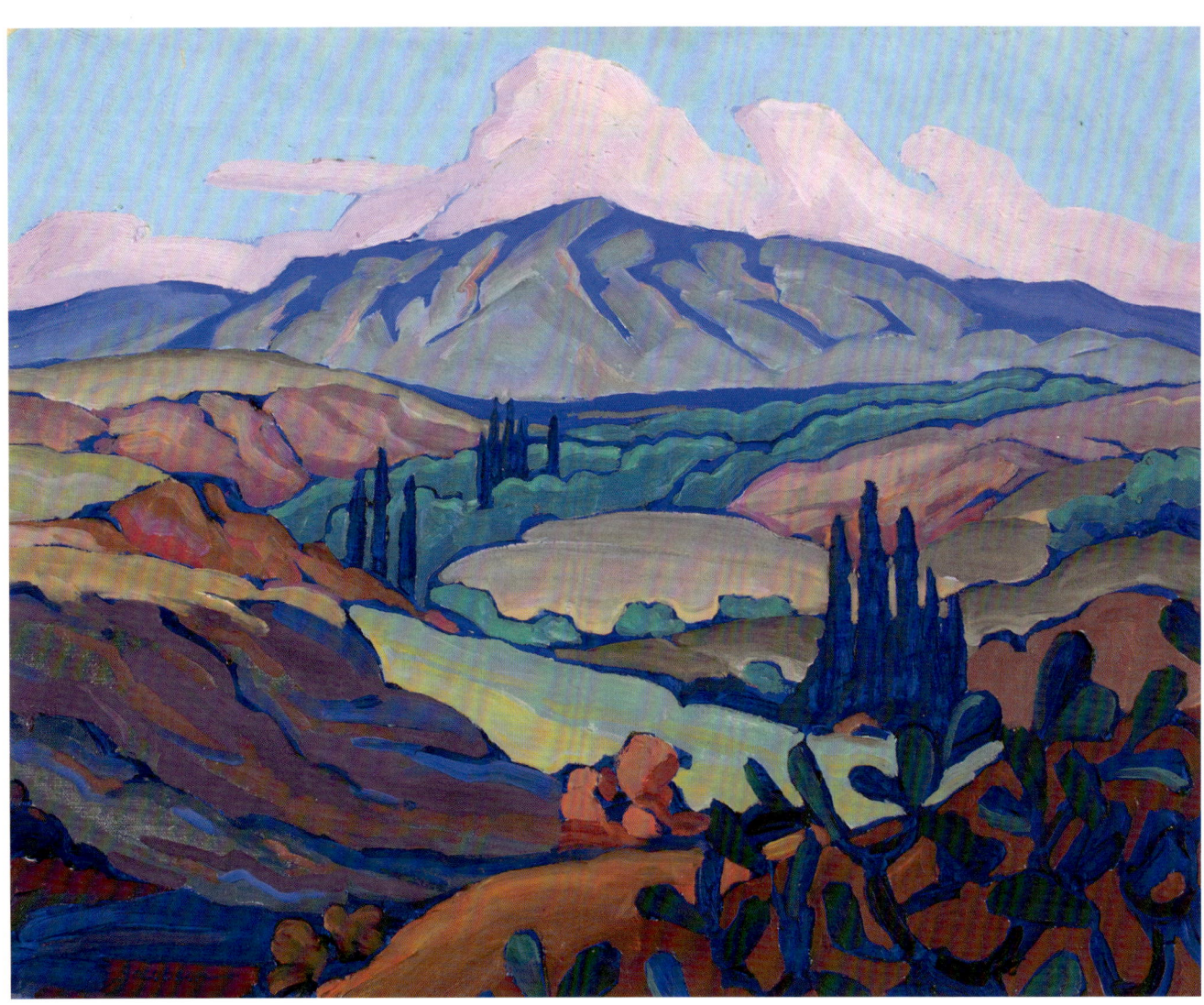

Fig. 10   Oscar Jacobson

U.S., born Sweden, 1882–1966

In Morocco, ca. 1925

Oil on canvas board, 20 x 26 in.

Oklahoma City Museum of Art.

Gift from the Kirkpatrick Foundation, 1999.021

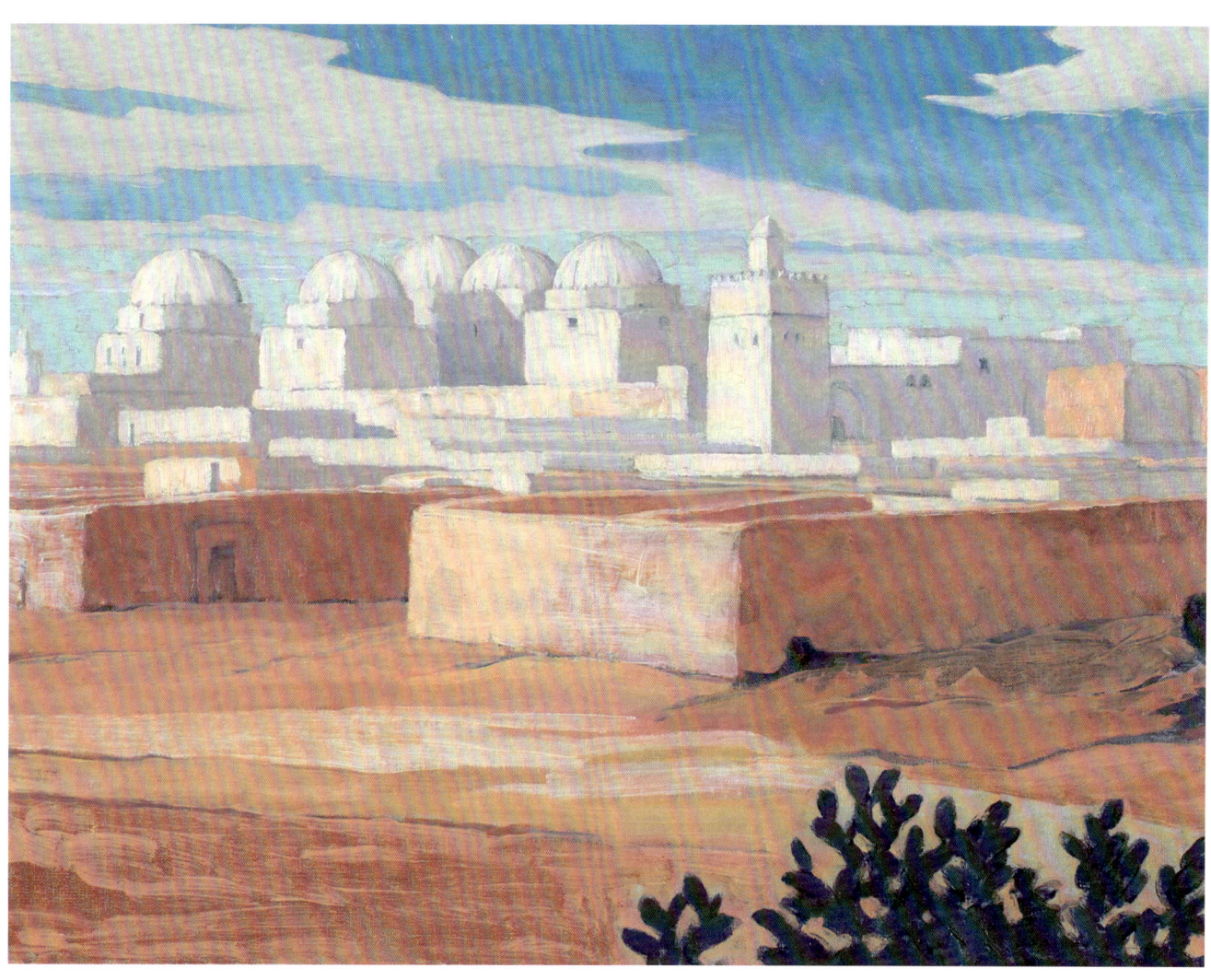

Fig. 11   Oscar Jacobson

U.S., born Sweden, 1882–1966

Kairouan, Tunis, Africa, 4th Holy City, Great Mosque, ca. 1925

Oil on canvas, 19$\frac{1}{2}$ x 25$\frac{1}{2}$ in.

Pierson Gallery, Tulsa, Oklahoma

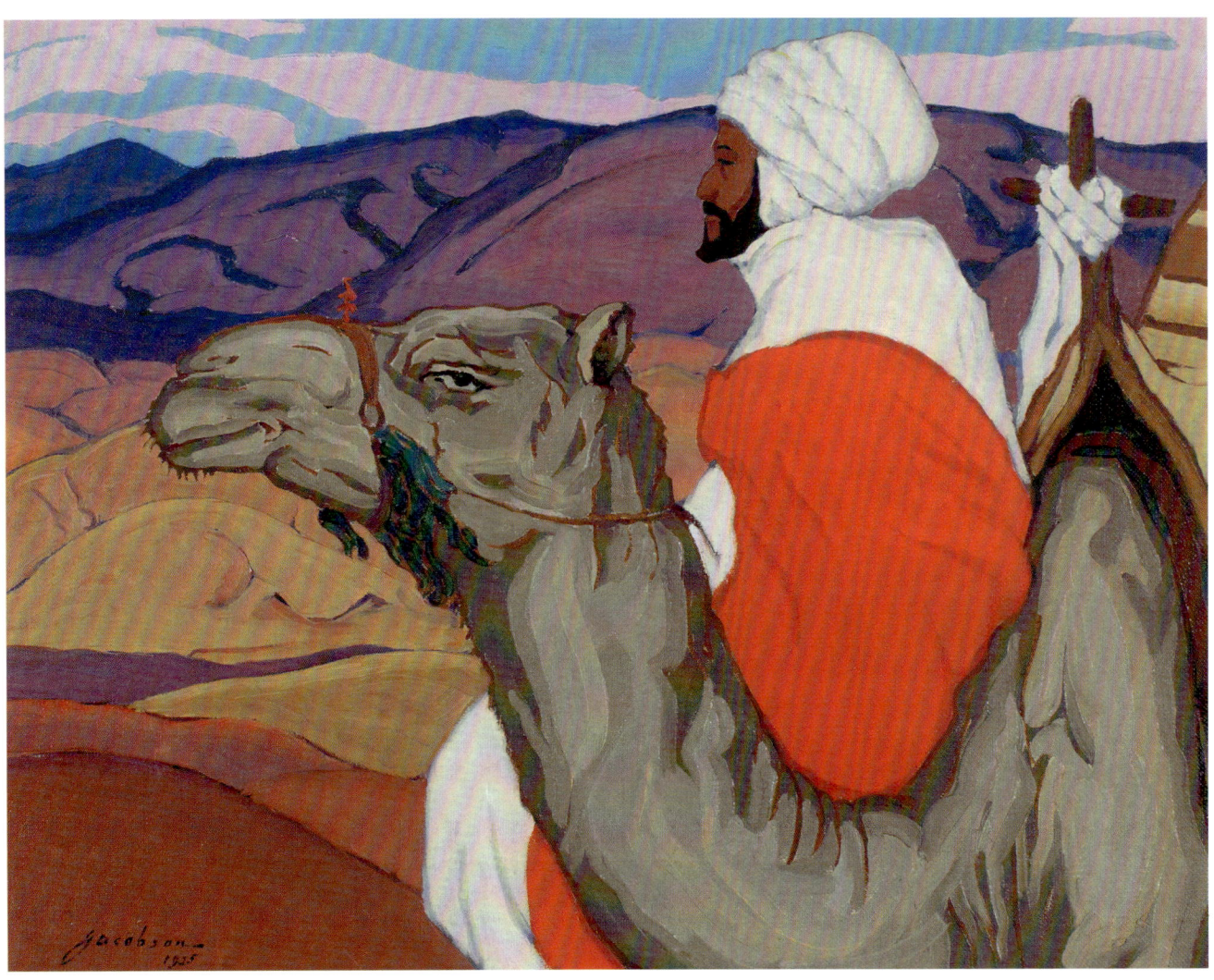

Fig. 12   Oscar Jacobson

U.S., born Sweden, 1882–1966

Untitled [Man on Camel], 1925

Oil on canvas, 20^1$_{16}$ x 26^1$_8$ in.

Oklahoma City Museum of Art.

Gift of Mr. and Mrs. Richard G. Taft. 1970.007

After crossing the Mediterranean on the French commercial liner Timgad, the Jacobsons spent much of their time in Algeria, wintering in Algiers, but also visited Morocco (fig. 10) and Tunisia. Islamic culture did have an appeal to the Jacobsons, and they visited some of the major sites of the Muslim faith, including the Great Mosque of Kairouan (also known as the Mosque of Uqba) in Al-Qayrawan, Tunisia (ca. 1925; fig. 11). Along the way, the artist had the opportunity to sketch caravans en route to the Saharan oases (fig. 12), and Oscar and Jeanne began to acquire pottery, jewelry, and textiles from the Imazighen (Berber) during the course of their travels.[28] Upon their return, they convinced President William Bennett Bizzell and Dean Fredrik Holmberg to purchase the collection for eight hundred dollars. Although Jacobson had not yet succeeded in establishing a museum on campus, the North African material became part of the nascent collection.[29] Jacobson offered several illustrated lectures to civic and professional groups in the following years with titles like "Fording Algeria" and "On the Trail of Berber Art" (fig. 13), and he organized numerous exhibits from the collection in 1929–30.

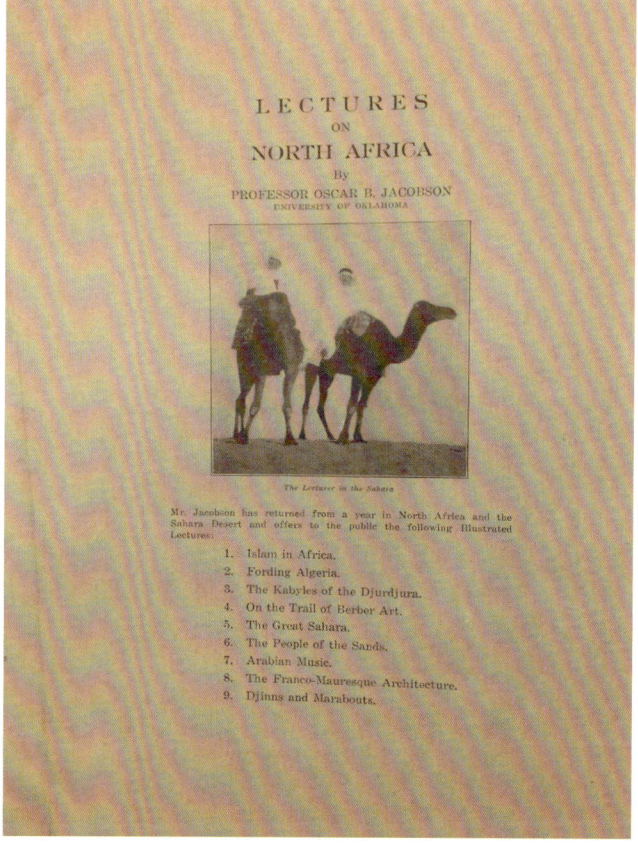

Jacobson's work with non-Western cultures accelerated after his return from Africa. He also began working with contemporary Native American artists, following his introduction to six Kiowa artists in 1926–27: Spencer Asah, James Auchiah, Jack Hokeah, Stephen Mopope, Bou-ge-tah Lois Smokey, and Monroe Tsatoke. The Kiowas worked in Mahier's office, secluded from the rest of the art students, and Jacobson began looking for ways to promote their work. Jacobson acted primarily as a cultural broker between Indian artists and art markets, museums, and, later, New Deal art projects. A close bond developed between Jacobson's family and his Indian students, primarily because the Kiowas viewed his ongoing efforts on their behalf as both genuine and sincere, but also because his high regard for Indian people in general remained readily apparent.[30]

Mahier and Jacobson were quick to exhibit the works of Asah, Hokeah, Mopope, and Tsatoke at the university in February 1927, but exhibitions outside Norman soon followed.[31] After an exhibition at the annual convention of the American Federation of Arts in Lincoln, Nebraska, Jacobson sent a traveling

Fig. 13

"Lectures on North Africa by Professor Oscar B. Jacobson," in Oscar Brousse Jacobson and Jeanne d'Ucel scrapbooks, volume 4, "1926–1932"

exhibition of the four men's works to the University of Missouri in Columbia, the Denver Art School, the University of Kansas in Lawrence, the Kansas City Art Institute, and his alma mater, Bethany College.[32] The exhibition at the convention also attracted the attention of Royal B. Farnum, director of Art Education for the state of Massachusetts, who helped arrange for an additional exhibition of the Kiowa paintings at the International Congress for Art Education in Prague, Czechoslovakia during the summer of 1928.

That same summer, the Kiowa tribe wanted to demonstrate their appreciation for Jacobson's contributions and his personal respect for their people and culture. In a ceremony in Anadarko, they officially and fully adopted him into the tribe as a war chief, the highest rank, giving him the name Nah-go-ey. With over one thousand American Indians in attendance, the induction pow-wow was an enormous affair. Although other tribes were present, the Kiowas wanted the dedication and dances to be strictly Kiowa. The Jacobsons and their domestic worker were the only non-Indians allowed to attend.[33]

By 1931, Jacobson was teaching art history exclusively, and he organized a course in American Indian art history, the first of its kind in the nation. As he saw it, Indian art was to be appreciated "as a living force and from the esthetic point of view, not merely as an anthropological and ethnological study."[34] Over the next few years, students with many tribal affiliations decided to take courses under Jacobson's direction at OU, including Acee Blue Eagle (Pawnee-Creek), Woody Crumbo (Potawatomi), Franklin Gritts (Cherokee-Potawatomi), Oscar Howe (Yanktonai Nakota), and Walter Richard "Dick" West (Cheyenne). As the first post-secondary Indian art curriculum in the United States, the American Indian art program at the University of Oklahoma gained national recognition.

Jacobson's concern for the promotion and encouragement of Native American art continued in the 1930s, when the U.S. Treasury Department asked him to serve as technical advisor for the Public Works of Art Project (PWAP) in Oklahoma. Part of President Franklin Delano Roosevelt's New Deal, the PWAP was a program designed to decorate public buildings with murals while providing needed relief to artists. After the dissolution of the PWAP in June 1934, Jacobson's supervisory role continued as a technical advisor to the Treasury Relief Art Project (TRAP) in Region XII, which included both Oklahoma and Texas. He ensured that Native artists received some of the commissions within the state; for example, Auchiah and Mopope completed two murals, *Kiowa Buffalo Dance* and *Kiowa Buffalo Hunt*, at the Cherokee Female Seminary (now Northeastern State University) at Tahlequah in 1934, and Blue Eagle painted a cycle of six murals for the gymnasium of the Oklahoma College for

Fig. 14
Unknown (facing page)
Gandhara, Trajanic Period
Buddha, 100–200
Schist, 17^1⁄$_2$ x 12^3⁄$_8$ x 6 in.
Fred Jones Jr. Museum of Art, The University of Oklahoma, Norman;
Wentz-Matzene Collection, 1936

Women (now the University of Science and Arts of Oklahoma) in Chickasha that same year. Other Native artists, like Dick West and Solomon McCombs, received TRAP commissions within the state in later years, as did Mahier and a few other Oklahoma colleagues.[35] Equally important, Jacobson also seems to have been instrumental in securing allocations of artwork from the PWAP and TRAP for the University of Oklahoma on four separate occasions, in 1935, 1938, 1942, and 1943, including Native American paintings from the Santa Fe Indian School Studio, prints from the PWAP workshops, and oils from notable artists such as Stuart Davis, Joseph Hirsch, and Jacobson's personal friends Lloyd Moylan and Josef Bakos. A total of 143 works of art, most of which were produced by Coloradan and New Mexican artists, became part of an OU collection that would expand dramatically in 1936.

Jacobson had announced his hope for a university art museum in 1921, but it was not until 1936 that a gift from photographer Richard Gordon Matzene led to the creation of the OU Museum of Art. Matzene began talking with Jacobson in 1934 about a partial gift of his collection of Asian art, since he could no longer pay the high storage costs. Much of it was apparently stored in Honolulu, and Matzene's personal friend, oilman Louis Haines "Lew" Wentz, had offered to pay for the shipment. The gift was comprised of 785 objects ranging from Persian manuscript pages to Chinese painting and Gandharan objects from Taxila and other historic sites in central Asia (fig. 14).[36] The Wentz-Matzene Collection, as it soon became known, was central to Jacobson's plan for a campus museum. When combined with the PWAP and TRAP allocation and other acquisitions since Jacobson's arrival, the collection of the new OU Art Museum numbered close to 1,000 works of art, and Jacobson was named director of the institution.

By 1940, Jacobson was not only a prolific artist with a lengthy exhibition record, but had also succeeded in increasing the visibility of the fine arts in Oklahoma through an aggressive exhibition program featuring the art and design of diverse cultures from across the globe, not to mention his promotion of Native American artists, and his work with the PWAP and TRAP. Fittingly, Nan Sheets, director of the WPA Oklahoma Art Center (now the Oklahoma City Museum of Art), helped to organize Jacobson's first retrospective in 1941, which traced the development of his career from 1912. A reproduction of his 1923 *Ocatilla and Barrel Cacti* (fig. 15) graced the silkscreened cover, alluding to Jacobson's fondness for the desert. The exhibition included seventy-four paintings, mostly of the American West and Africa, a testament to his summer travels.

Over the course of the 1940s, Jacobson received further accolades for his promotion of culture. His alma mater, Bethany College, honored him with a Doctor of Fine Arts degree in 1941, and he received the International Business Machine Corporation Medal for Notable Contribution to the Art World the following year. He reached the mandatory retirement age for faculty in 1945 and stepped down as the director of the School of Art after thirty years of service. Jacobson continued to direct the art museum, however, and even a partial list of the exhibits for 1946 indicates his continuing interest in diverse cultures: *Lithographs by Artists from 18 Latin American Countries, Graphic Arts from Poland, Exhibition of Paintings by Indians of North American,* and *Masks of the World.*

As director of the OU Museum of Art, Jacobson also assisted in a major acquisition in 1948 from the controversial U.S. State Department exhibition, *Advancing American Art.* The State Department intended to showcase the breadth and diversity of contemporary American art for international audiences and sent the exhibition in two sections to Eastern Europe and the Caribbean. As a form of cultural diplomacy, the exhibition was intended to showcase the freedom of expression under American democracy. A scandal erupted in early 1947, unfortunately, when Congress learned that the State Department had not only sent modern art abroad but had also used taxpayer funds to purchase the paintings. The exhibition was ultimately recalled that same year by Secretary of State George C. Marshall.[37]

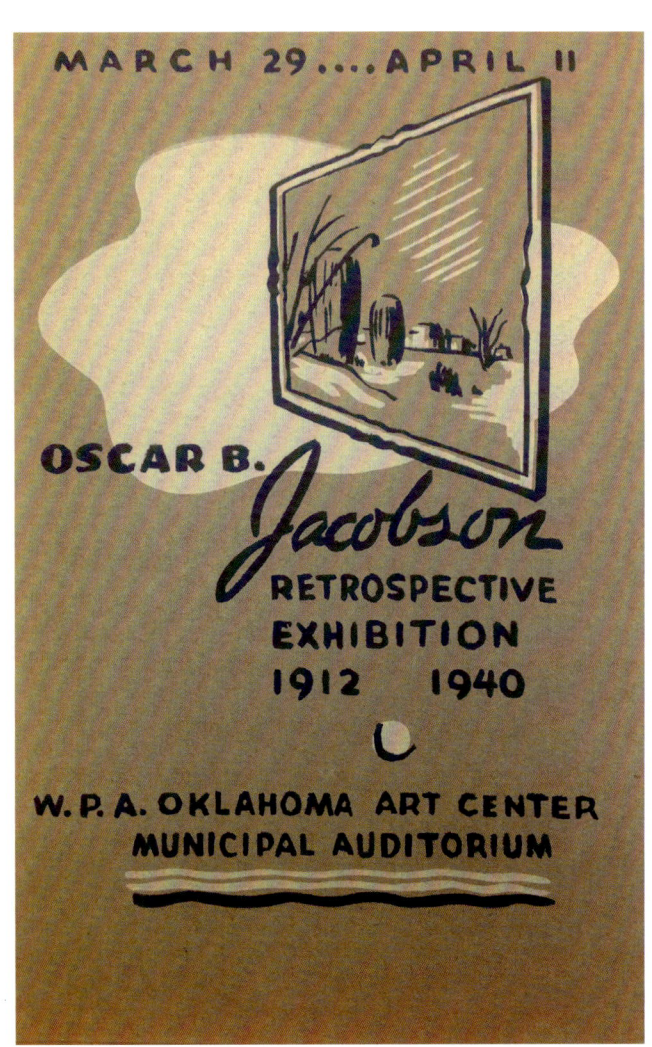

The works were auctioned through the War Assets Administration in 1948, and OU, with the encouragement of Jacobson and the new director of the School of Art, William Harold Smith, bid on the entire offering of 117 paintings. The university won 36 lots, the highest number of any bidder until Alabama Polytechnic Institute (now Auburn University) was awarded an extra painting at a later date making their total 36 as well. Paintings by William Baziotes, Romare Bearden, Adolph Gottlieb, Edward Hopper, Georgia O'Keeffe, and Ben Shahn entered the museum collection, although Jacobson was less enthusiastic than expected about all of the acquisitions. When asked for his opinion on the State Department paintings after their arrival in September 1948, Jacobson complained that modern art "is shrouded in a prevailing gloom and is not 'happy' as art should be." He suggested some of the paintings "might have been done by some displaced persons from Europe," since Americans seemed to have a more positive disposition.[38] A former advocate for modernist experimentation, Jacobson found the pessimism, anxiety, and alienation of postwar art contrary to the optimism and buoyancy of spirit he believed that the visual arts should express. He had become the rearguard.

Oscar and Jeanne remained active in the arts in the 1950s, especially in the promotion of Native American and Oklahoman art. In 1950, they published the two-volume set *Les Peintres Indiens d'Amerique (American Indian Painters)* and followed in 1953 with the article "Early Oklahoma Artist," which traced the art history of the state from George Catlin's 1834 visit to Indian Territory to Heinrich Balduin Möllhausen's drawings for the 1853 transcontinental survey conducted by Amiel W. Whipple. And in 1952, Jacobson collaborated on the portfolio *North American Indian Costumes, 1564–1950* with Yanktonai Nakota artist Oscar Howe, who was completing his Master of Fine Arts at the OU School of Art.[39]

When Jacobson decided to retire in 1952, the university recognized the value of his contributions by renaming the art museum building for him. Jacobson Hall continued to house the museum until the completion of the Fred Jones Jr. Memorial Art Center in 1971 and now serves as the Visitor Center for the campus.[40] At seventy, Jacobson's career as both a painter and culture broker had slowed, but his legacy was very much apparent. The Philbrook Art Center hosted solo exhibitions in October 1957, during the semi-centennial of the state, for Jacobson and three other significant Oklahoma artists: Doel Reed, Adah Robinson, and Pauline Townsend. Jacobson was unable to attend the opening because of ongoing poor health, having suffered from a cerebral hemorrhage in March 1955. The solo exhibitions were part of a much larger program that included the installation *Artists of Early Oklahoma*, a survey that focused on painting in the territory and state from 1896 to 1934.[41] Within this context, Jacobson's solo exhibition implicitly acknowledged his role in fostering the arts in Oklahoma.

The OU Museum of Art mounted the most ambitious exhibition of Jacobson's career since 1941, with the 1961 *Oscar Brousse Jacobson Retrospective Exhibition* (fig. 16), which included forty-six paintings and drawings that traced Jacobson's career from his days at Yale to his recent work. One of the most important paint-

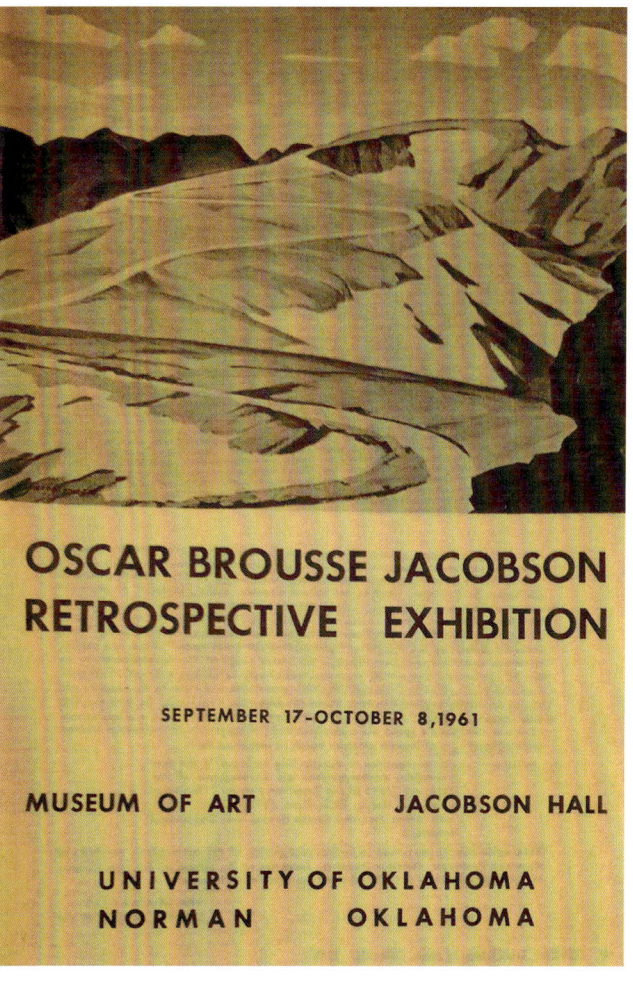

Fig. 16

Cover of *Oscar Brousse Jacobson Retrospective Exhibition*, 1961, Museum of Art, Jacobson Hall, University of Oklahoma

ings of his career, *Trail Ridge Road in June* (fig. 58), appeared on the cover and spoke to Jacobson's affection for Colorado. The retrospective was the last major event of Jacobson's career prior to his death in 1966 at the age of eighty-four.

With Jeanne's passing in 1967, Yolande and Yvonne hired Heldenbrand and Anderson Auctioneers, Inc. to offer a public sale of Jacobson's remaining inventory of 143 paintings. The highest price went to Jacobson's 1920 *Enchanted Mesa* (fig. 22), which was valued at twenty-five hundred dollars but went for a thousand. Many of the paintings went for less than estimated, but auctioneer Andy Anderson considered the auction a success with a total sale value between twenty-five and thirty thousand dollars. Craig Sheppard, Yolande's husband, opined, "We might have done better in San Francisco or Los Angeles or somewhere else, but I feel, as my wife does, that the paintings belong in Oklahoma where he [Jacobson] lived and had so many friends."[42]

Jacobson had left an indelible mark on the state. For fifty years, Oscar Jacobson had been a key figure in the cultural development of Oklahoma. He had increased the faculty and student enrollment at the OU School of Art dramatically, established an art museum on campus, and generally encouraged the visibility of the arts in the state through his participation in organizations such as the Association of Oklahoma Artists. Jacobson was a prolific artist and was largely sympathetic to modernist experimentation, even though his own work was somewhat conservative in its adherence to Post-Impressionist techniques. However, his role in promoting a cosmopolitan awareness of global cultures, especially Asian, Middle Eastern, and Native American, is, arguably, the most significant aspect of his career. Through lectures and exhibitions, he introduced Oklahoma audiences to the complexity of different cultures and encouraged his audience to appreciate and find value in the unfamiliar. As a culture broker, Oscar Brousse Jacobson contributed greatly to the enrichment of both Oklahoma and the Southwest, and his artistic legacy lives on—today and for future generations—through his paintings, his advancement of Native American art and art history, public art murals across Oklahoma and Texas, and the University of Oklahoma's Fred Jones Jr. Museum of Art. ✤

Notes

1 The primary defense of modernism may be found in Oscar Brousse Jacobson, "The Meaning of Modernism in Art," *American Magazine of Art* 15, no. 1 (January 1924): 697-703.

2 Jacobson's official full name was Anders Oskar Jakobson, according to his baptismal records, but for most of his life he went by Oscar Brousse Jacobson, abandoning his first name and taking his wife's maiden name for his middle. For clarity, he will be addressed here as Oscar Brousse Jacobson. O. R. Landelius, "Oscar B. Jacobson, pedagog och konstnar," *Utlandessvenskarna Forening* (Nov. 11, 1955): 15, in the Oscar B. Jacobson Collection, Western History Collections Library, University of Oklahoma, Norman, Oklahoma. The Oscar B. Jacobson Collection at the Western History Collection (WHC) consists of three archival boxes, J-1, J-13, and J-18, that hold eighty-nine folders ranging from published documents to government records, and Jacobson's typed manuscripts.

3 Landelius, "Oscar B. Jacobson," 14–16; Jeanne d'Ucel, *Memoir and Biographical Writings*, ca. 1962, box 1, folder 1, Oscar B. Jacobson Collection, Oklahoma Historical Society (OHS), Oklahoma City, 33. This collection consists of scrapbooks containing published information regarding Oscar Jacobson's life and accomplishments. The sources include thousands of articles from newspapers, magazines, journals, and pamphlets, in addition to other primary and secondary sources. Most of the time, each source's origin is indicated on the document itself, but almost no page numbers are provided. Box 1–4 of the Jacobson Collection at OHS contains biographical notes in eight folders, most of which were typed by Jacobson's wife, Jeanne. Her manuscript closely follows the chronology of the scrapbooks and can almost be used interchangeably. The fifth box includes miscellaneous items and an additional scrapbook.

4 d'Ucel, *Memoir and Biographical Writings*, 35.

5 Ibid., 33.

6 Ibid., 37.

7 d'Ucel, "About Indians," box 1, folder 5, 1.

8 d'Ucel, *Memoir and Biographical Writings*, 37.

9   Ibid.; "Program for the Fourth," *Lindsborg News-Record*, July 2, 1902, in Jacobson and d'Ucel scrapbooks, vol. 1, "1902–11," box 1.

10   Untitled newspaper clipping, *Lindsborg Record*, June 1, 1903, in Jacobson and d'Ucel scrapbooks, vol. 1, "1902–11," box 1.

11   d'Ucel, *Memoir and Biographical Writings*, 39–40. May Frank, "A New Story of Oil on Oklahoma," *Daily Oklahoman*, Feb. 24, 1924, D-1.

12   d'Ucel, *Memoir and Biographical Writings*, 39–40; George Souris, "Globe-Trotting O. B. Jacobson Sticks to Landscape Painting," *Sooner Magazine* 19, no. 10 (June 1947): 6–7; and Frank, "A New Story."

13   d'Ucel, *Memoir and Biographical Writings*, 39.

14   d'Ucel, *Memoir and Biographical Writings*, 40, and Frank, "A New Story."

15   d'Ucel, *Memoir and Biographical Writings*, 42 and untitled newspaper clipping, *Lindsborg News-Record*, June 27, 1905, in Jacobson and d'Ucel scrapbooks, vol. 1, "1902–11," box 1.

16   "'Sunset' a Success," *New Haven Palladium*, Dec. 21, 1907, and other articles review the performances in Jacobson and d'Ucel scrapbooks, vol. 1, "1902–11," box 1.

17   "Real Thing in these Costumes," *Lindsborg News-Record*, Dec. 1907, in Jacobson and d'Ucel scrapbooks, vol. 1, "1902–11," box 1. The article mentions that Jacobson got the headdress at great danger since he stole it from a tipi; however, Jacobson wrote that the claim was a lie next to the article in the scrapbook.

18   d'Ucel, *Memoir and Biographical Writings*, 64.

19   Ibid., 45–46.

20   d'Ucel, "About Indians," 1.

21   Paul A. F. Walter, secretary of the School of American Archaeology, to Jacobson, Dec. 6, 1917, and Sheldon Parsons to Jacobson, Jan. 8, 1918, Jacobson Papers, box J-1, folder 13, WHC.

22 d'Ucel, "About Indians," 42–43.

23 "Western Artists Displaying Pictures," *Oklahoma Daily*, Jan. 14, 1916, 1; "Faculty Club Meets," *Oklahoma Daily*, Dec. 10, 1917, in Jacobson and d'Ucel scrapbooks, vol. 2, "1911–18," box 2.

24 "Crude Oil Means Crude Art; Professor Mourns Because Oklahoma Is Not Refined," *Daily Oklahoman*, May 17, 1919, 1.

25 "Art Department Shows Remarkable Increase," *Oklahoma Daily*, Oct. 19, 1920, 1, and "Jap Uniforms Art Feature," *Oklahoma Daily*, Jan. 14, 1921, 1.

26 G. M., "Group of Asiatic Art Works Shown," *Norman Transcript*, Feb. 1925, in Jacobson and d'Ucel scrapbooks, vol. 3, "1918–26," box 3.

27 d'Ucel, *Memoir and Biographical Writings*, 101.

28 See Janet Catherine Berlo's essay in this volume for further information on the Jacobsons' North African collection.

29 d'Ucel, *Memoir and Biographical Writings*, 152.

30 Ibid.

31 "Art Work of Kiowa Indians is Exhibited," *Oklahoma Daily*, Feb. 17, 1927, in Jacobson and d'Ucel scrapbooks, vol. 4, "1926–32," box 4.

32 "State Indians' Art to Be Shown Nationally," *Daily Oklahoman*, Aug. 7, 1927, A-11; "Indians' Art Work Gains Recognition," *Oklahoma Daily*, Nov. 29, 1927, 2.

33 d'Ucel, "About Indians," 11–13, and "Indian Tribe Adopts Artist as Member," *Christian Science Monitor*, Aug. 20, 1928, in Jacobson and d'Ucel scrapbooks, vol. 4, "1926–32."

34 D'Ucel, box 4, folder 3, p. 184.

35 See Nicholas A. Calcagno, *New Deal Murals in Oklahoma: A Bicentennial Project* (Miami, OK: Pioneer Print, 1976) and Alyson Greiner and Mark White, *Thematic Survey of New Deal Era Public Art in Oklahoma, 2003–04* (Oklahoma City: Oklahoma Historical Society, 2004).

36   d'Ucel, *Memoir and Biographical Writings*, box 1, folder 3, 217, and "Glimpses," box 4, folder 6, 62.

37   For further information on *Advancing American Art*, see Dennis Harper, Paul Manoguerra, and Mark Andrew White, *Art Interrupted: Advancing American Art and the Politics of Cultural Diplomacy* (Athens: The Georgia Museum of Art, 2012).

38   Riley Wilson, "Modern Art Is Too Gloomy, O.U. Professor Maintains," *Norman Transcript*, Sept. 21, 1948, 8.

39   See Berlo's essay in this volume for more information on the portfolios.

40   "Jacobson Hall Named to Honor Retired Teacher," *Norman Transcript*, Dec. 12, 1952, 1.

41   "Philbrook Observes Semi-Centennial with Exhibitions of Oklahoma Art," *Tulsa World*, Oct. 1, 1957, 15.

42   Jon Denton, "Jacobson Art Sale a Buyer's Market," *Daily Oklahoman*, June 24, 1968, 1–2.

Detail, see Fig. 12, page 22
Oscar Jacobson
U.S., born Sweden, 1882–1966
Untitled [Man on Camel], 1925

Fig. 17 (pages 33–34)
Oscar Jacobson
U.S., born Sweden, 1882–1966
The Pacific, 1952
Oil on canvas, 20 x 26¼ in.
Kirkpatrick Foundation, Oklahoma City

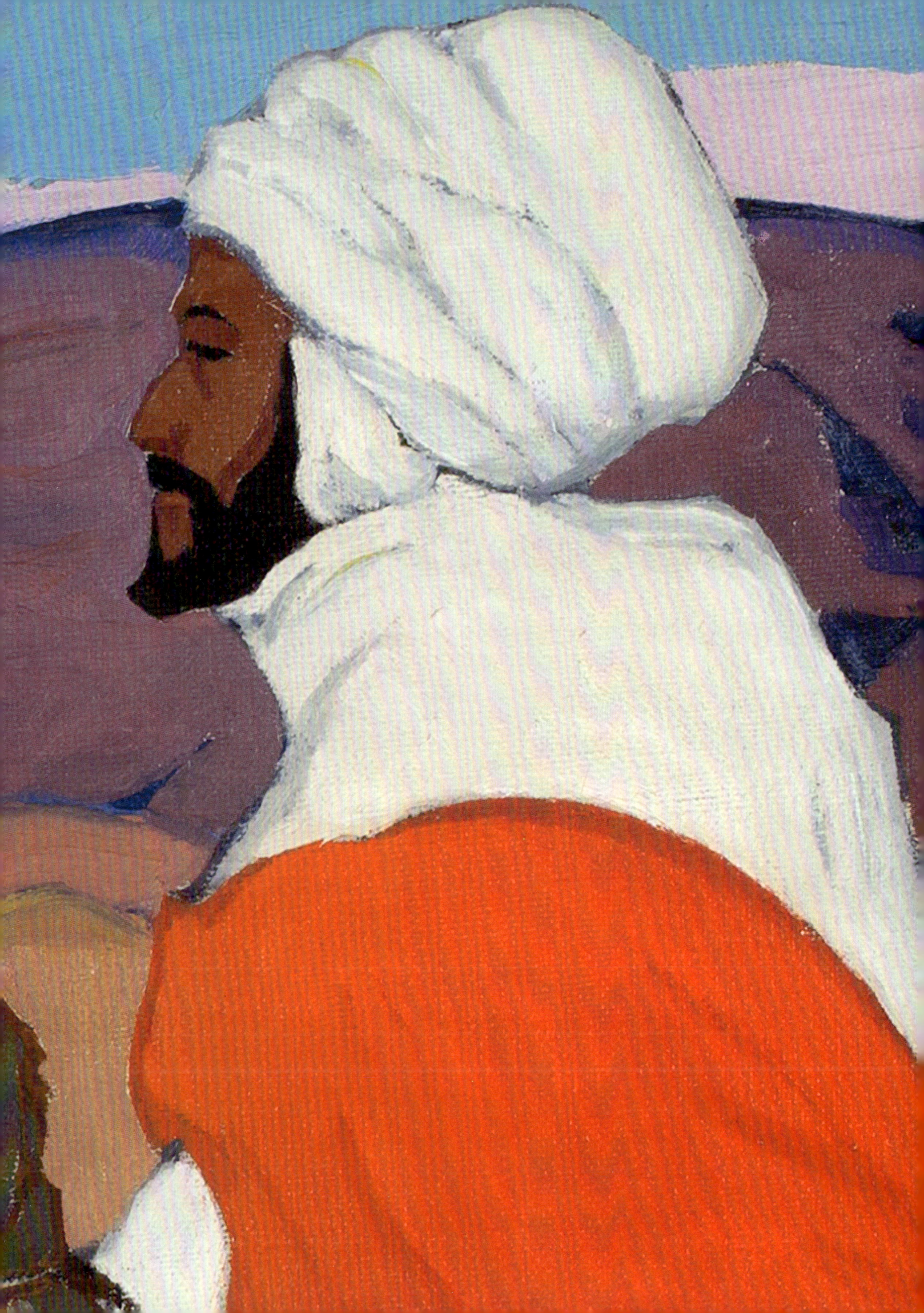

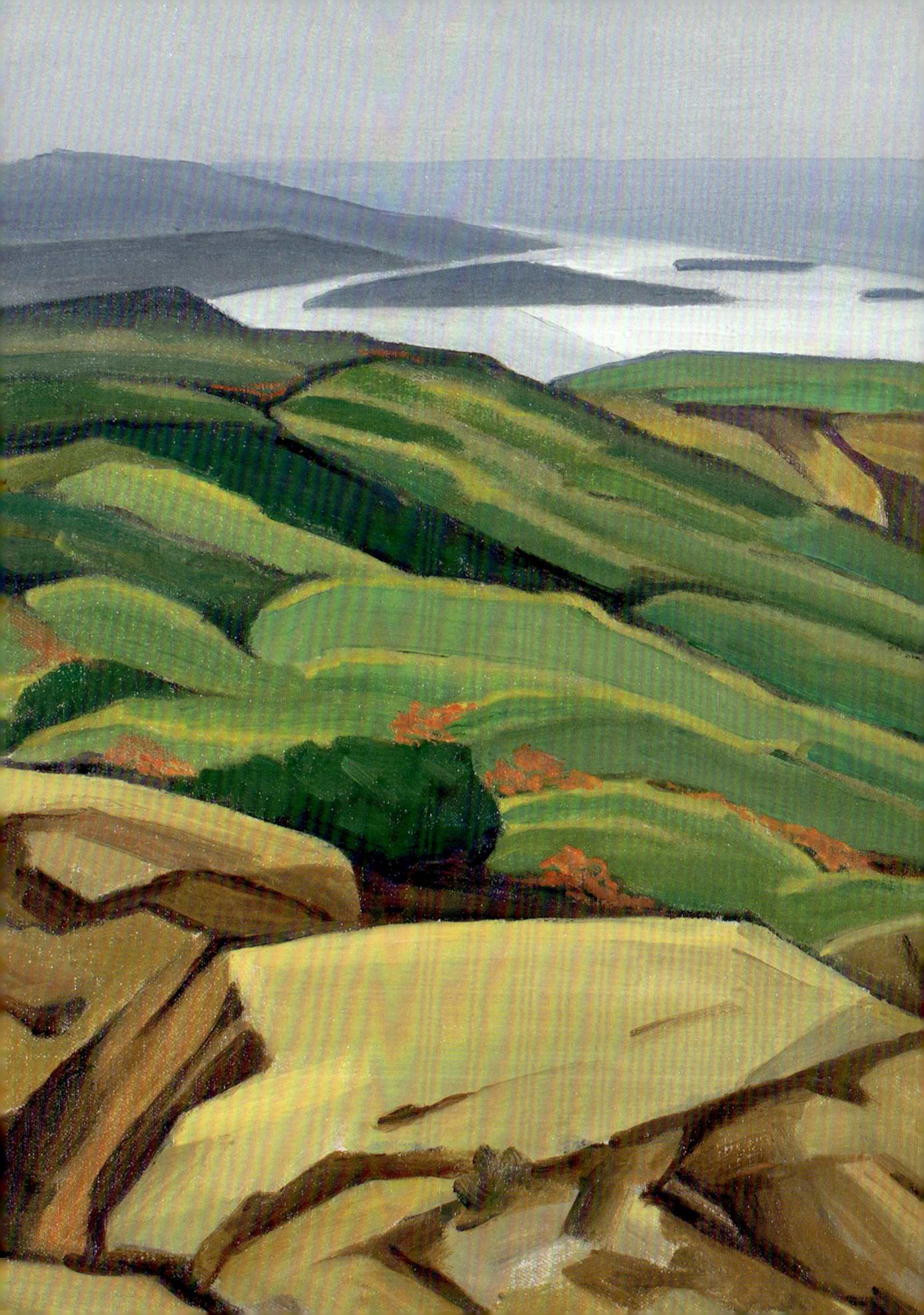

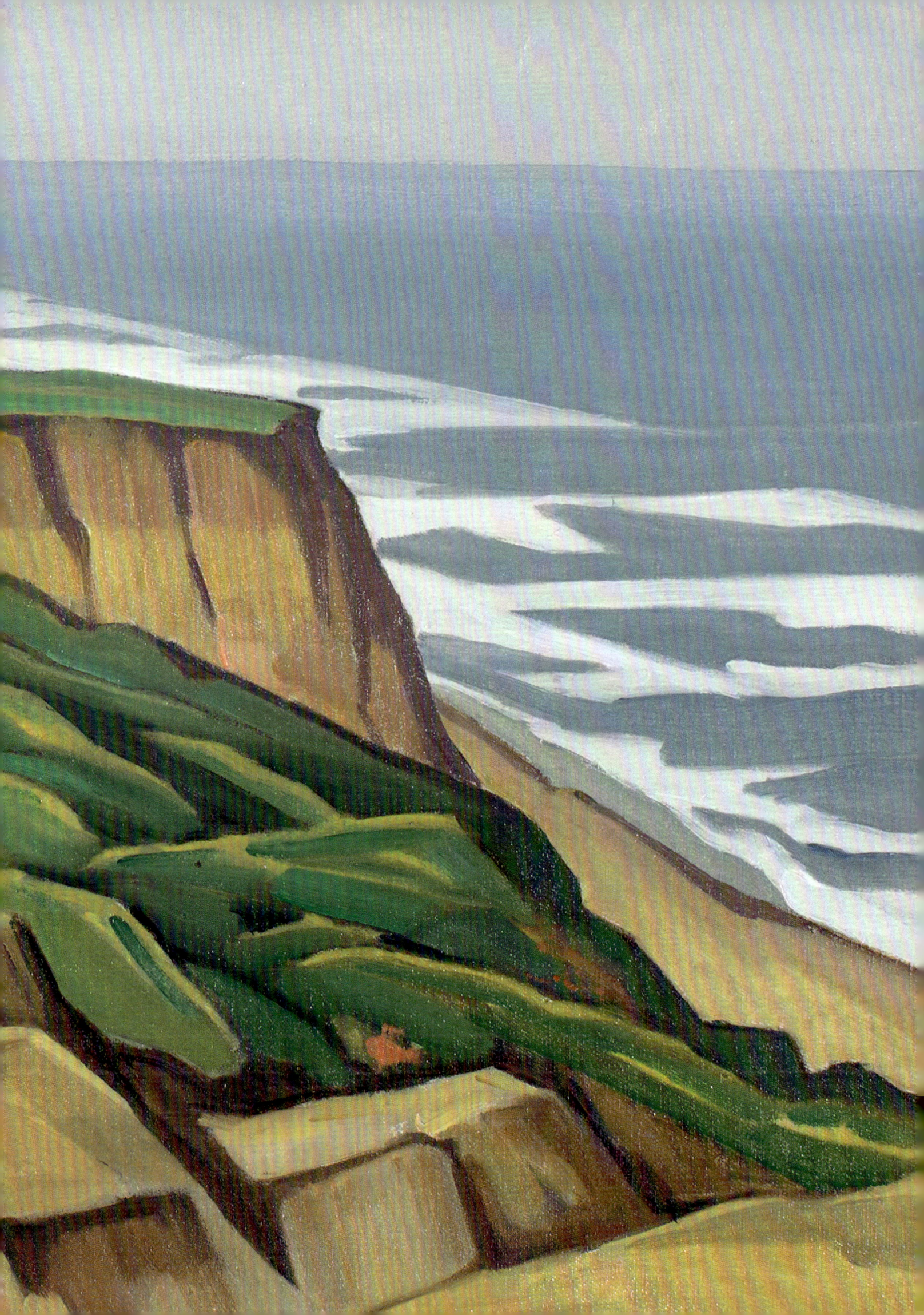

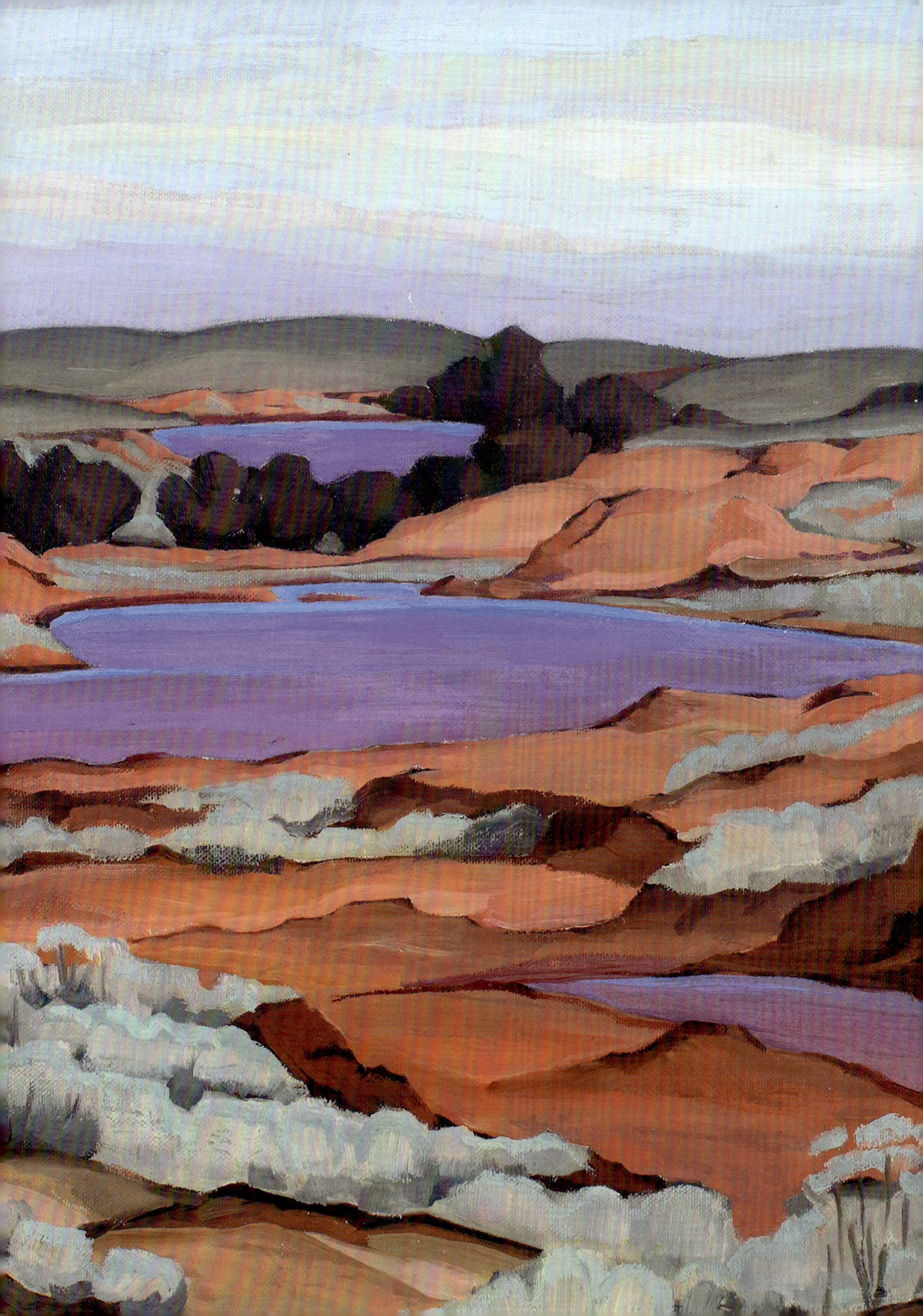

An Artist in the Wilderness

Oscar Brousse Jacobson and Worlds Unconquered

Mark Andrew White

O SCAR BROUSSE JACOBSON BEGAN HIS CAREER OSTENSIBLY AS A FIGURAL artist and devoted his early career to portraiture following his study at Yale University. But Jacobson gradually depopulated his paintings in the 1910s, after a trip through the American Southwest and just prior to his faculty appointment at the University of Oklahoma in fall 1915. Increasingly, in subsequent years, he looked to areas outside human settlement for inspiration and found solace in what he perceived as the uncorrupted and sometimes desolate wilderness of the West: the arid deserts and austere topography of Arizona and New Mexico, the grandeur of the Colorado Rockies, and the Spartan prairies of Oklahoma. This affection for the uninviting, and even inhospitable, spaces of the West eventually inspired Jacobson in 1926 to paint the Sahara, arguably one of the most antagonistic places on the planet.

Later, in 1948, Jacobson explained his seemingly hermitic relationship with the wilderness: "It may now be considered old fashioned but I seem to prefer to paint the world unconquered by man, unviolated by human greed, a world untouched by misery and despair. Every summer for 30 years or more, I have wandered over the south-western States attempting as best I may, by means of paint, to interpret their dramatic beauty, not neglecting the lyrical melancholy charm of Oklahoma's winters."[1]

As his comments make clear, Jacobson deliberately sought subjects that implied a lack of human presence or influence, partly as a condemnation of human greed and capitalist exploitation. He found sublime satisfaction in spaces still considered by many to be unusable, uninteresting, or uninhabitable wastelands, and he was among the vanguard of those hoping to change popular

Detail, see Fig. 46, page 69

Oscar Jacobson

U.S., born Sweden, 1882–1966

Oklahoma Mosaic, 1936

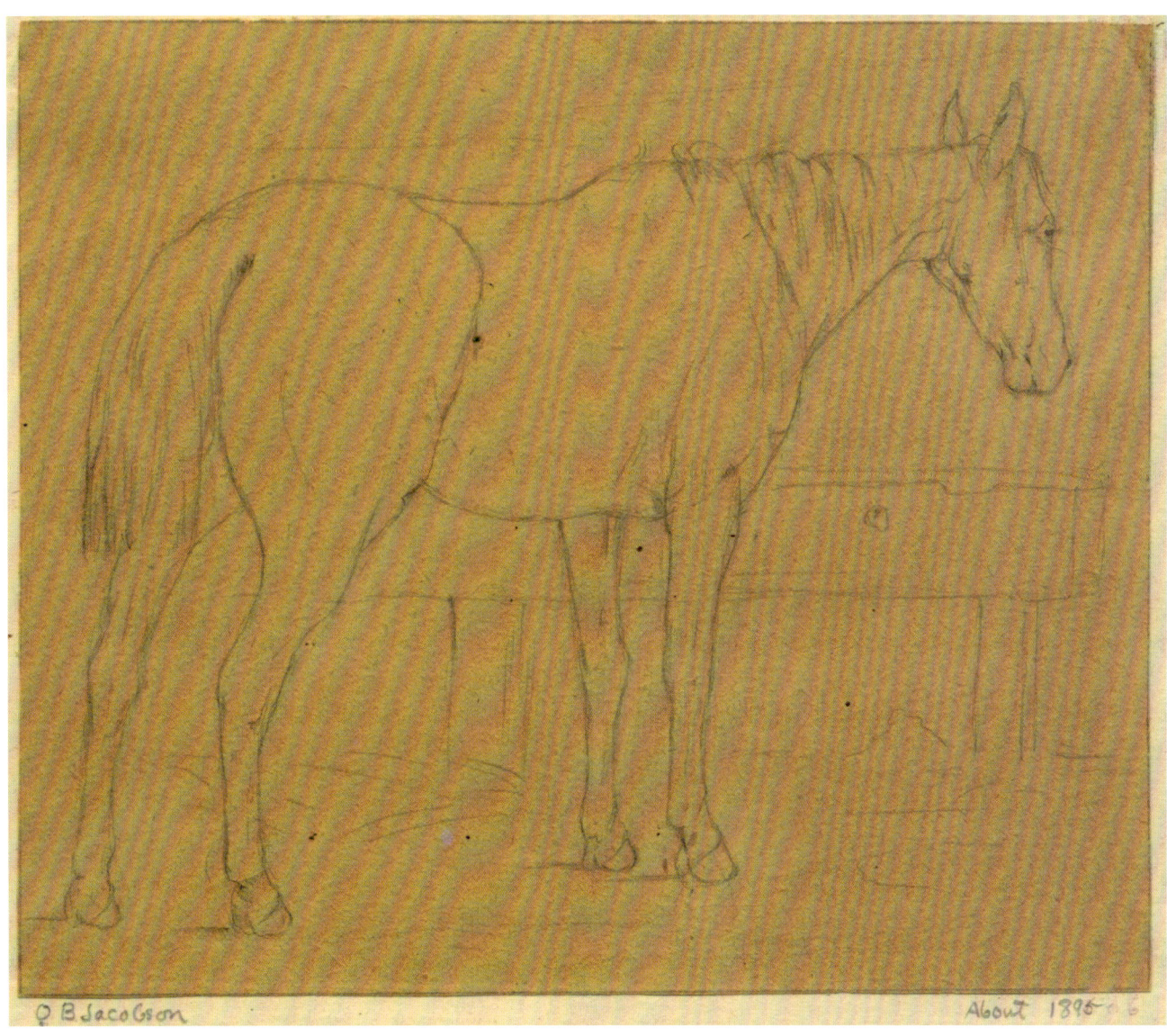

Fig. 18   Oscar Jacobson

U.S., born Sweden, 1882–1966

Untitled, 1895

Graphite on paper, $5\frac{11}{16}$ x $6\frac{7}{8}$ in.

Western History Collection, University of Oklahoma Libraries

opinion regarding the merits of the wilderness. To some degree, he followed the direction taken by his former teacher at Bethany College, Birger Sandzén, who achieved regional fame for his landscapes of western Kansas and Colorado. Yet Jacobson opted for a more severe approach, ultimately eschewing the thick impasto and kaleidoscopic brilliance of his mentor, in favor of an angular, planar aesthetic reminiscent of Paul Cézanne and akin to that of colleagues such as B. J. O. Nordfeldt and Jozef Bakos. Jacobson's ongoing fascination with the wilderness speaks to his lament for a bygone, boundless West, the product of a boyhood enthusiasm for the Old West mythos, and to his concerns for environmental preservation, which dovetailed with national efforts to establish parks, monuments, and reserves. Sympathetic to the conservationist ideals of Theodore Roosevelt, Jacobson valued nature untamed as a necessary spiritual relief from the debilitating effects of civilization, and his paintings demonstrate a sympathy with similar efforts to protect natural spaces that ultimately culminated in the Wilderness Act of 1964.

Jacobson's upbringing and education certainly informed his love for the wilderness. Jacobson's family relocated from Sweden to Lindsborg, Kansas, in 1890 after the eldest son extolled the agricultural potential of the land. Jacobson's father, aware that young Oscar longed for the sea that now seemed so remote, gave his son a horse that became the boy's companion. Jeanne d'Ucel, wife of the artist, reflected, "Together [Jacobson and his horse] roamed until, little by little, Oscar transferred some of his love of the sea to the long horizons of the Plains."[2] With his mustang Brady, who may be the subject of an 1895 drawing (fig. 18), Jacobson began to wander the West, embracing the lifestyle of a cowboy. He went so far as to organize his friends into a group variously titled the Crazy Ridge Wild West Riders, or Jakobson's Rough Riders out of homage to Theodore Roosevelt and his volunteer cavalry.[3] As an aspiring artist, Jacobson collected clippings of Western Americana that included everything from reproductions of the work of Charles Schreyvogel and Edwin Deming to program covers for Buffalo Bill Cody's Wild West.

His studies under Birger Sandzén at Bethany College fostered Jacobson's emerging talent, leading him ultimately to modernism, and further encouraged his aesthetic interest in the wilderness. Sandzén joined the faculty of Bethany College in 1894 after training with Swede Anders Zorn and French Symbolist Edmond François Aman-Jean, who introduced Sandzén to divisionism. Jacobson enrolled at Bethany College in 1895, and he began accompanying his instructor on hunting and sketching trips.

Although Sandzén's divisionist approach to landscape would not manifest in the work of his pupil until the 1910s, Jacobson demonstrated an early interest in portraying traits associated with the wilderness, such as isolation and inhospitality, in *At the Freezing Point (Vyd Fryspunkten)* (1901; fig. 1). Given the Swedish title, he likely based the painting on fishing communities near the family home in Västervik, but genre was not his primary interest. Frigid gray and blue tonalities and a stark composition emphasize the hostility of the climate and anticipate the Coloradoan subjects of his mature career. By the time he returned to Sweden as a subject in the 1910s, Sandzén's influence, with its expressive brushstroke and bright palette, dominated paintings such as *Winter Forest in Sweden* (ca. 1914; fig. 19).[4] An empathetic interpretation of light and color seem to have been Jacobson's primary interest, and vigorous, linear strokes in the secondary colors acknowledge not only Sandzén's impact, but also that of Vincent van Gogh. Apart from the stylistic change, *Winter Forest in Sweden* emphasizes a solitary experience of nature, in which no trace of human habitation appears. The viewer, like the artist, communes silently with the visual beauty of a pristine winter setting.

Understandably, the stylistic direction of *Winter Forest in Sweden* and other works of the period acknowledge Jacobson's embrace of the aesthetic thought of Post-Impressionism and other early modernist styles. A painting is not a faithful reproduction of everyday optical experience, Jacobson argued, but an arrangement of color and form that encourages an emotional and spiritual response. Using the term "pure art," he likened painting to music in its subjective appeal. Painting was the result of an exceptional, transcendent experience, as he claimed in a 1915 lecture: "It is the artist's duty to watch for the rare mood when nature wafts aside the commonplace and shows us her inner soul of sublime vision of beauty, and then try to reproduce it on canvas." He sought the spiritual in nature, but not in accord with a single spiritual tradition. A keen student of philosophy and religion, Jacobson apparently boasted knowledge of multiple religious traditions, although he never seems to have embraced a theosophical viewpoint. His rhetoric links him not only with Post-Impressionist ideas, expounded by artist Maurice Denis and the critic Roger Fry, but also contemporary modernist camps in the United States like the Stieglitz Circle; however, Jacobson was unprepared aesthetically to abandon his strong ties to representation, unlike his contemporaries Arthur Dove and Georgia O'Keeffe.[5] Jacobson's lofty beliefs in the spiritual and emotional import of painting were anchored in a tangible experience of nature, specifically the pristine wilds of western North America. Given his youthful admiration for Theodore Roosevelt's

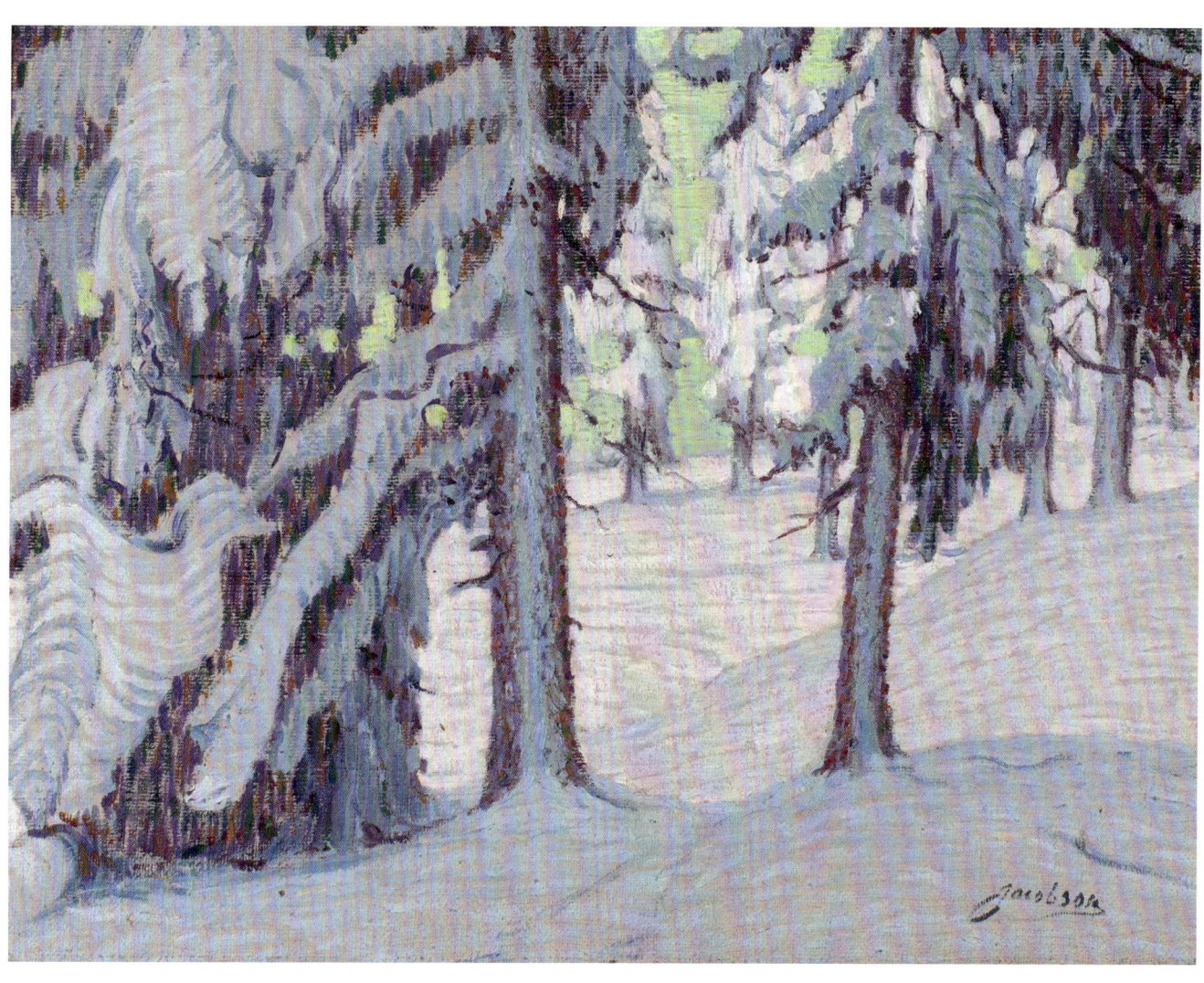

Fig. 19   Oscar Jacobson

U.S., born Sweden, 1882–1966

Winter Forest in Sweden, ca. 1914

Oil on canvas, 18 x 24 in.

Fred Jones Jr. Museum of Art, The University of Oklahoma, Norman;

Gift of Hal Johnson, 1983

military exploits, it is not surprising that Jacobson also subscribed readily to similar notions of art, nature, and conservation. Roosevelt's travels in the West convinced him of the need to protect natural resources and cultural heritage from potential destruction, leading eventually to the passage of the American Antiquities Act in 1906 and the creation of national monuments across the region. Fearful that Americans did not fully understand the legacy with which they were entrusted, Roosevelt implored his contemporaries to protect the sanctity of the wilderness for future generations: "Surely our people do not understand even yet the rich heritage that is theirs. There can be nothing in the world more beautiful than the Yosemite, the groves of giant sequoias and redwoods, the Canyon of the Colorado, the Canyon of the Yellowstone, the Three Tetons; and our people should see to it that they are preserved for their children and their children's children forever with majestic beauty unmarred."[6]

Preservation of that majestic beauty meant not only conservation but also the prevention of misuse, implicitly by industrial and business interests that sought to despoil for financial gain. Roosevelt condemned both destruction and commercialization of the landscape, arguing, "It is also vandalism wantonly to destroy or to permit the destruction of what is beautiful in nature, whether it be a cliff, a forest, or a species of mammal or bird. Here in the United States we turn our rivers and streams into sewers and dumping-grounds, we pollute the air, we destroy forests, and exterminate fishes, birds and mammals—not to speak of vulgarizing charming landscapes with hideous advertisements."[7]

Jacobson later echoed Roosevelt's rhetoric in his desire for "a world unconquered by man," and the artist expressed his sympathy for the former president in other ways. For example, the pamphlet for Jacobson's 1923 exhibition at the University of Oklahoma quoted Roosevelt's admission that "Art, or at least the art for which I care, must present the ideal through the temperament and the interpretation of the painter. I do not greatly care for the reproduction of landscapes which in effect I see whenever I ride or walk. I wish 'the light that never was on land or sea' in the pictures that I am to live with."[8] Taking nature as inspiration, the artist should express his or her sensibilities independent of any naturalistic impulse or didactic intention. Jacobson maintained his attachment to place, often giving his paintings geographically specific titles, yet the landscape always remained a platform for artistic invention. From the 1910s throughout his career, he used the western landscape as a vehicle for emotional and spiritual expression and gravitated increasingly to sites of isolation and inhospitality, free of overt human influence.

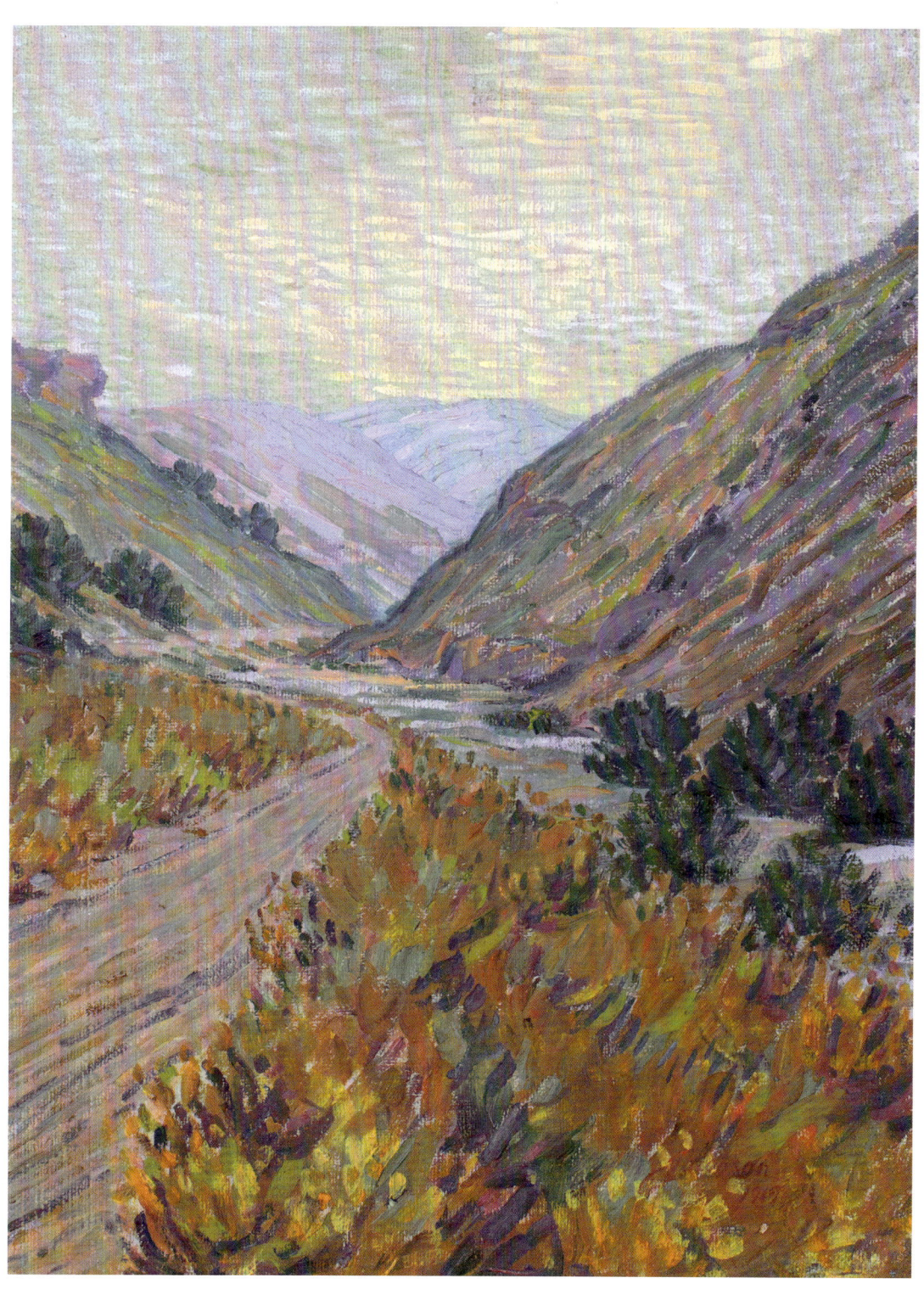

Fig. 20   Oscar Jacobson

U.S., born Sweden, 1882–1966

Snake River Cañon, ca. 1912

Oil on canvas, 24 x 18 in.

Collection of Kelly Knowlton

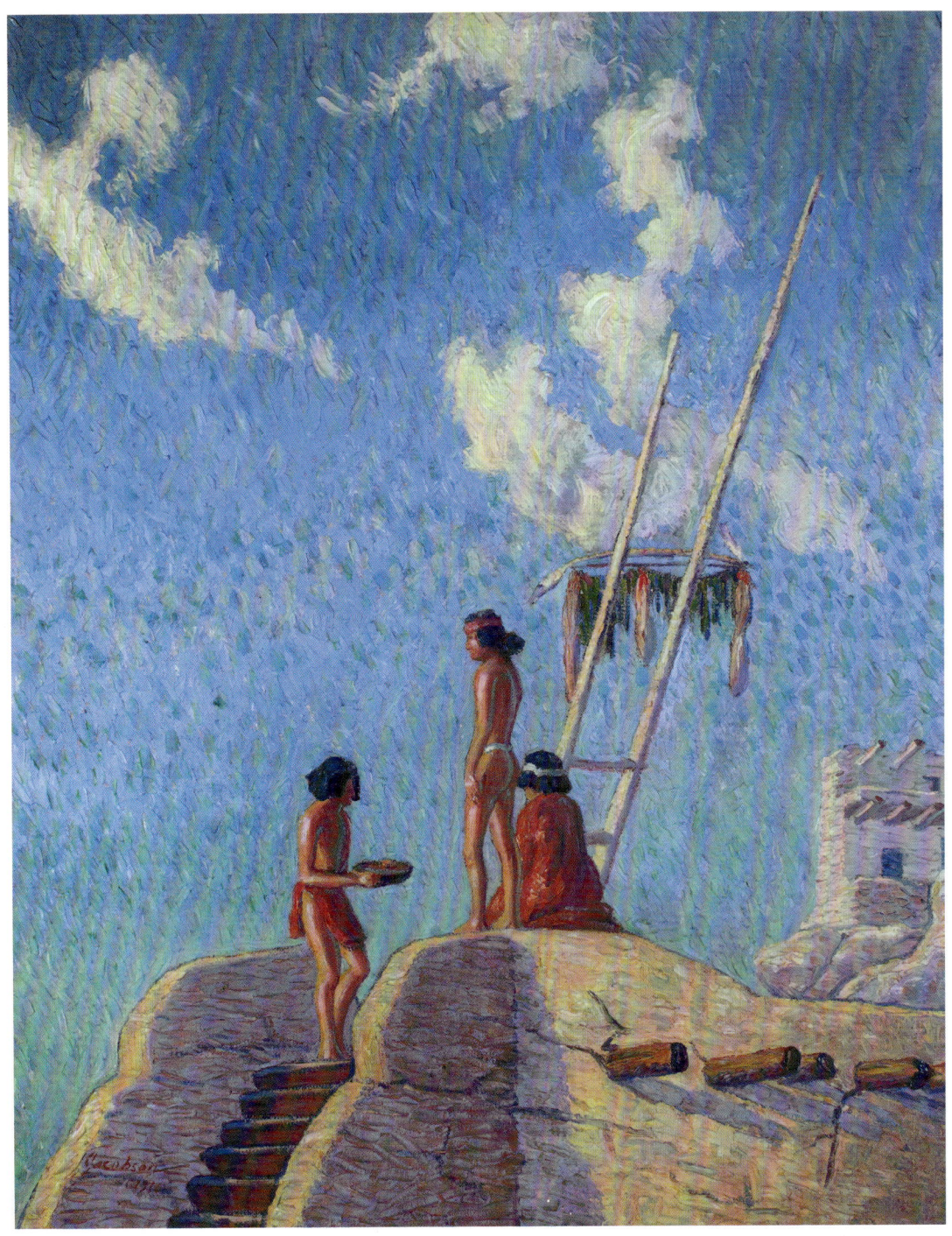

Fig. 21   Oscar Jacobson

U.S., born Sweden, 1882–1966

A Prayer for Rain, 1916

Oil on canvas, 34 x 28$\frac{1}{8}$ in.

McPherson, Kansas, School District #418

The Western landscape assumed increasing importance for Jacobson in the early 1910s, following his appointment at Washington State College in 1911. During his tenure there, he painted *Snake River Cañon* (ca. 1912; fig. 20) in southeastern Washington. Organized through a tension of parallel and perpendicular diagonals, *Snake River Cañon* suggests the dynamism of nature over the centuries, from the tectonic uplift of rock to the erosive power of water, which runs roughly through the center of the composition and created the canyon that inspired Jacobson's depiction. Jacobson invites the viewer to explore the flora and geology of the canyon via a worn trail at left that promises an immersive and solitary experience of the wilderness.

Clearly comfortable with the direction his work was taking, Jacobson included *Snake River Cañon* in his first exhibition at OU in October 1915.[9] He had accepted the position earlier that spring and, over the summer, he and his wife Jeanne d'Ucel drove leisurely through California, Arizona, and New Mexico to visit both national landmarks and the Panama-California Exposition in San Diego. They were taken especially with the New Mexico Building, designed by Isaac Hamilton Rapp and inspired largely by the San Estevan del Rey Mission Church at Acoma. D'Ucel recalled, "The exhibits inside were also chosen with unusual taste and discrimination. We studied these exhibits and we secured information about the Indian country where we spent the second half of the summer."[10] Although the Jacobsons visited other sights along the way, such as the Grand Canyon, their experience at the exposition led them to Acoma, and they spent much of the remaining summer in northwestern New Mexico.

Acoma provided countless opportunities for painting, and Jacobson painted the portrait of the Governor of Acoma (now lost), as well as ceremonial scenes such as *A Prayer for Rain* (1916; fig. 21).[11] Katzimo or Mesa Encantada also attracted Jacobson's attention, and he would paint the megalithic butte numerous times in subsequent years. His 1915 nocturne (fig. 6) may be the earliest, and Jacobson employed the stippling of Georges Seurat to animate the night sky. The evocative atmosphere likely alludes to the sense of mystery accorded to the Pueblo and its origins, and Acoma oral tradition insists on an earlier settlement atop the butte, the access to which was washed away in a flood.[12] Cultural lore aside, the ambiance of the painting suggests something of the ineffable, or that inner soul Jacobson sought in nature. He considered the arrangement of color and form analogous to music and even titled one of his images of the mesa *Largo*, out of homage to Antonín Dvorák's *New World Symphony*. The same holds true of a later, more ambitious treatment of the subject (1920; fig. 22), painted in the vein of van Gogh. *Enchanted Mesa* steps back in space to include more of

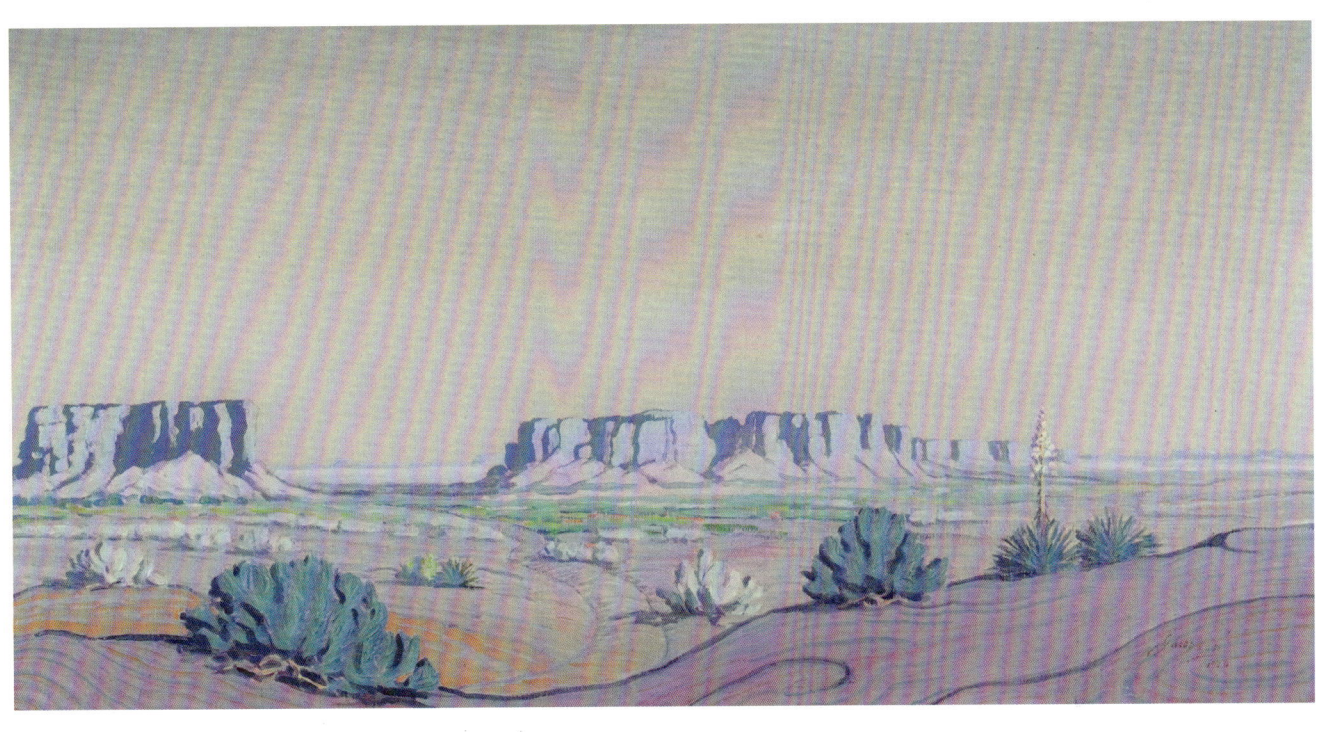

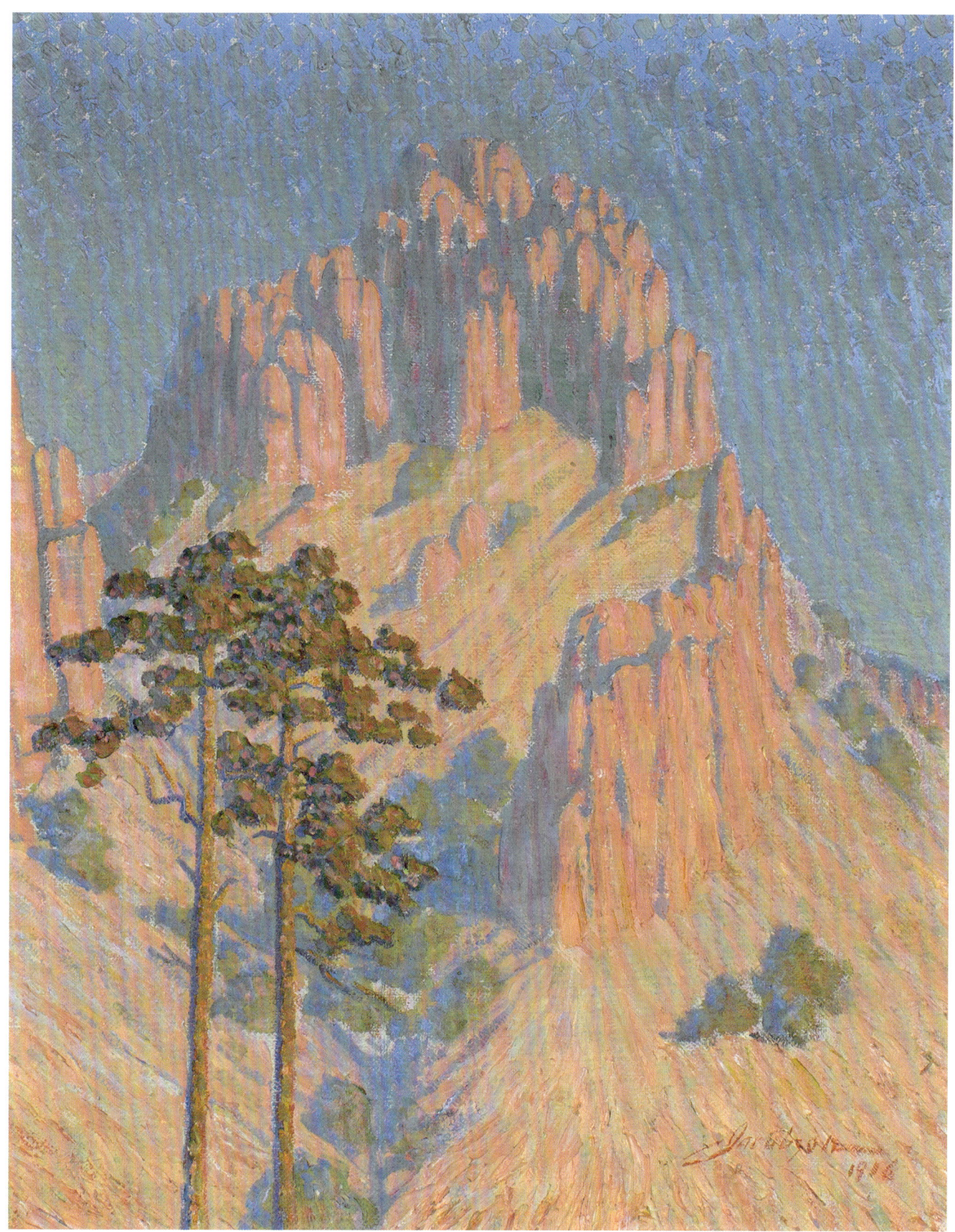

Fig. 23   Oscar Jacobson

U.S., born Sweden, 1882–1966

Pink Mountain, 1916

Oil on canvas, 22¹⁄₂ x 18 in.

Kirkpatrick Foundation, Oklahoma City

the surrounding terrain, especially a pair of wagon ruts that provide the viewer a route for exploring space. Although the ruts serve as a trace of human habitation, they are vacant of traffic, and the desert scrub has begun to grow across the tracks, implying disuse.

Over the next few years, Mesa Encantada and other images of the desert such as the so-called Pink Mountain, outside Sedona (1916; fig. 23), and the Grand Canyon came to dominate his interests. The pointillist stippling apparent in his depictions of Mesa Encantada gradually gave way to a broader stroke and angular approach to form akin to that of Sandzén, who shared his pupil's interest in the western landscape. *In the Painted Desert, Arizona* (1915; fig. 24), a painting that Jacobson owned, had a clear influence on his *Grand Canyon* (ca. 1920; fig. 25) with its masses of vibrant color, fluid lines, and simple masses.

Both Jacobson and Sandzén joined a growing group of artists interested in the aesthetic possibilities of the desert. Like the members of the Santa Fe and Taos art colonies, with whom they were friendly, the protégé and master believed that the desert possessed what Jacobson had called the sublime vision of beauty. The Southwestern deserts no longer lacked artistic appeal thanks in part to art historian John C. Van Dyke's influential 1901 book, *The Desert: Further Studies in Natural Appearances.* The product of a three-year exploration of the western deserts, Van Dyke's book championed the distinctive geography, vivid coloration, and perceived vacancy as aesthetic virtues worthy of investigation:

> In sublimity—the superlative degree of beauty—what land can equal the desert with its wide plains, its grim mountains, and its expanding canopy of sky! You shall never see elsewhere as here the dome, the pinnacle, the minaret fretted with golden fire at sunrise and sunset; you shall never see elsewhere as here the sunset valleys swimming in a pink and lilac haze, the great mesas and plateaus fading into blue distance, the gorges and canyons banked full of purple shadow. Never again shall you see such light and air and color; never such opaline mirage, such rosy dawn, such fiery twilight. And wherever you go, by land or by sea, you shall not forget that which you saw not but rather felt—the desolation and the silence of the desert.[13]

Van Dyke's picturesque descriptions of the topography and its hues, which betray a literary sympathy to the vibrant palettes of both Impressionism and Post-Impressionism, had an unquestionable influence on a younger generation of painters including Jacobson, whose desire to express the sublimity of the

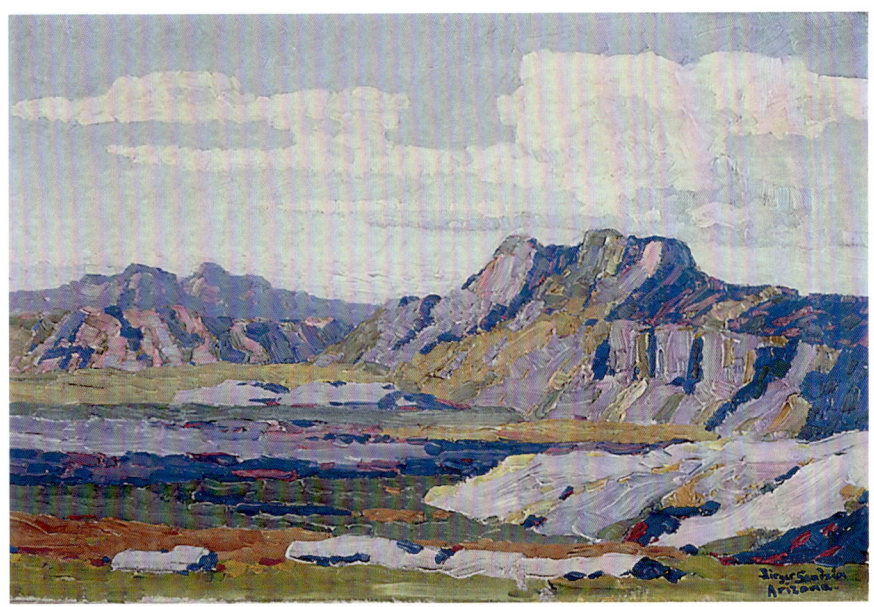

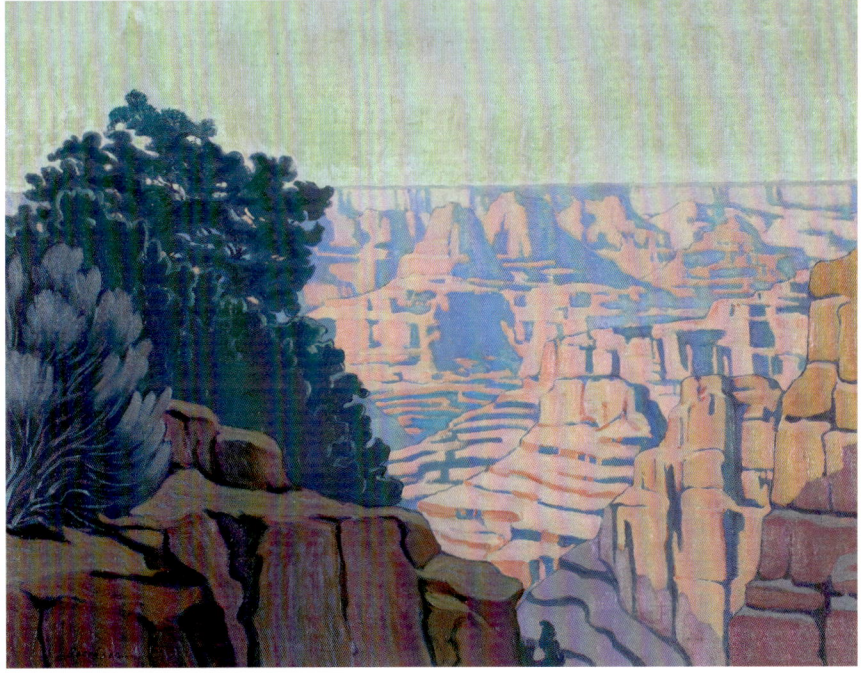

Fig. 24

Sven Birger Sandzen

U.S., born Sweden, 1871–1954

In the Painted Desert, Arizona, 1915

Oil on canvas, 16 x 24 in.

Fred Jones Jr. Museum of Art,

The University of Oklahoma, Norman;

Gift of the Oscar B. Jacobson Estate, 1977

Fig. 25

Oscar Jacobson

U.S., born Sweden, 1882–1966

Grand Canyon, ca. 1920

Oil on canvas, 26 x 34 in.

Fred Jones Jr. Museum of Art,

The University of Oklahoma, Norman;

Gift of Shirley McMillian

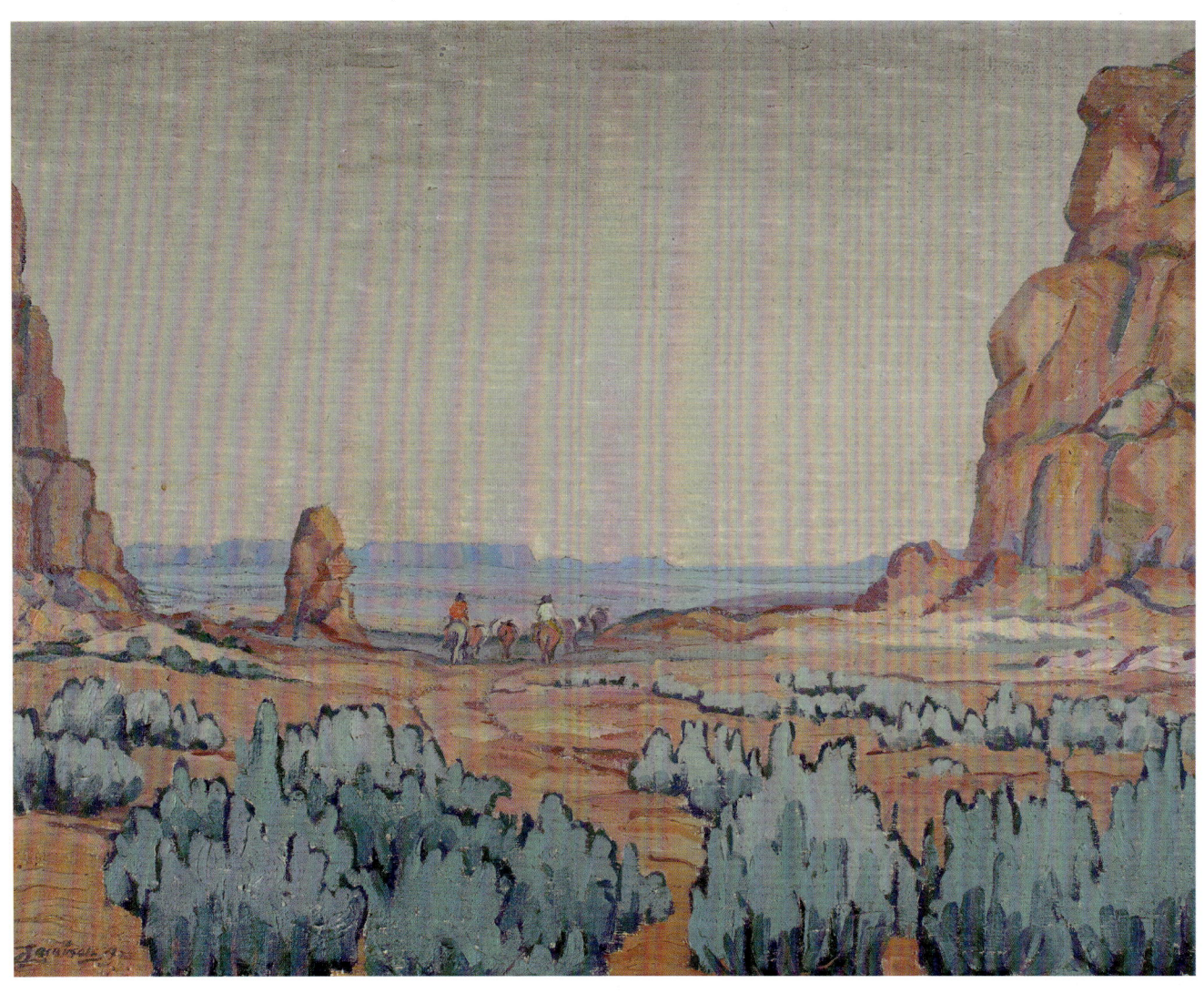

Fig. 26   Oscar Jacobson

U.S., born Sweden, 1882–1966

Navajo Going to the Snake Dance, 1922

Oil on canvas, $28\,^1{}_4$ x $36\,^1{}_8$ in.

Collection of Charity Burkhart

desert would echo pictorially Van Dyke's language. In a 1919 interview, Jacobson characterized his principal subject as the "great silent places of the wilderness."[14] The salient qualities of desolation and silence, which Van Dyke deemed an unforgettable experience, would gain greater expression in Jacobson's work as he continued to explore the West in search of subject matter.

During a period of intense activity in the early 1920s, Jacobson sought those desolate qualities among the angular yet vaguely sinuous contours of eroded washes, horizons broken by monumental mesas, and the extraordinary forms of the desert flora, especially sagebrush and saguaro, cholla, and ocatillo cacti. Paintings of the Arizona deserts such as *Navajo Going to the Snake Dance* (1922; fig. 26), *White Shadows—Among the Navajos* (1922; fig. 27), *Giant Cacti* (1922; fig. 28), *Apache Night* (1923; fig. 29), *The Garden of Allah* (1923; fig. 30), *Painted Desert—Northern Arizona* (fig. 31), *The Needles, Colorado Desert* (1923; fig. 32), and *Orabai Wash* (1925-26; fig. 33) evoke a palpable stillness, likely a product of Jacobson's solitary communion with the landscape. Critic Harry R. Burke likened Jacobson to a pioneer, who has confronted in his paintings the "vast spaces" and "elemental forces" of the West, effectively "settling the very spirit of that land before you." An unnamed critic for the *St. Louis Globe-Democrat* also perceived "the virility of an untamed and uncultivated new country" but lamented in those images the foreboding of change, that notion that all wilderness might be settled.[15]

Jacobson hoped to convey the sensations and moods of the wilderness through form and color and saw his project as inherently modernist. All of the aforementioned paintings, save for *Navajo Going to the Snake Dance*, *The Needles*, and *Orabai Wash*, were illustrated in his 1924 article, "The Meaning of Modernism in Art," which was adapted from a 1923 lecture for the American Federation of Arts. By including his own work in an article that spoke broadly of modernist art history and its ideology, he signaled his allegiance to its ideals. Jacobson acknowledged a formalist emphasis on aesthetic issues over content and associative ideas when he explained, "The ideal [modernists] are trying to realize is to relieve painting of the barnacles of literature, illustration, anecdote, history, and make it a purer art of color; to express ideas and emotions rather than facts and sentiment."[16] Valuing color and its arrangement over other concerns, Jacobson looked not only to Roger Fry, but also to James McNeill Whistler and the notions of aestheticism or "art for art's sake." Whistler's influence is apparent in Jacobson's affection for the nocturne, which remained popular among artists in the West into the 1920s.

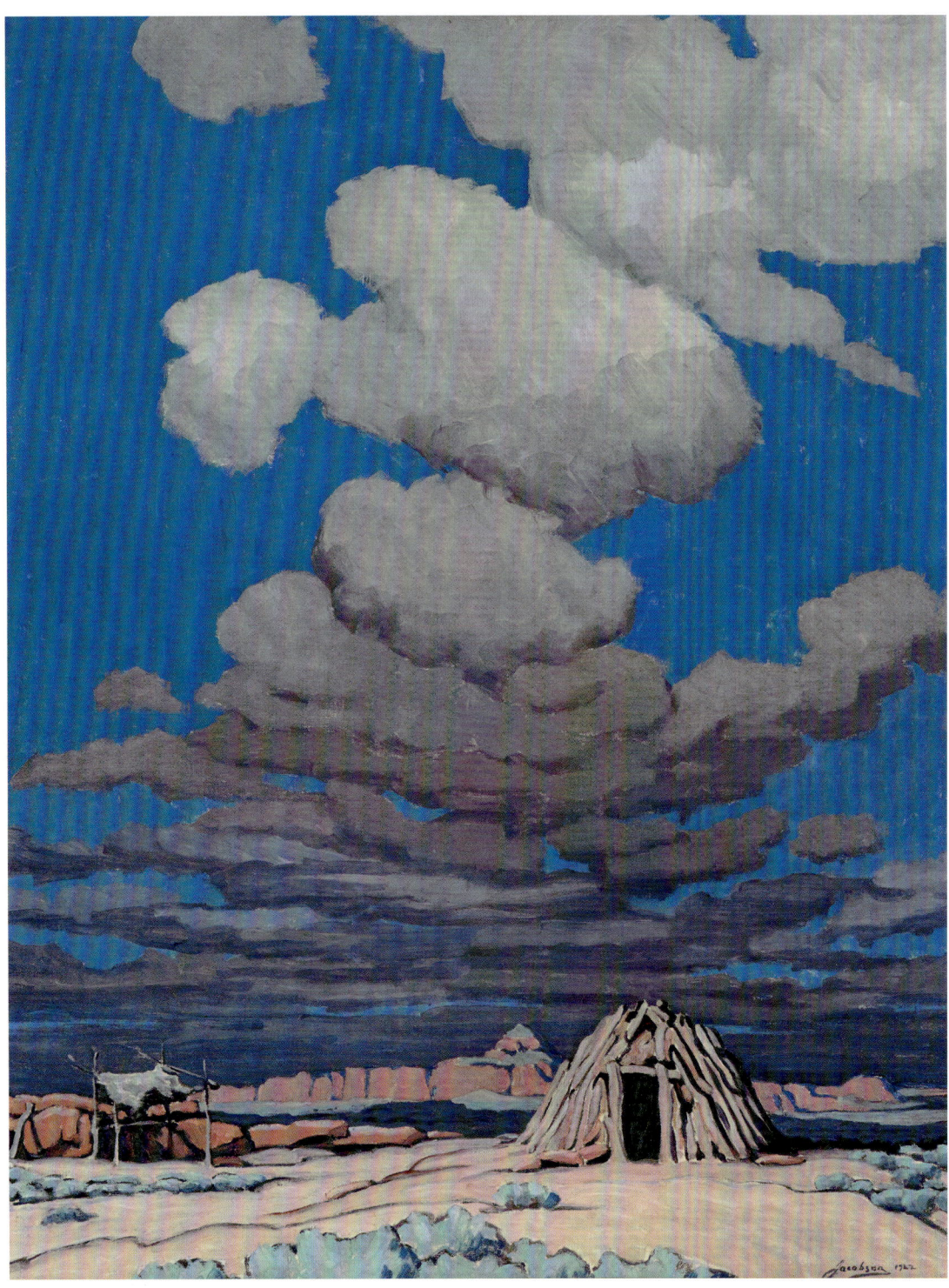

Fig. 27   Oscar Jacobson

U.S., born Sweden, 1882–1966

White Shadows—Among the Navajos, 1922

Oil on canvas, 48 x 38¾ in.

Gilcrease Museum, Tulsa, Oklahoma

#01.2535

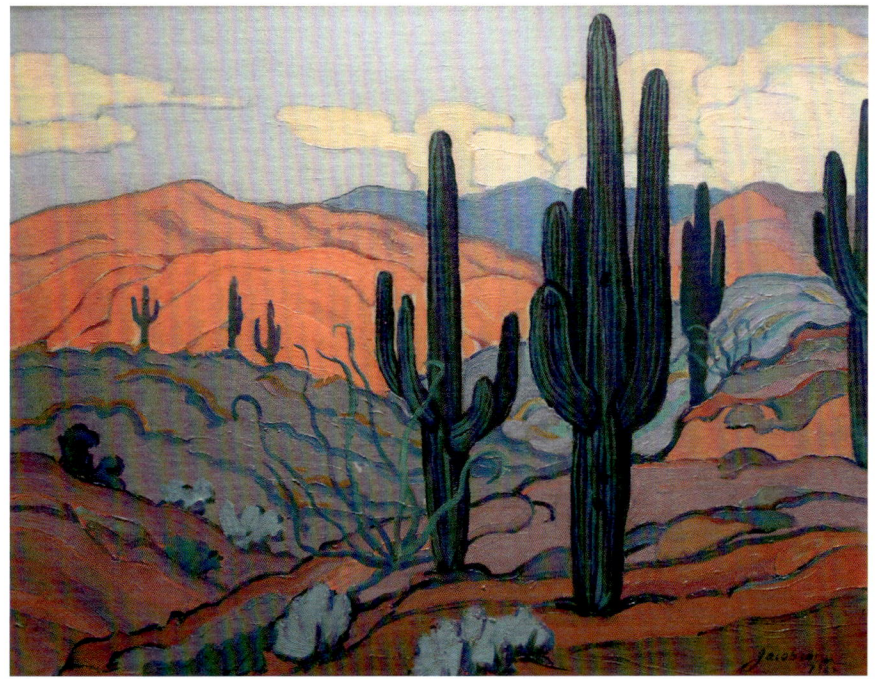

Fig. 28

Oscar Jacobson

U.S., born Sweden, 1882–1966

Giant Cacti, 1922

Oil on canvas board, 20 x 25 ¾ in.

Mabee-Gerrer Museum of Art, Shawnee, Oklahoma

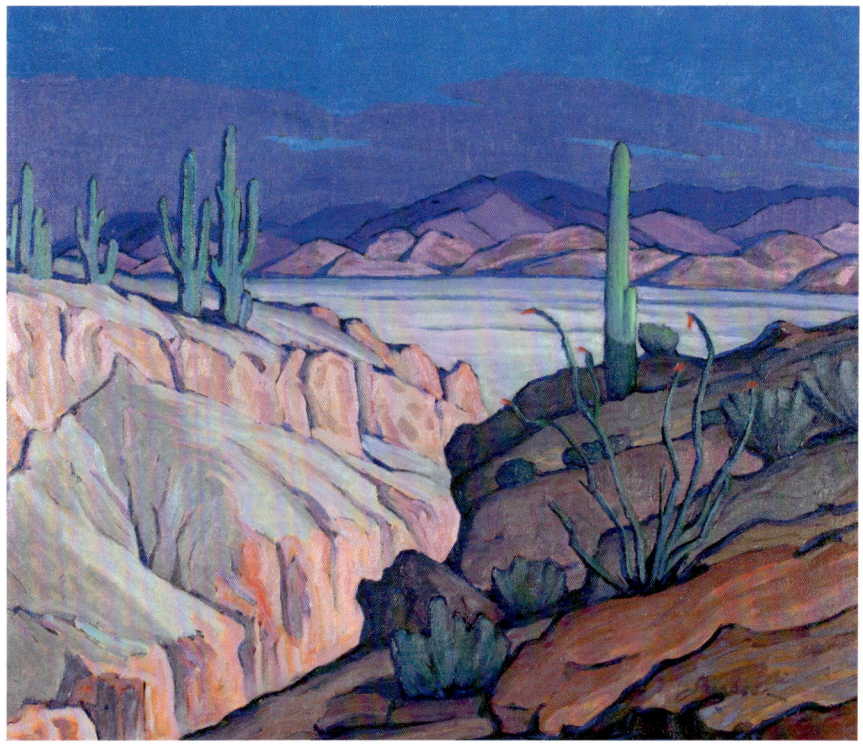

Fig. 29

Oscar Jacobson

U.S., born Sweden, 1882–1966

Apache Night or *Arizona Night*, 1923

Oil on canvas, 28 x 34 in.

Private collection

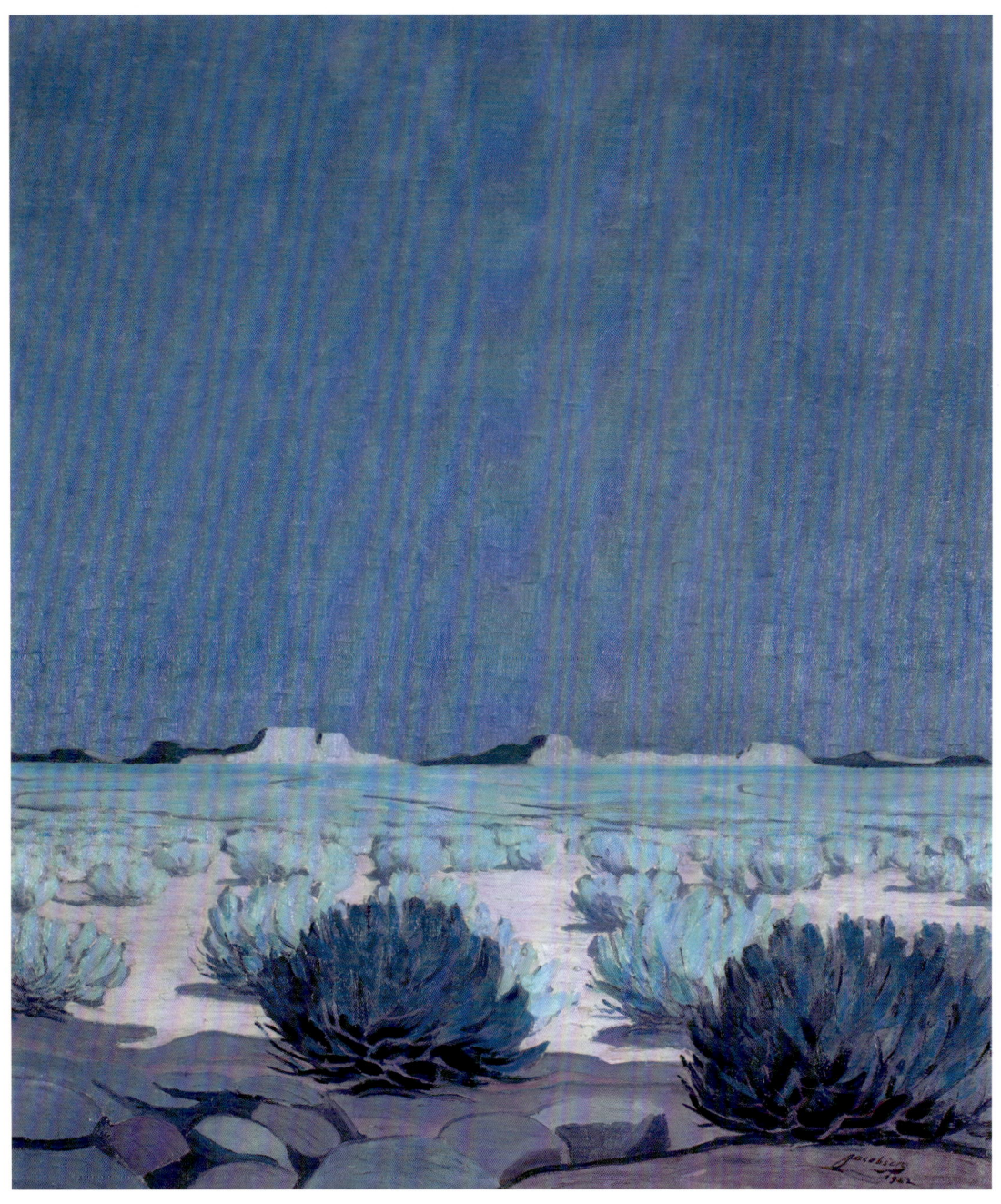

Fig. 30   Oscar Jacobson

U.S., born Sweden, 1882–1966

The Garden of Allah, 1923

Oil on canvas, 40 x 34 in.

Private collection

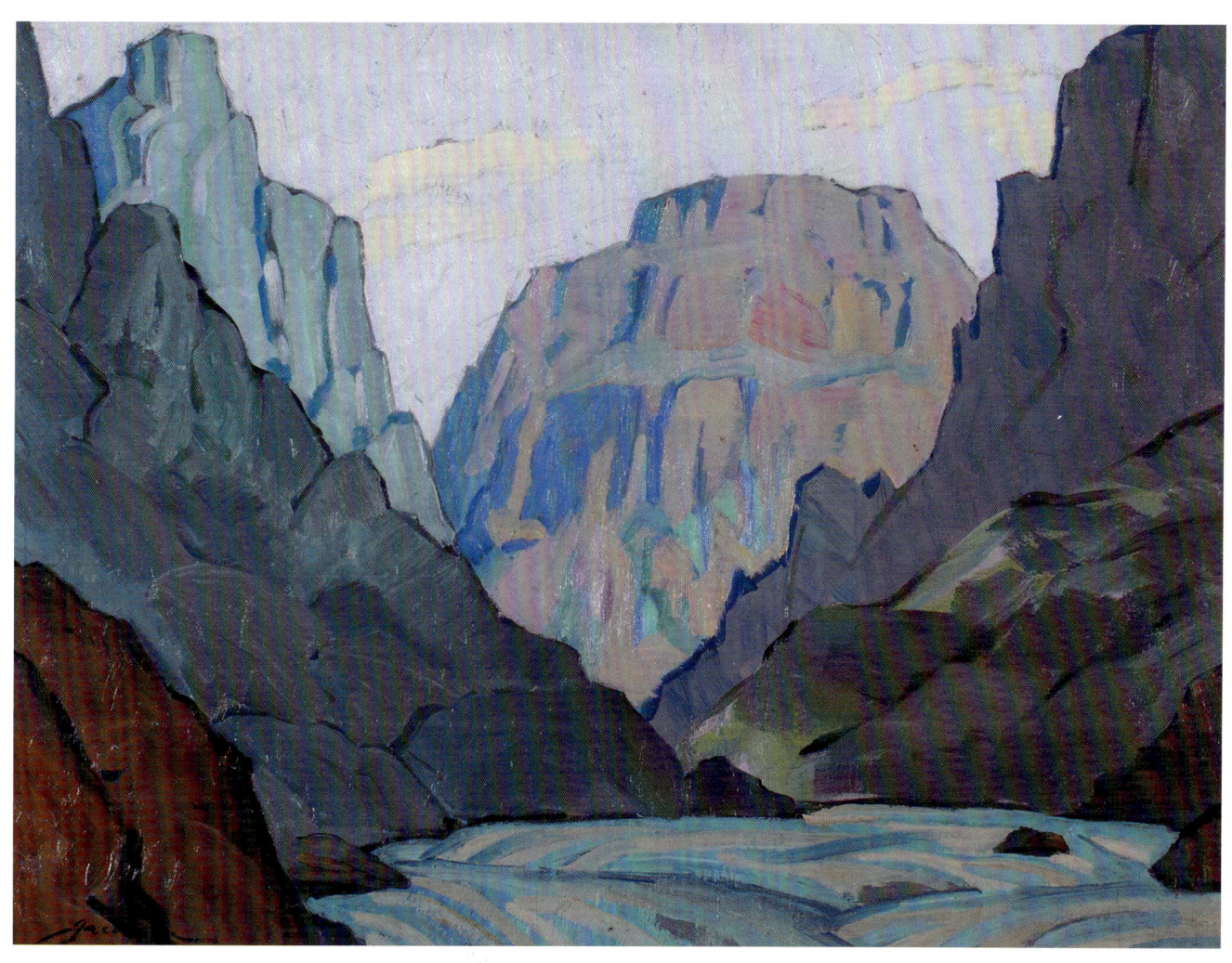

Fig. 31   Oscar Jacobson

U.S., born Sweden, 1882–1966

Painted Desert—Northern Arizona or *Down in the Canyon*, 1923

Oil on canvas board, 22³⁄₄ x 28³⁄₄ in.

Kirkpatrick Foundation, Oklahoma City

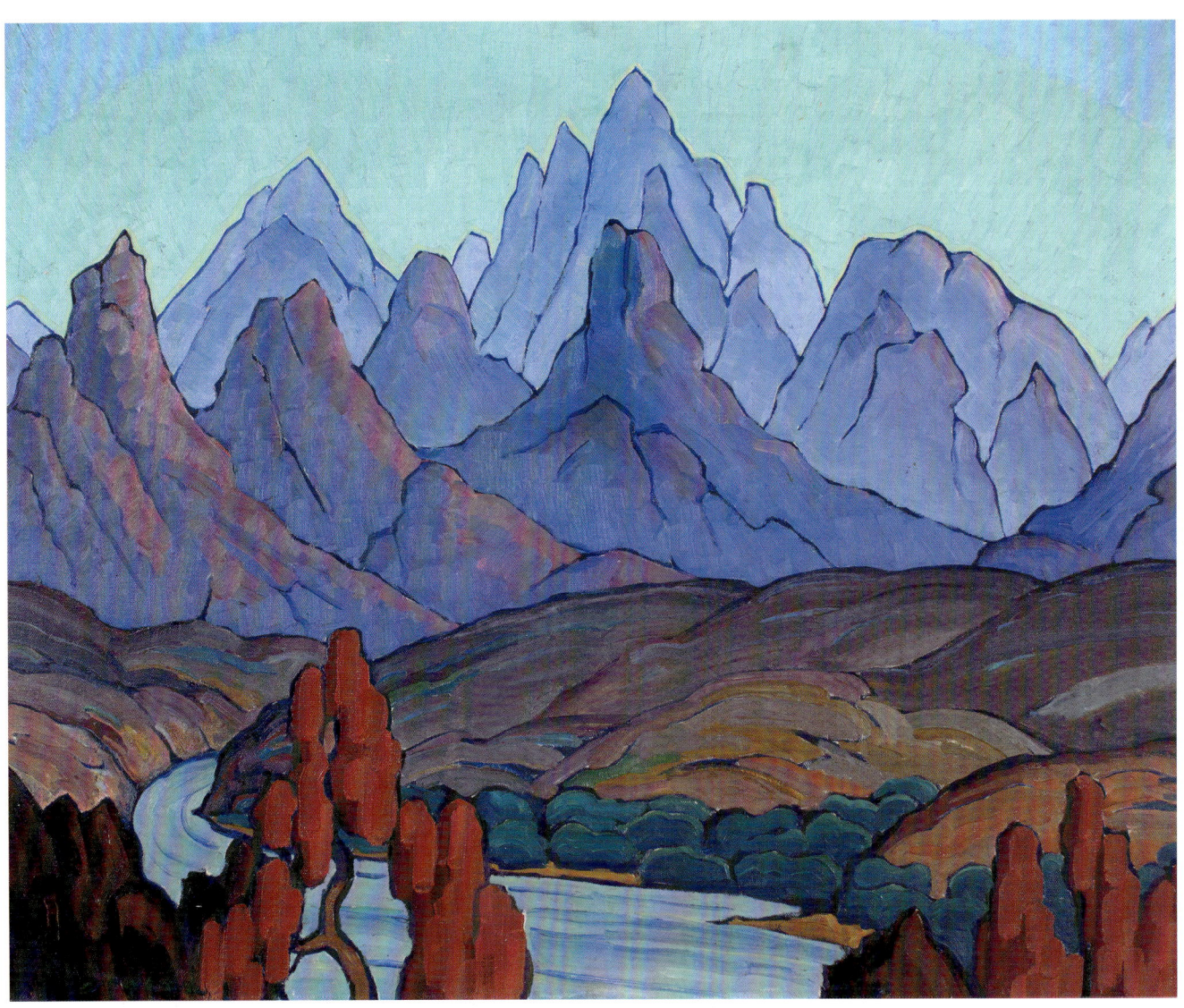

Fig. 32   Oscar Jacobson

U.S., born Sweden, 1882–1966

The Needles, Colorado Desert, ca. 1923

Oil on canvas, 29 x 36 in.

Oklahoma City Museum of Art.

Gift from the Oklahoma Art League, 1966.013

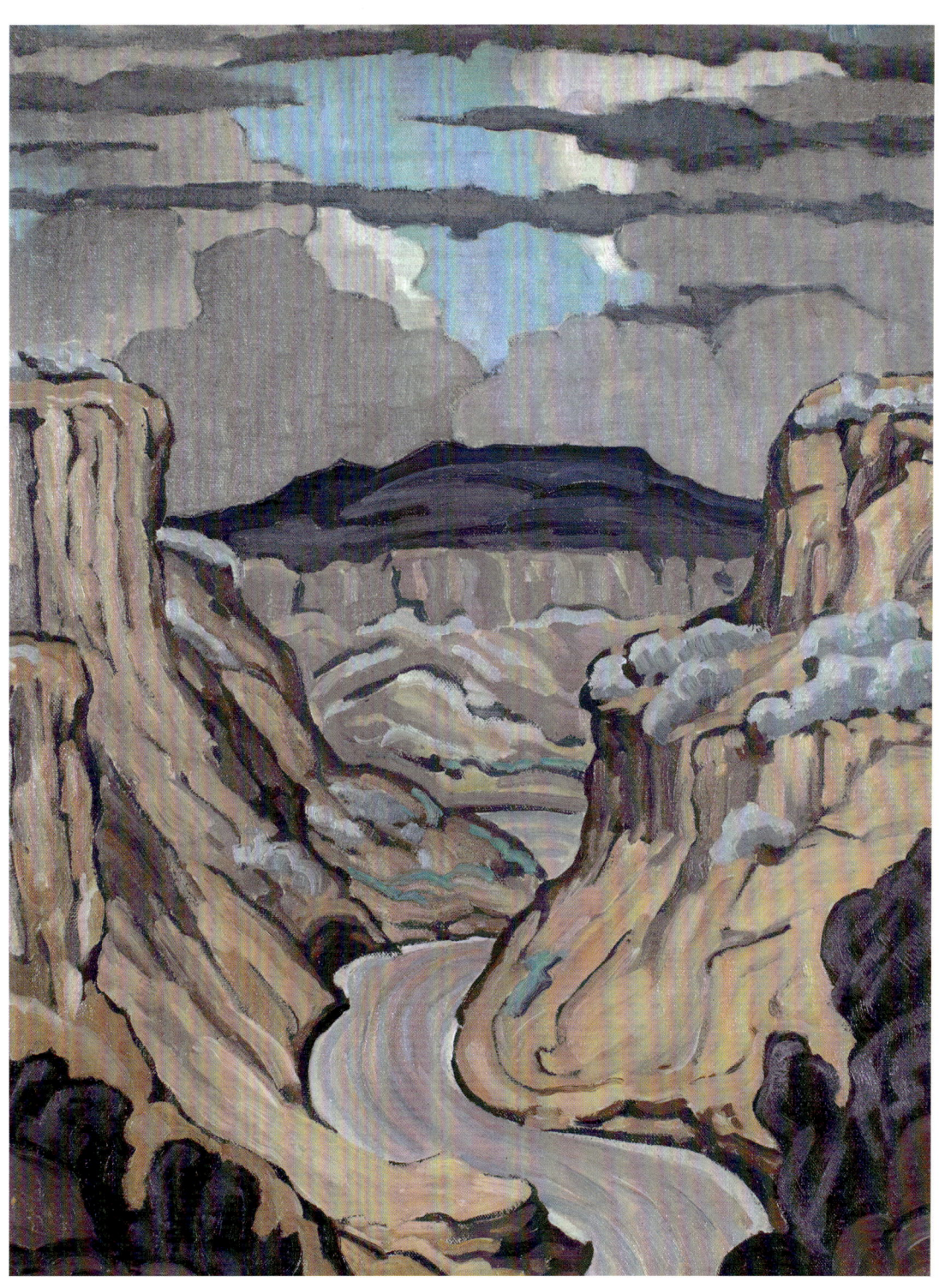

Fig. 33   Oscar Jacobson

U.S., born Sweden, 1882–1966

Orabai Wash, 1925–26

Oil on canvas board, 21⅝ x 27¾ in.

University of Oklahoma, Elaine Bizzell Thompson Study Room,
University of Oklahoma Libraries

Most of Jacobson's paintings of this period depict the desert landscape not as a backdrop for narrative but as the principal subject. Both *Giant Cacti* and *The Needles* revel in the distinctive flora and striking geology of Arizona in a manner uncommon for artists of the period. Most artists working in the Southwest like Jacobson's Santa Fe colleague, Gerald Cassidy, had an unquestionable interest in the desert but frequently used the arid climate as a setting for modest narratives, as in his *Road in the Desert* (n.d.; fig. 34). In the early 1920s, Jacobson's persistent fascination with the desert as an aesthetic end unto itself was matched only by Maynard Dixon, who began to treat the desert in similar ways following a 1923–24 visit to the Hopi. The latter's *Evening and Afterthought* (1924; fig. 35) offers an impression of the expansive sky, theatrical light, and seemingly immeasurable spans of the deserts surrounding Hopiland. Dixon, like Jacobson, sought a similar effect of silence and vacancy, as though the artist's experience (as well as that of the viewer) is solitary and unfettered.

Jacobson's formalist approach to the desert notwithstanding, political and literary ideas emerged in some of his paintings of this period. The vast expanses and dramatic atmospherics in *White Shadows—Among the Navajos* are mediated by the suggestive title and the seemingly abandoned hogan and corral. Jacobson, like many of his colleagues in Santa Fe and Taos, was concerned about encroachment on Indian lands, the most egregious example of which was the 1922 Bursum Bill.[17] New Mexican Senator Holm Olaf Bursum proposed legislation that would recognize in state court the land claims and water rights disputes of non-Indians residing on Puebloan lands. Although the Navajo were less threatened by the Bursum Bill, Jacobson's general concern for Native sovereignty was manifested in *White Shadows—Among the Navajos*, as d'Ucel reflected: "In the case of the Pueblos the trouble was due to knavery, white knavery. Dad's first painting after the trip showed a typical Beautiful Southwestern landscape: large horizons, subtle color harmonies, topped by a heavy white cloud, an ominous thunder head. He called this canvas WHITE SHADOWS and his meaning was figurative as well as literal."[18] The looming white cumulonimbus cloud serves as a veiled indictment of greed and the political injustices Native Americans faced in the Southwest, a polemic only accentuated by the vacant dwelling that suggests the specter of removal.

In contrast, literary allusions informed *The Garden of Allah*, named for Robert Hichens' popular novel that had been adapted for both stage and screen. The sensationalist tale of a British woman traveling through the Algerian desert and her affair with a Trappist monk seems to have little to do with Jacobson's nocturne of the northern Arizona desert, save for a vaguely romantic

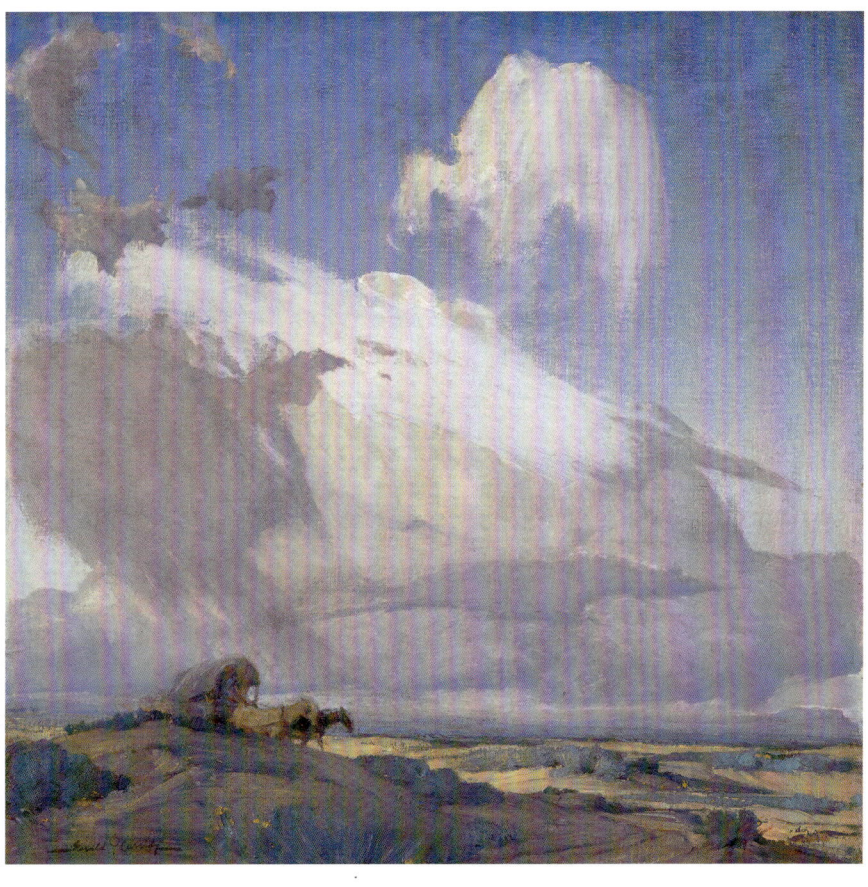

Fig. 34

Gerald Cassidy

U.S., 1879–1934

Road in the Desert, n.d.

Oil on canvas, 28 x 30 in.

The Eugene B. Adkins Collection at the Fred Jones Jr. Museum of Art,
The University of Oklahoma, Norman, Oklahoma, and the Philbrook Museum of Art, Tulsa, Oklahoma

Fig. 35

Maynard Dixon

U.S., 1875–1946

Evening and Afterthought, 1924

Oil on board, 25 x 30 in.

The Eugene B. Adkins Collection at the Fred Jones Jr. Museum of Art, The University of Oklahoma, Norman, Oklahoma, and the Philbrook Museum of Art, Tulsa, Oklahoma

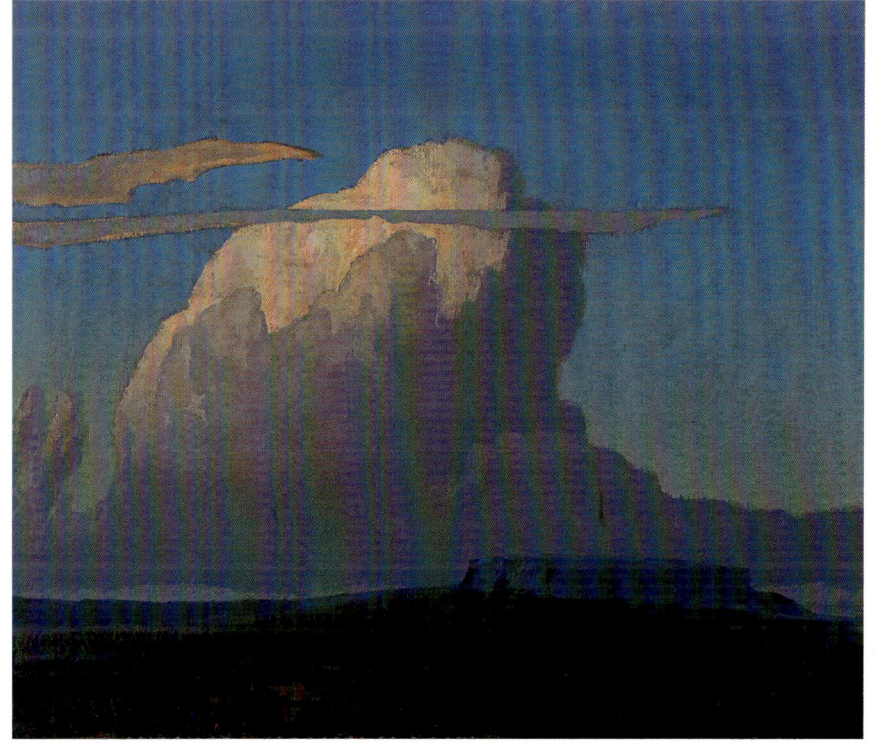

sentiment, yet the title reveals the orientalist fascination with northern Africa that would lead Jacobson to the continent in 1925–26. Some indication of Jacobson's perception of North Africa is apparent in his admiration of Matisse, which led him to acquire the lithograph *Odalisque à la Coupe de Fruits (Odalisque with a Bowl of Fruit)* (1925; fig. 36). Matisse's odalisques of the 1920s likely informed Jacobson's perceptions of Islamic North Africa, even though the figure was a rarity in Jacobson's work by 1925.

For an artist inspired by both nature untamed and the romance of the Orient, northern Africa and especially the Sahara proved irresistible. D'Ucel recalled that Jacobson, "[who] had already made a reputation as a painter of the desert, wanted to see how the light of the Sahara compared with that of the American Southwest."[19] They began their trip in France in June and visited the *L'Exposition internationale des arts décoratifs et industriels modernes* in Paris, where Jacobson encountered Art Deco.[20] The influence, combined with that of Cézanne, would result in a break with Jacobson's expressionist tendencies of the 1910s in favor of a planar, angular style suitable to the representation of the severe landscapes of both North Africa and the American West. A glimpse of that new direction appeared in *Olives in Provence* (1925; fig. 37), which acknowledged the influence of Cézanne and van Gogh, both of whom had painted the olive orchards of the region.

After completing their trek through southern France, the Jacobsons crossed the Mediterranean, docking in Algiers. The family crossed the Mitidja Valley into the Atlas Mountains, eventually arriving in Tizi-Ouzou. Inspired by Matisse's earlier trips to Biskra, Jacobson approached the local landscape with an eye towards Fauvism in his *Olive Orchard in Grande Kabylie* (1926; fig. 38). The painting lacks the ornamental line that Matisse drew from Islamic design but employs radiant color, with penetrating oranges and reds balanced by opulent blues and greens. His palette borders on nonrepresentational, yet Jacobson maintained a tie with naturalism in the simplified gnarled olive trees and surrounding scrub. Given his sultry palette, *Olive Orchard in Grande Kabylie* remains one of his boldest experiments in color, possessing little of the restraint he demonstrated in later paintings.[21]

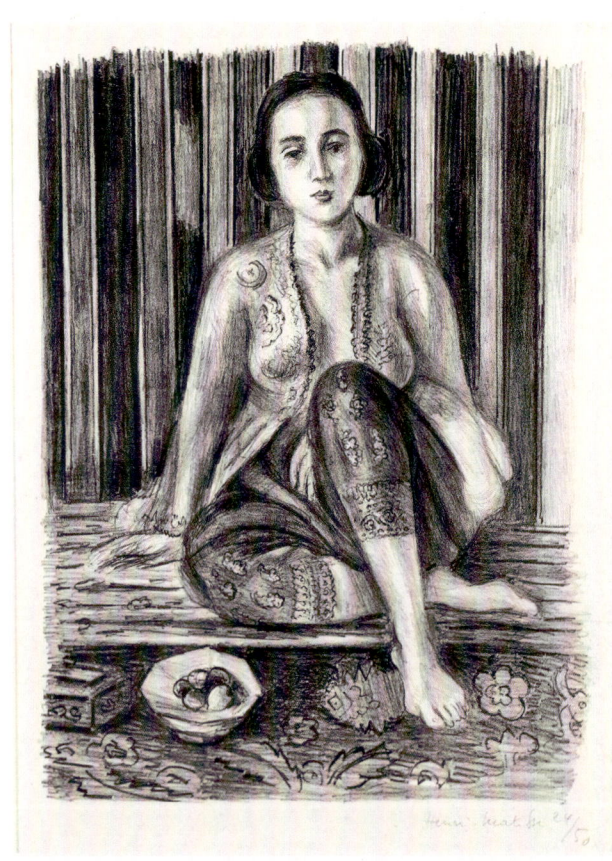

Fig. 36

Henri Matisse

France, 1869–1954

Odalisque à la Coupe de Fruits

(Odalisque with a Bowl of Fruit), 1925

Lithograph, 14 x 11 in.

Fred Jones Jr. Museum of Art, The University of Oklahoma, Norman;

Gift of O. B. Jacobson

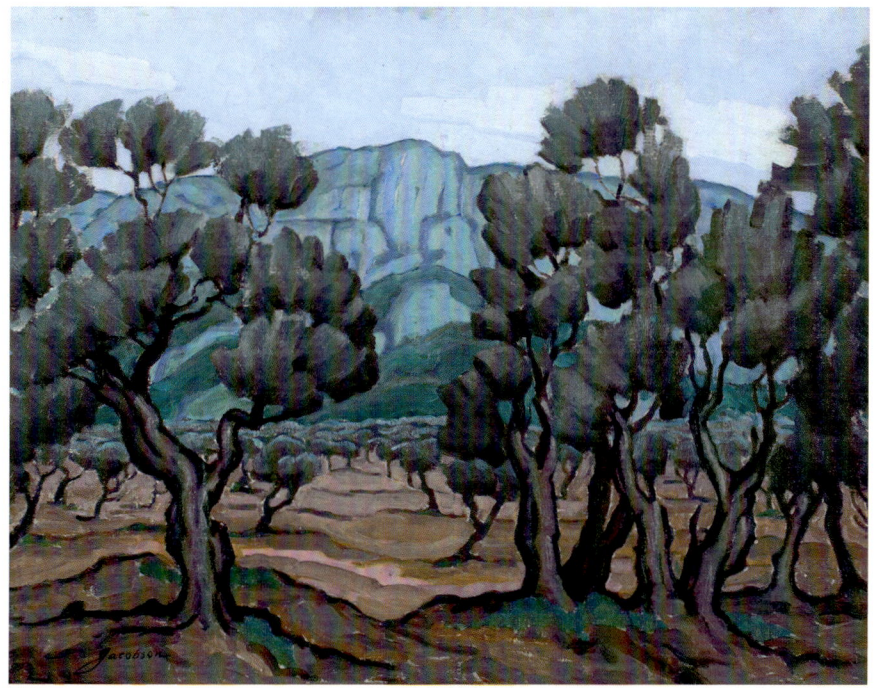

Fig. 37

Oscar Jacobson

U.S., born Sweden, 1882–1966

Olives in Provence, 1925

Oil on canvas board, 20^{1}4 x 26^{1}8 in.

Collection of Doctors Julia and Derek Irwin

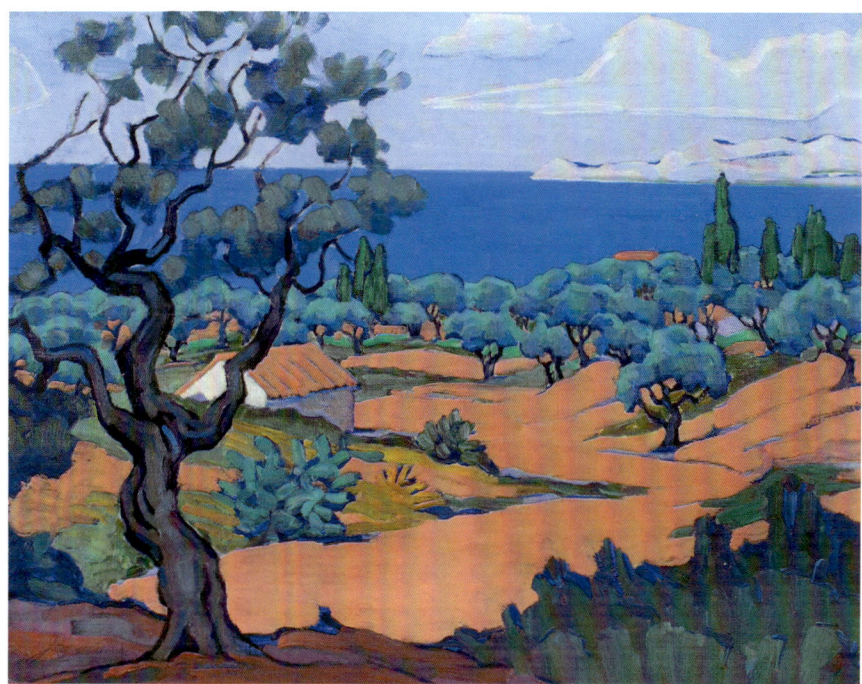

Fig. 38

Oscar Jacobson

U.S., born Sweden, 1882–1966

Olive Orchard in Grande Kabylie, ca. 1926

Oil on canvas board, 20 x 26 in.

Collection of Judge and Mrs. Ralph G. Thompson and the family of Dr. William Bennett Bizzell

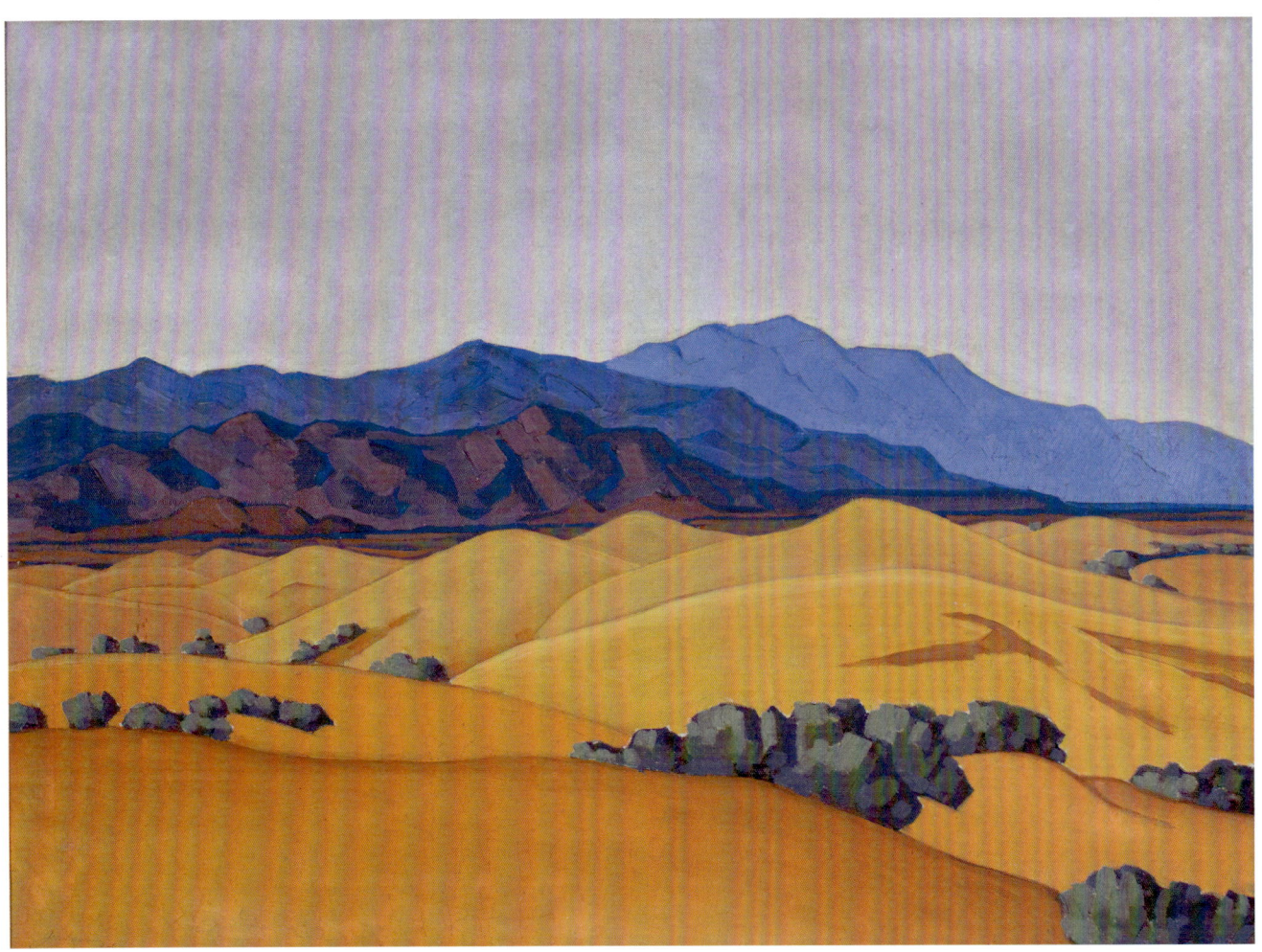

Fig. 39   Oscar Jacobson

U.S., born Sweden, 1882–1966

Sahara Desert Near Biskra, Algeria or

North of Biskra (Edge of Desert), 1925

Oil on canvas, 26 x 36 in.

Private collection

Facing page:

Fig. 40

Bror Julius Olsson Nordfeldt

U.S., born Sweden, 1878–1955

Thunder Dance or *The Pinion Dance*, ca. 1919

Oil on canvas, 34 x 43 in.

Fred Jones Jr. Museum of Art, The University of Oklahoma, Norman;
Gift of Oscar B. Jacobson, 1966

Fig. 41

Paul Cézanne

France, 1839–1906

Les Baigneurs (The Bathers), 1896–97

Lithograph, $11\frac{1}{8}$ x 14 in.

Fred Jones Jr. Museum of Art, The University of Oklahoma, Norman;
Gift of O.B. Jacobson, 1930s

The remainder of the trip took the Jacobsons through Setif, Timgad, El Kantara, Touggourt, and finally Biskra. Upon their arrival in Biskra, Jacobson finally realized the purpose of the trip in painting *Sahara Desert Near Biskra, Algeria*, alternatively titled *North of Biskra (Edge of Desert)* (1925; fig. 39). The intensity of *Olive Orchard in Grande Kabylie* is largely absent, although the yellows and oranges of the dunes are vibrant, especially in contrast to the ruddy browns and cobalt blues of the distant Atlas Mountains. Simplified, planar forms dominate the painting in the undulating, sensuous dunes, the angular foliage, or the brawny mountains. Cézanne's approach to rendering volumes, paired with the stylized forms of Art Deco, must have seemed suitable to the severity of the Sahara and encouraged Jacobson to break with the expressionist tendencies that had characterized his earlier career, particularly when considering he was unquestionably familiar with the technical approach prior to 1925. In 1919, Jacobson purchased *Thunder Dance* by colleague B. J. O. Nordfeldt (ca. 1919, fig. 40), an American disciple of Cézanne, and prior to 1932, Jacobson owned a copy of Cézanne's *Les Baigneurs (The Bathers)* (1896–97; fig. 41). The rugged muscularity of the bathers appears in heaving dunes and jagged shrubs, while the Atlas Mountains are reminiscent of Mont Sainte-Victoire.[22]

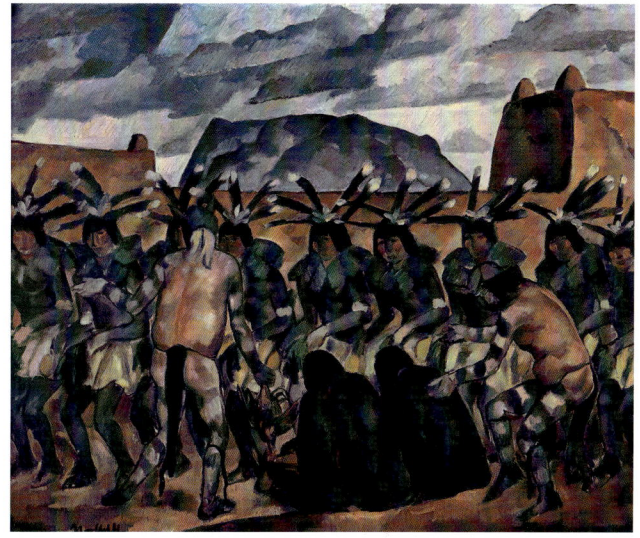

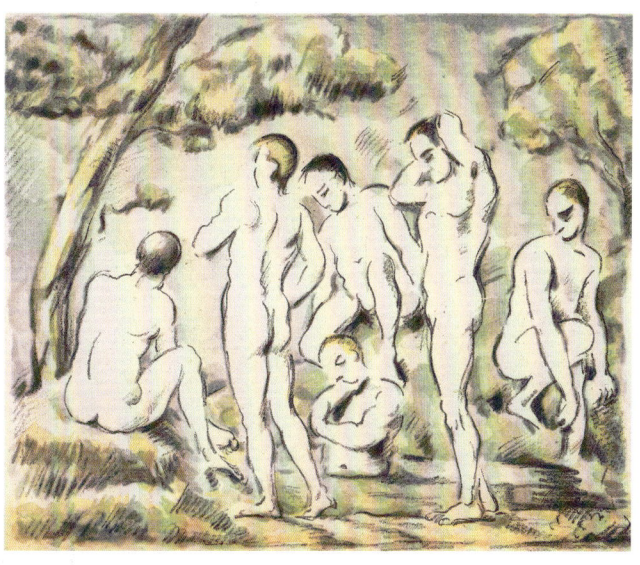

That stylistic shift is even more apparent in a painting from the following year, *Djedjelli, Algeria* (1926; fig. 42) which was variously titled *Djedjelli (A Cape Near Bougie)* and *Djedjelli (the Coast of Algeria)*. Painted on his return to Algeria after a visit to Tunisia, the work depicts a view of the Mediterranean from a cape near Béjaïa (formerly Bougie) near the city of Jijel (formerly Djidjelli). Jacobson must have considered it one his best, since he exhibited it more than any other painting from his early career and submitted it to the Society of Independent Artists in 1928. *Djedjelli, Algeria* exemplifies the stylistic direction initiated in *Sahara Desert Near Biskra, Algeria*. He reduces rock, water, and cloud to simple forms and employs a repetition of patterns and rhythms loosely drawn from the ornamental qualities in Art Deco. An outcropping of rock provides a vantage point to gaze across a sea of chevrons at a backdrop of cobalt, spavined mountains and an overcast sky luminous with cumulus and stratocumulus clouds. Jacobson drew formal parallels between the peaks of waves, clouds, and mountains, suggesting the elemental relationship between water, whether sea or rain, and the gradual erosion of coast and rock. As if to emphasize his interest in nature and its processes, unadulterated by

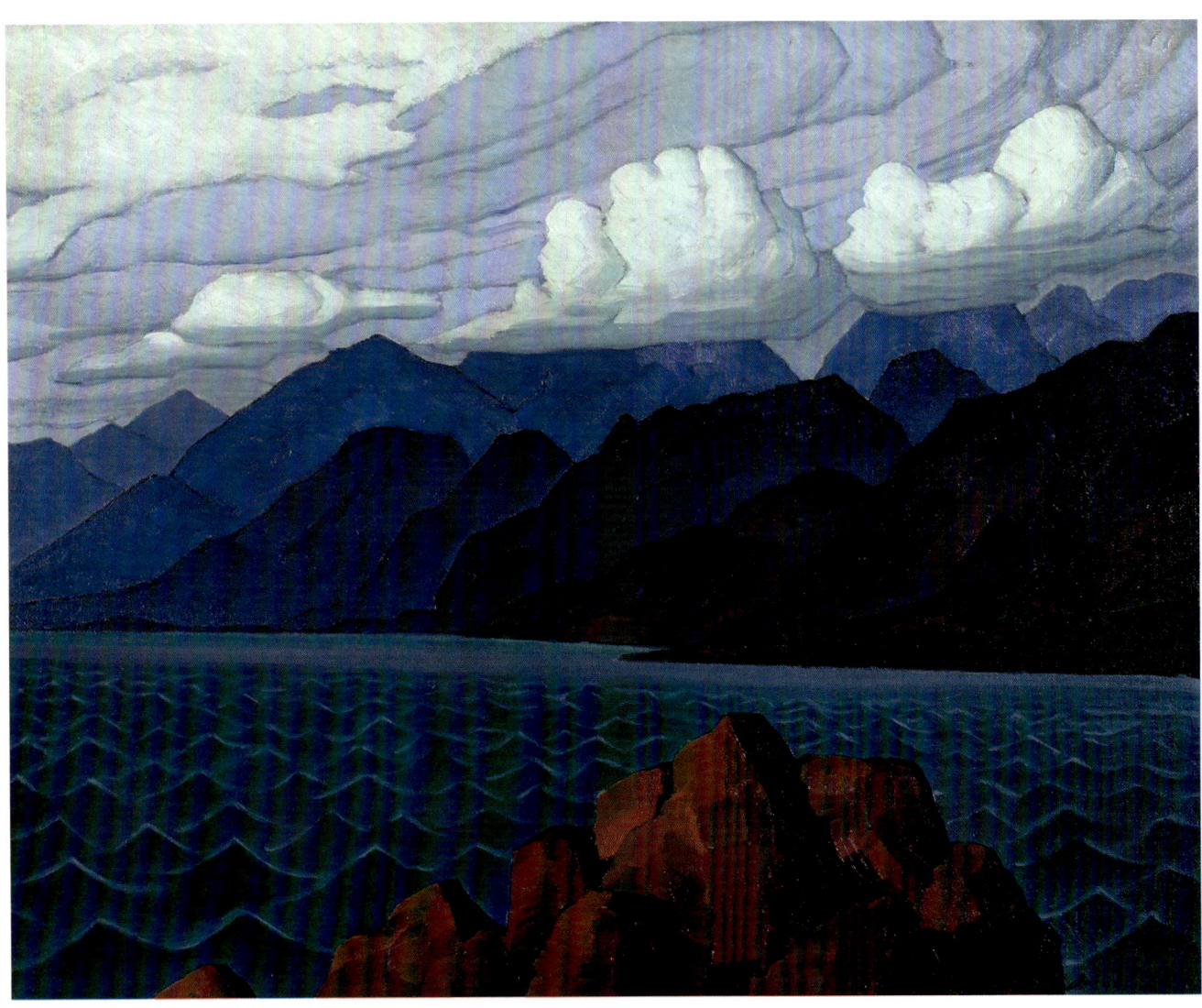

Fig. 42   Oscar Jacobson

U.S., born Sweden, 1882–1966

Djedjelli, Algeria or *Djedjelli (A Cape Near Bougie)* or

Djedjelli (the Coast of Algeria), 1926

Oil on canvas, 28 x 36 in.

Oklahoma State University Museum of Art,

Gardiner Permanent Art Collection, Stillwater, Oklahoma

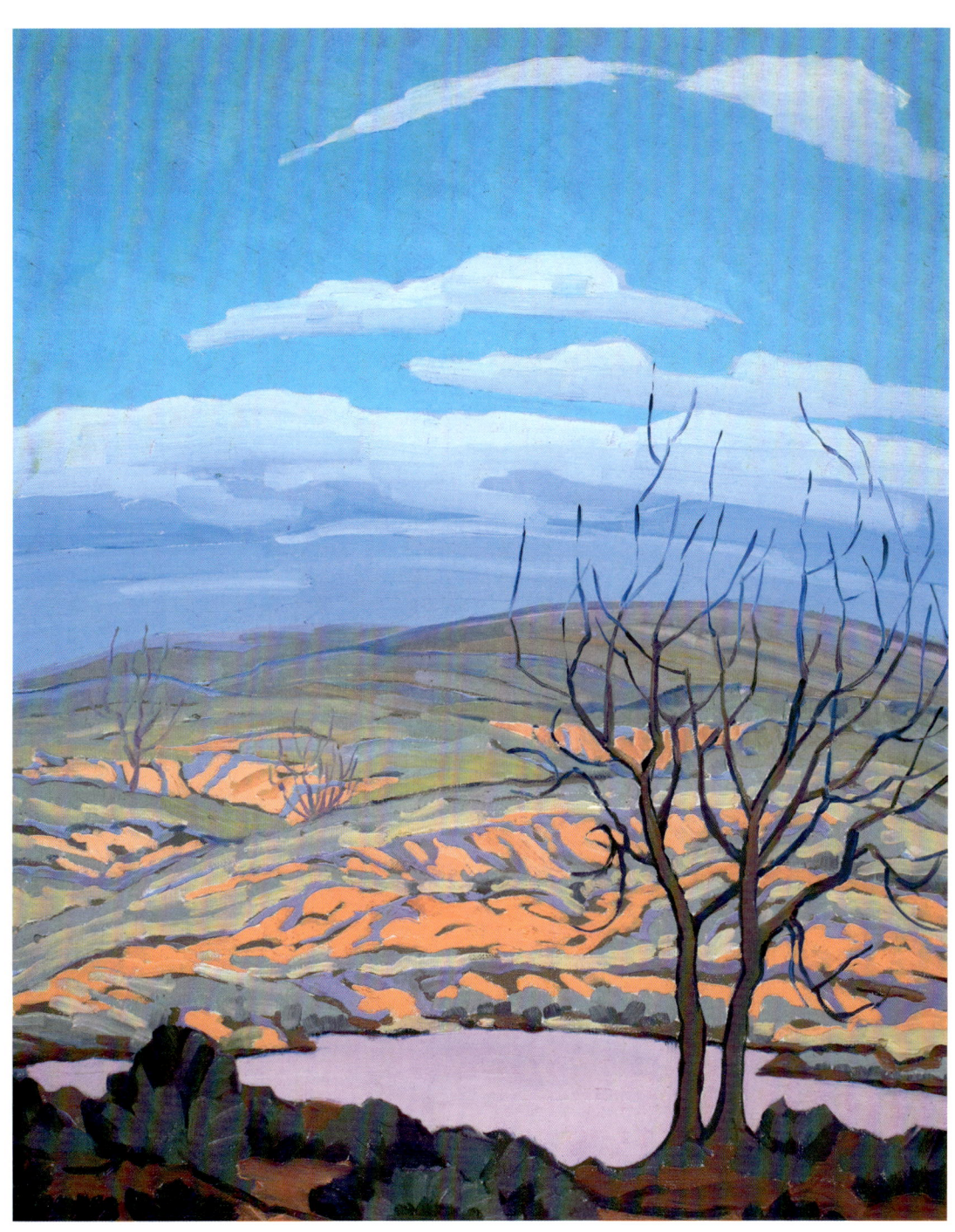

Fig. 43   Oscar Jacobson

U.S., born Sweden, 1882–1966.

Purple Waters, 1927

Oil on canvas, 32^{1}4 x 26^{1}2 in.

Collection of Jim Gasaway

human presence, he later described the Algerian coast as "like that of our own California, only more beautiful and without real estate billboards."[23] A naturalist curiosity drew him in coming decades to consider the "dramatic beauty" of elemental forces in a world unconquered. In turn, writer William Cunningham, in a review of Jacobson's art, emphasized the geotic in his palette, which depended heavily on old copper, mauve, amethyst, ultramarine, emerald, and vermilion.[24]

Upon Jacobson's return to the U.S. in 1926, he lectured widely on his trip and, when asked about his reasons, he expanded on the allure of northern Africa: "The towering spread of peaks are grand in their loneliness. At night they are made beautiful with the cloudless sky glittering her thousands of golden stars above them. Then daylight streaming down through these peaks next morning shows us not fanciful and meaningless beauties, but the very handiwork of God, and like the cathedral spires, they point up through Africa's cloudless sun, to God, their maker."[25] The religious overtones with which he associated both the loneliness and the sublimity of the African landscape harkens back to the rhetoric frequently used among Thomas Cole, Frederic Edwin Church, and other Hudson River School artists. In this respect, Jacobson may have seen the wilderness from a paradisiacal perspective, equating the despoliation of nature with sacrilege.

Paintings from the late 1920s and 1930s feature landscapes from Oklahoma, Colorado, and New Mexico with little to no trace of human presence and an emphasis on the contours of the western landscape and its geological and floral diversity, with an occasional nod to the atmospheric details. Spending much of each year in Oklahoma, he became intrigued by the austerity of the landscape, particularly its undulating eroded hills and battered mountains. *Purple Waters* (1927; fig. 43), painted in June of that year, could be an image of the previous winter given the denuded trees, but may be Jacobson's interpretation of the harsh extremes of the Oklahoma climate. When native Will Rogers quipped, "If you don't like the weather in Oklahoma, wait a minute and it'll change," he effectively characterized the unpredictability of rainfall and drought, cold and heat, and wind and dead calm.[26] The patchy turf, eroded slopes, and presumably dead trees reference the past effects of that unpredictability, although Jacobson's emphasis on the purple reflection on the pond serves to beautify what might be considered desolate otherwise.

These qualities appear in Jacobson's other Oklahoma landscapes of the period, including *Medicine Park* (ca. 1925; fig. 44), *The Quartz Mountains* (1928;

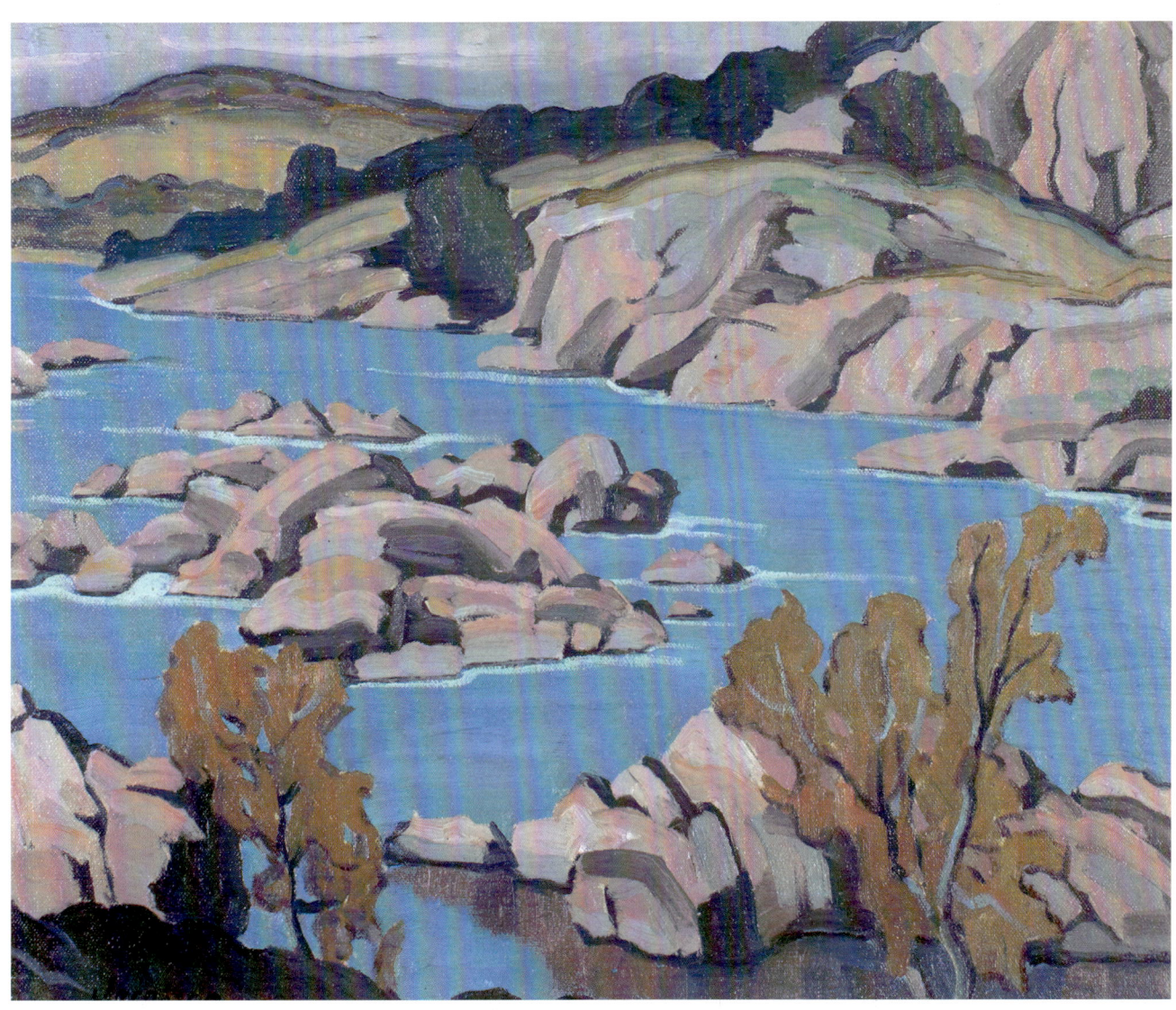

Fig. 44   Oscar Jacobson

U.S., born Sweden, 1882–1966

Medicine Park, 1925

Oil on canvas board $17^5/_8$ x $22^7/_8$ in.

Kirkpatrick Foundation, Oklahoma City

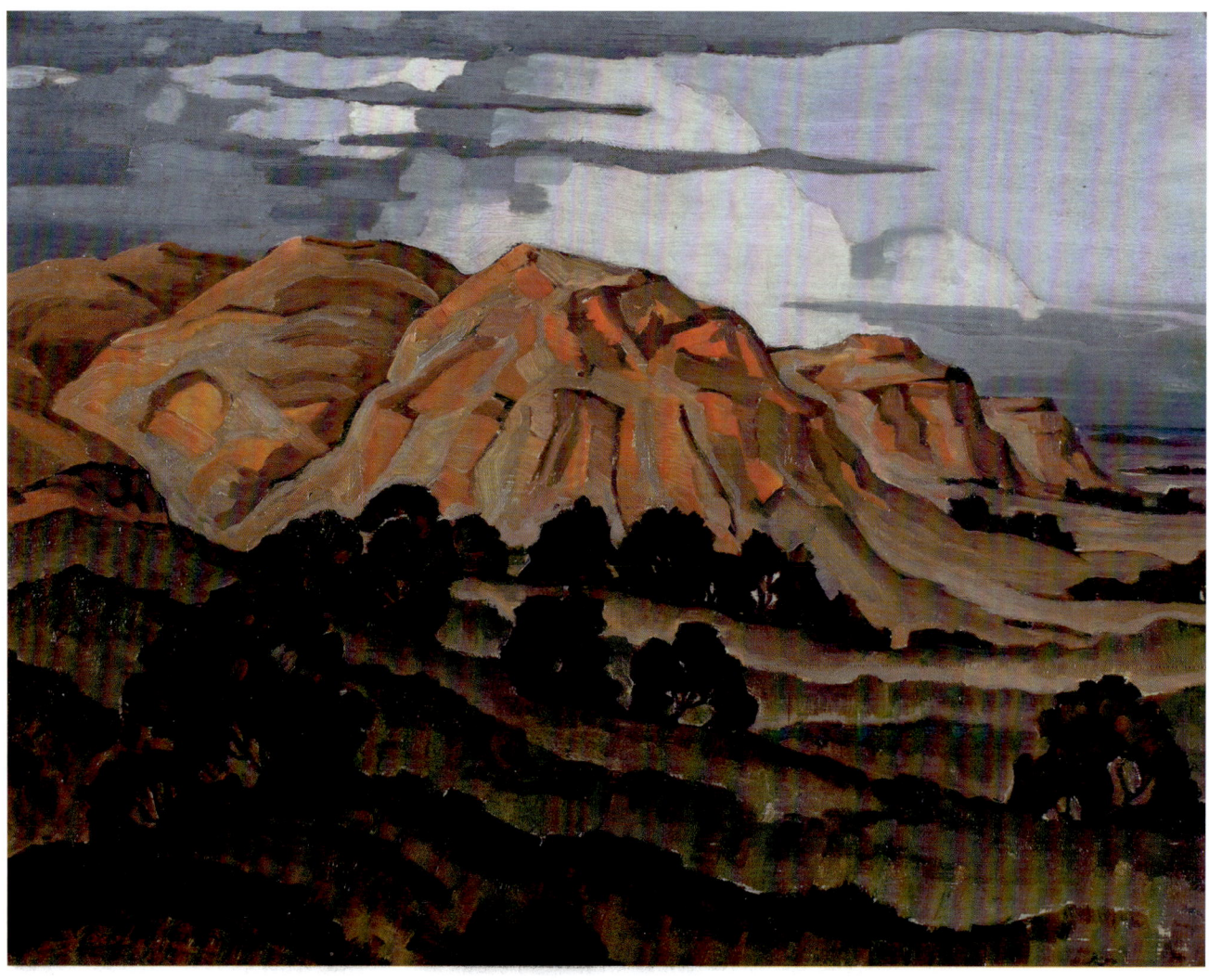

fig. 45), *Oklahoma Mosaic* (1936; fig. 46), and *The Red Tank* or *Indian Pool* (1940; fig. 47).[27] It is no surprise that Jacobson might have been attracted to the resort community of Medicine Park near the Wichita Mountains. Centuries of erosion and spheroidal weathering had produced the oddly rounded rocks of Medicine Park, and the shaded stream had led to the construction of a health spa and bathhouse by the 1920s. Jacobson paid little attention to the resort in favor of the broken and smooth rocks that spoke to the geological age of the Wichitas.[28]

He approached the Quartz Mountains, which are outliers of the Wichitas, in a similar fashion. In *The Quartz Mountains*, the eroded outcroppings of red

Fig. 45

Oscar Jacobson

U.S., born Sweden, 1882–1966

The Quartz Mountains, 1928

Oil on canvas board, 20 x 26 in.

Private collection

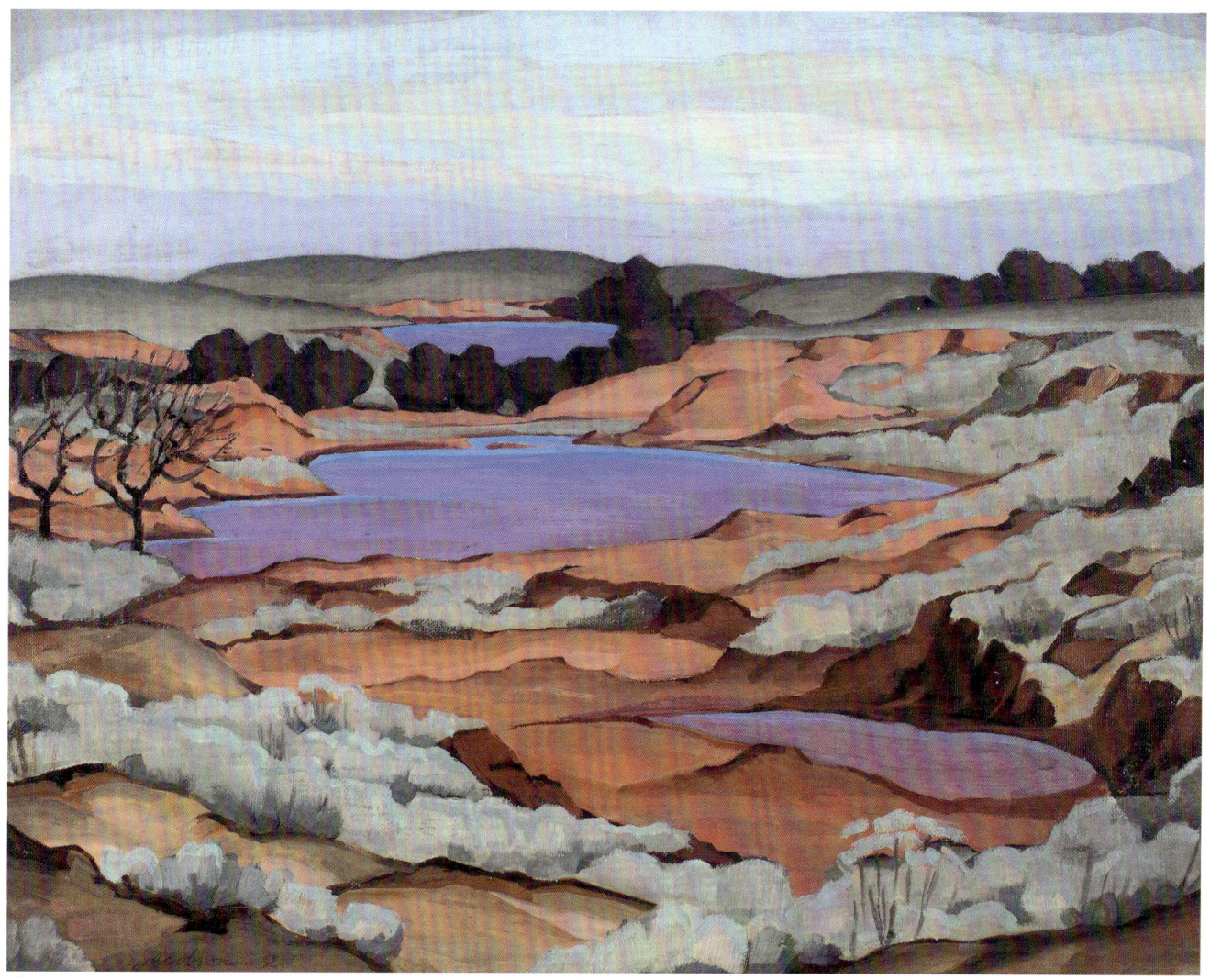

granite project from the surrounding greenery in stark contrast. He painted the area prior to their designation as a state park in 1935 and the subsequent efforts of the Civilian Conservation Corps to construct trails and picnic areas the following year. Although the Quartz Mountains saw tourism in 1928, Jacobson paints them free of human presence. Using Cézanne's planar technique to depict both foliage and rock, the landscape seems perceptibly animate, as though Jacobson hoped to capture the essence of change in both the growth of plant life and the slow erosion of the ancient mountains.

Fig. 46

Oscar Jacobson

U.S., born Sweden, 1882–1966

Oklahoma Mosaic, 1936

Oil on canvas board, 20 x 26 in.

University of Oklahoma, Elaine Bizzell Thompson Study Room.

University of Oklahoma Libraries

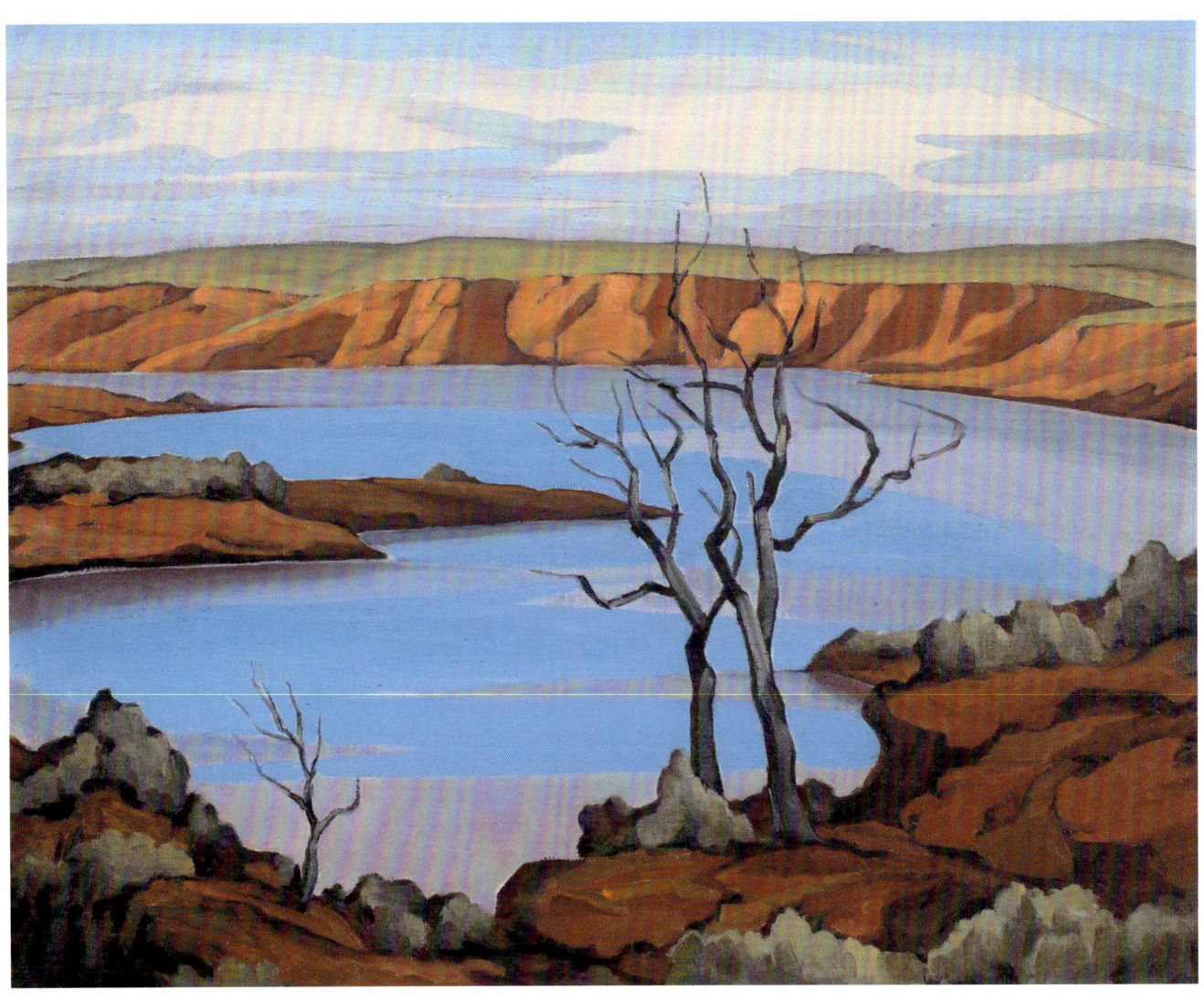

Fig. 47   Oscar Jacobson

U.S., born Sweden, 1882–1966

The Red Tank or *Indian Pool*, 1940

Oil on canvas, 22 x 28 in.

Fred Jones Jr. Museum of Art, The University of Oklahoma, Norman;

Gift of Robert Long

The contrast between fecundity and aridity is particularly apparent in *Oklahoma Mosaic*, which by virtue of its title expresses the diversity of the landscape. Barren, ruddy soil provides a counterpoint to both the scrub and the pasture beyond and to the ponds that punctuate the landscape. The watering holes of central Oklahoma ranchlands became a recurring subject for Jacobson in the 1930s and, for much of his career, he meditated on the disparity between water, erosion, and growth on the Oklahoma prairies. *The Red Tank* attempts to capture the essence of the Oklahoma landscape with its spindly trees and recessed pool encircled by the exposed, red dirt that has now become a part of the state's identity.

Given the environmental volatility of Oklahoma during the 1930s, Jacobson's interest in erosion seemingly associates him with colleagues such as Alexandre Hogue, who decried the poor farming practices that had helped produce the Dust Bowl. However, Jacobson never addressed the subject publicly and seems to have considered erosion a natural process, without commenting on human culpability. This is surprising since OU was also the academic home of botanist Paul B. Sears, one of the leading ecological voices during the 1930s. In his influential book *Deserts on the March* (1935), Sears considered the Dust Bowl the result of greed, lawlessness, and "freedom without a strong code of responsibility." It was imperative, he argued, to recognize the interdependence of all living things to prevent environmental conditions from worsening and resulting in irrevocable change. Variation in climatic patterns is "the rule and not the exception," he insisted, but he added that "variation between wet and dry, hot and cold, forms a reasonably orderly pattern to which human enterprise can and must be adjusted."[29] Jacobson certainly agreed with Sears' indictment of greed as a central cause of environmental degradation and, although it is unclear whether the former ever embraced an ecological view of interdependence, paintings such as *Oklahoma Mosaic* and *The Red Tank* depict an environmental diversity suggestive of the variations Sears considered fundamental to any climate. In this respect, Jacobson's paintings of Oklahoma were not precisely topical, but he must have recognized at some level that an ecosystem was shaped by a range of conditions over long periods of time. Conservation, an idea he clearly supported, depended on a managed relationship with the environment, and his paintings sought to express the sublimity of the natural world, preserved unmarred for future generations and as a paean to the divine.

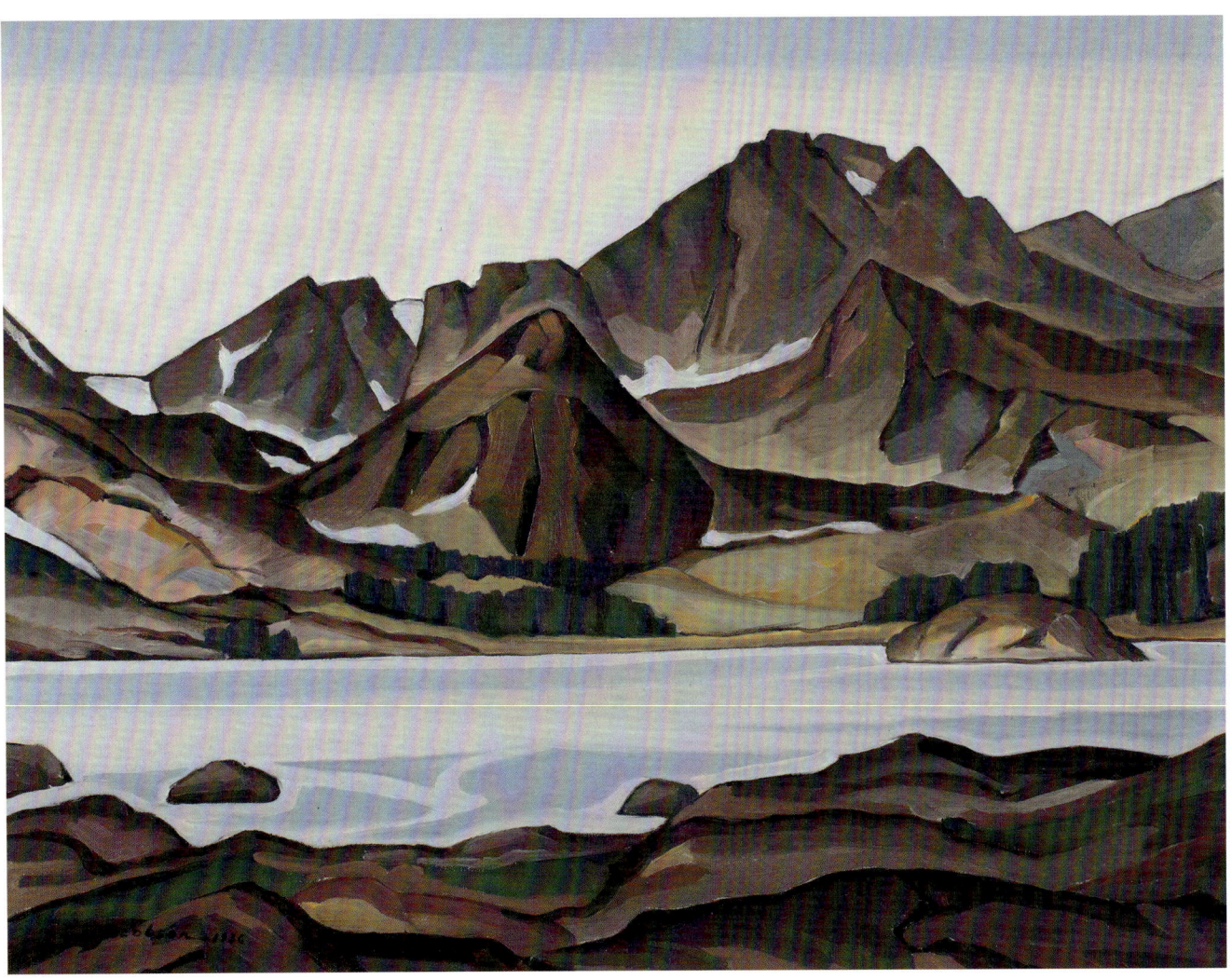

Fig. 48   Oscar Jacobson

U.S., born Sweden, 1882–1966

In Brown and Grey, 1936

Oil on canvas board, 20 x 26 in.

Fred Jones Jr. Museum of Art, The University of Oklahoma, Norman;

Gift of Mr. and Mrs. David H. Bridges

By the 1930s, Jacobson's style and his ideas about nature had matured considerably, and he found expression not only in the Oklahoma prairies but also in northern New Mexico and his future summer home in Colorado. His friendships with the artists in Taos and New Mexico rarely led him to paint in those areas, save for the occasional work such as *In Brown and Grey* (1936; fig. 48). He submitted the painting to the 1940 Coronado Quarto Centennial in New Mexico, celebrating Francisco Vázquez de Coronado's 1540 expedition through North America, but it is unclear whether the site of Jacobson's painting depicts anything specific to Coronado other than a stretch of the Rio Grande River backed by the Sangre de Cristo Mountains. Colleagues like Santa Fean William Penhallow Henderson had depicted similar scenes in prior years (fig. 49), and with a similar nod to Cézanne, although Jacobson excluded figures to focus on natural splendor.[30]

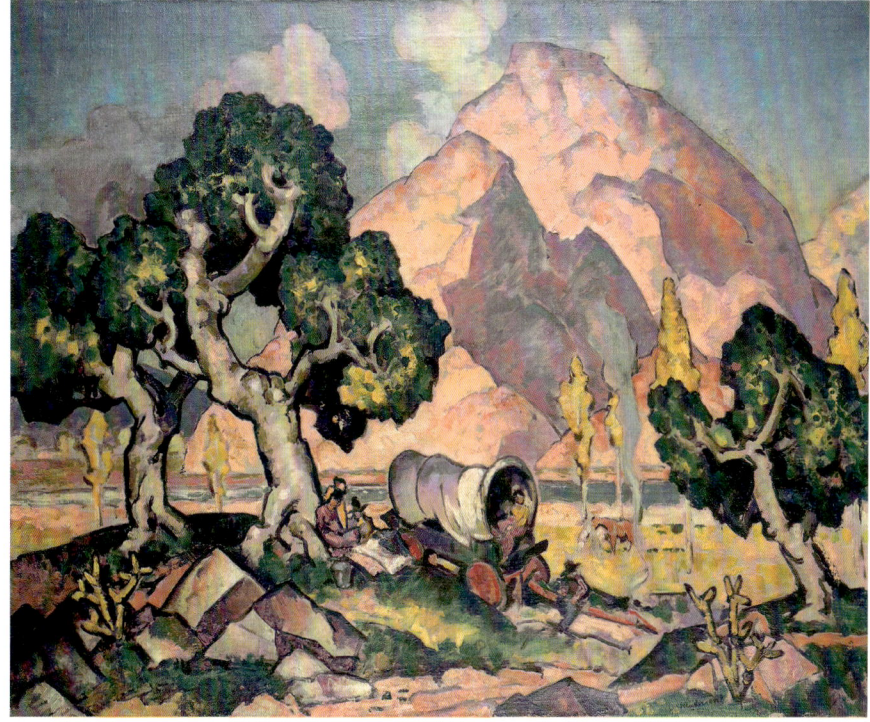

He preferred locations further afield from the art colonies such as Eagle Nest Lake or Therma, as it was known prior to the 1930s (1933; fig. 50). Therma drew fishermen more frequently than artists, and its sparse population appealed to the Jacobsons initially. As d'Ucel recalled, "While we liked Therma, its lake, its mountains, because they weren't commercialized, their being so primitive demanded too much time and energy just to live, get supplies. Friends told us of a beautiful spot in Colorado and we went there. It lacked some of the colorfulness of New Mexico but it was a pleasant place to be."[31] That spot was Allenspark, Colorado, located in the Rocky Mountain National Park northwest of Boulder. The family began building a cabin in 1932 and seems to have followed U.S. Highway 87 (now Interstate 25), with frequent trips through New Mexico. The Jacobsons passed through Raton regularly by 1934 on their way to and from Colorado. His *Below Raton* (1934; fig. 51) depicts Raton Mesa from a point to the south along the path of the Santa Fe Trail. Although the wagon ruts were largely gone by the 1930s, Jacobson certainly recognized the historical significance of the area and considered it a site worth depiction.

Fig. 49
William Penhallow Henderson
The Road to Taos at the Rio Grande, n.d.
Oil on canvas, 32 x 40 in.
Fred Jones Jr. Museum of Art, The University of Oklahoma, Norman;
Purchase, Richard H. and Adeline J. Fleischaker Collection, 1996

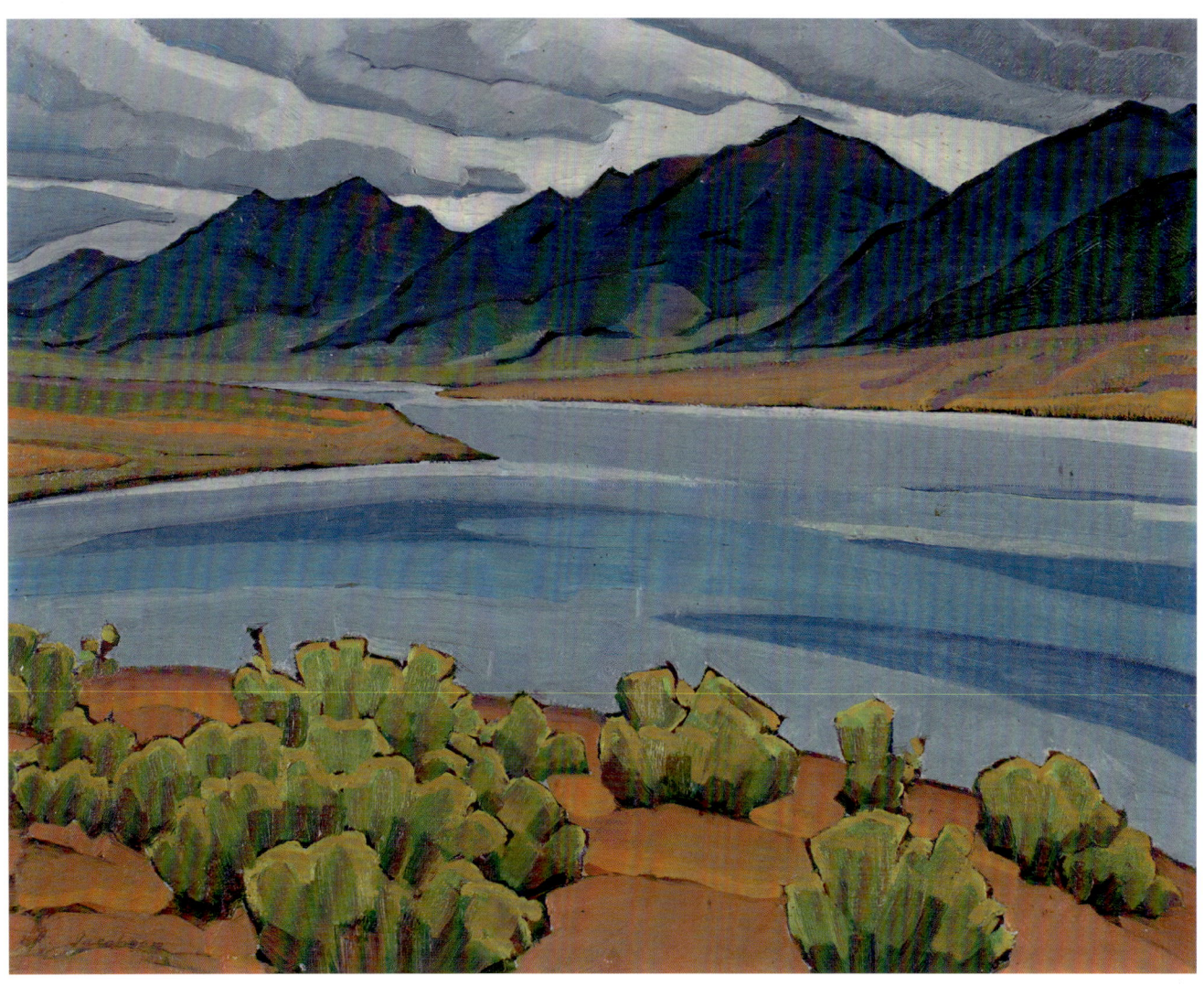

Fig. 50   Oscar Jacobson

U.S., born Sweden, 1882–1966

Eagle Nest Lake, 1933

Oil on canvas board, 20 x 26 in.

Private collection

Fig. 51

Oscar Jacobson

U.S., born Sweden, 1882–1966

Below Raton, 1934

Oil on canvas board, 20 x 26 in.

Collection of Doctors Julia and Derek Irwin

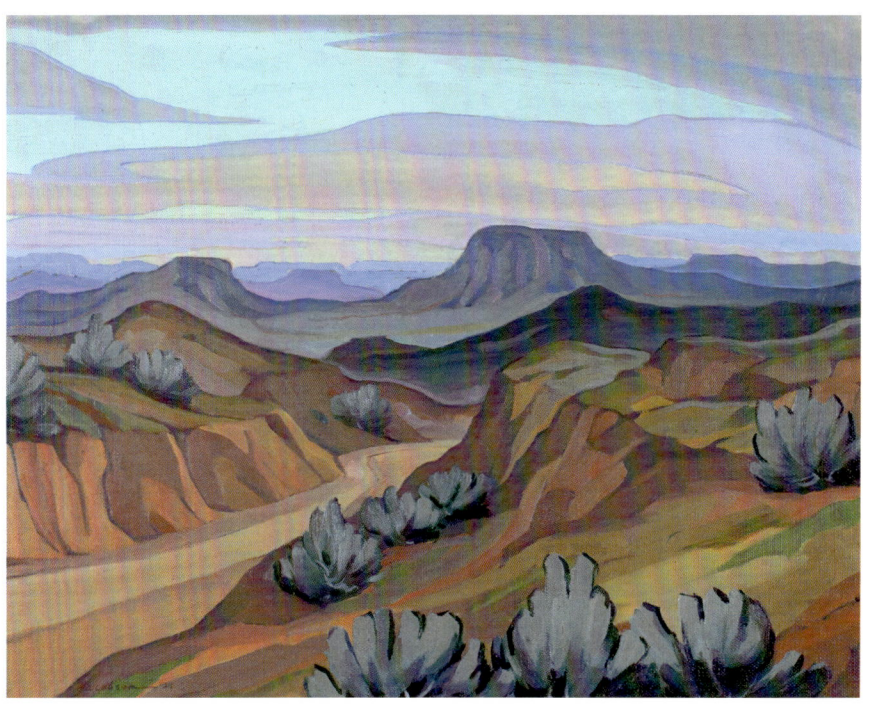

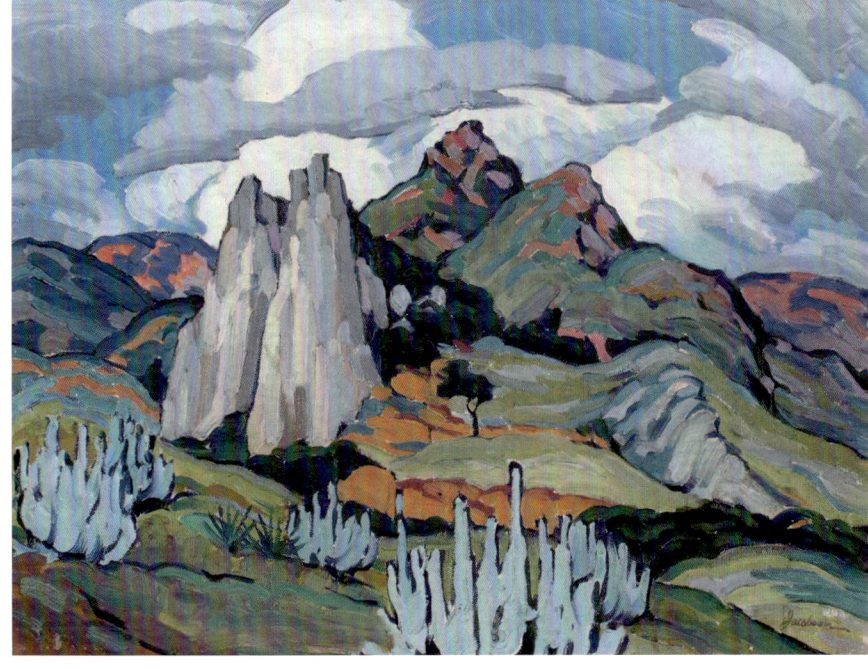

Fig. 52

Oscar Jacobson

U.S., born Sweden, 1882–1966

Entrance to the Garden of the Gods (Approaching the Garden of the Gods), 1924

Oil on panel, 17¾ x 23⅞ in.

Collection of William C. (Bill) Woods and Kay Woods

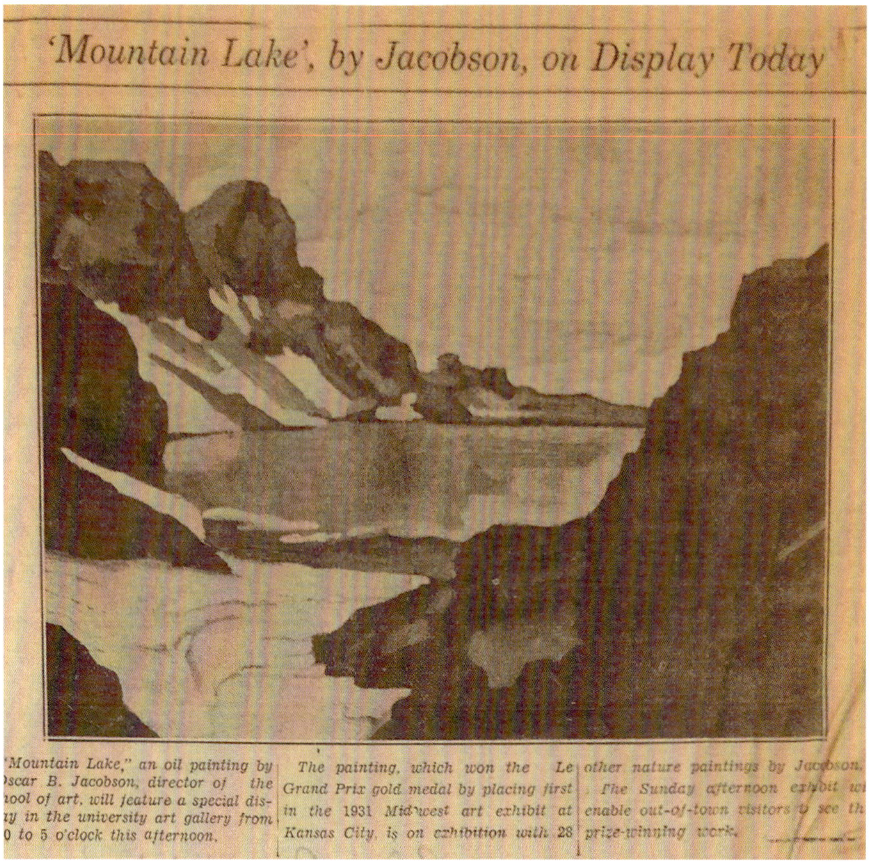

"Mountain Lake," an oil painting by Oscar B. Jacobson, director of the School of art, will feature a special display in the university art gallery from 0 to 5 o'clock this afternoon.

The painting, which won the Grand Prix gold medal by placing first in the 1931 Midwest art exhibit at Kansas City, is on exhibition with 28 other nature paintings by Jacobson. The Sunday afternoon exhibit will enable out-of-town visitors to see the prize-winning work.

Colorado would become the Jacobsons' second home, and the grandeur of the Rockies, the isolation of mountain trails, and the placid beauty of undiscovered lakes came to dominate much of Jacobson's mature work. He first treated the state artistically in 1924 when he served as director of the Broadmoor Art Academy, overseeing a faculty that included Sandzén, Lloyd Moylan, and Robert Reid. Jacobson painted the area around Colorado Springs during his tenure, focusing on burgeoning tourist attractions such as the Garden of the Gods. *Entrance to the Garden of the Gods* (1924; fig. 52) features Gateway Rock and other less notable geological formations, rendered in a fluid, energetic style as though he hoped to suggest the slow yet turbulent geological processes that formed the area. In *Entrance to the Garden of the Gods*, Sandzén's influence speaks loudly in the strata of brushstrokes that describe foliage, soil, and rock, and the work anticipates Jacobson's later paintings, such as *Oklahoma Mosaic*, with its environmental diversity.

Fig. 53

Reproduction of *Mountain Lake*, *Oklahoma Daily*, 1931

Jacobson only remained at the Broadmoor a year, but he returned to Colorado several additional times before 1932 and frequently took the opportunity to paint the landscape. In 1927, he lectured at the University of Colorado Chautauqua program, during which time he may have visited the area around Pikes Peak. He painted *Mountain Lake* (1928; fig. 53) following a hike in the mountains west of that landmark, and he considered the painting a clear success, given its distinguished exhibition record.[32] It won the gold medal at the Midwestern Artist Exhibition at the Kansas City Art Institute in 1931, and it was also his submission to the *Second National Exhibition of American Art* in 1937, which was organized by the Municipal Art Committee, City of New York at the American Fine Arts Society Galleries (fig. 54).

The 1928 version of *Mountain Lake* is lost, but Jacobson painted a later version with a few alterations in 1948 (fig. 55). *Mountain Lake* embodies the stylistic and thematic issues addressed earlier in *Djedjelli, Algeria* and the concerns that continued to interest Jacobson for the remainder of his career. He applied a reductive approach to form, which emphasizes angles and planes, to rock and cloud alike and used dark shadows and contours sparingly to add relief. A spare palette dominated by the complimentary colors of blue and orange reduces his representation of the scene to an elemental simplicity. *Mountain Lake* examines subtly how water has shaped rock over the centuries. Snow from past storms, to which Jacobson alluded in the breaking clouds, has melted not only forming the tranquil lake but also cutting away the rock. Drainage from

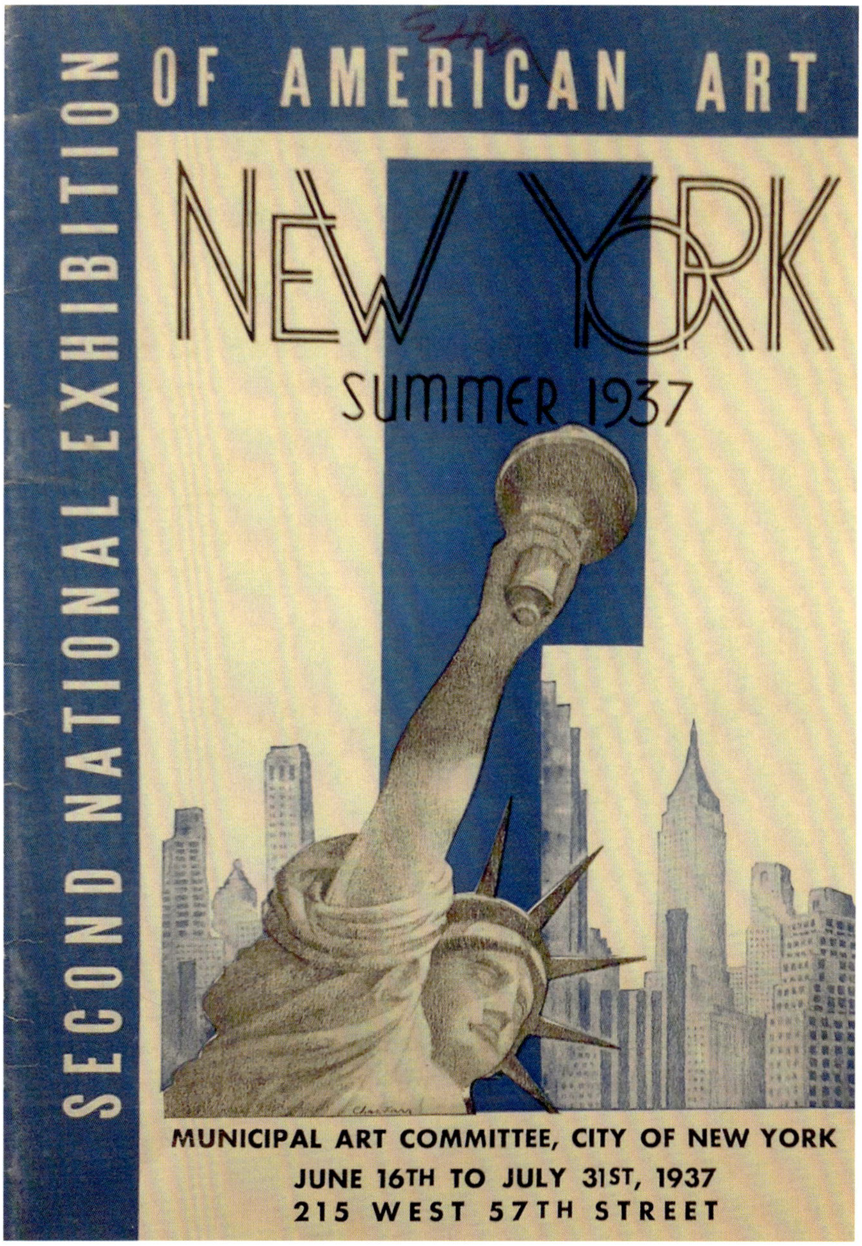

Fig. 54

Cover for the *Second National Exhibition of American Art*, the Municipal Art Committee City of New York, the American Fine Arts Society Galleries, 1937

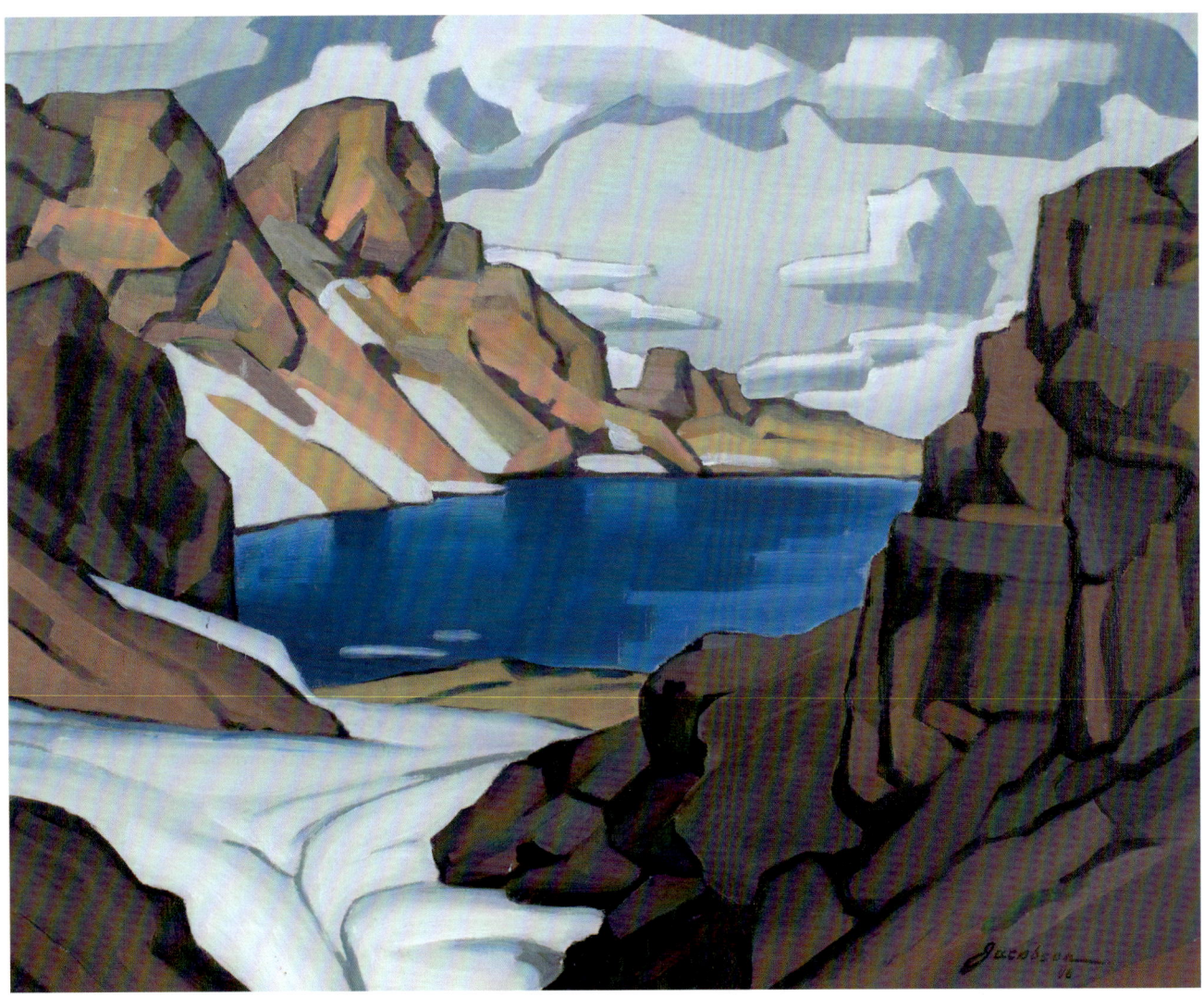

Fig. 55   Oscar Jacobson

U.S., born Sweden, 1882–1966

Mountain Lake (second version), 1948

Oil on canvas, 22 x 28 in.

Collection of Jim Gasaway

Fig. 57

Oscar Jacobson

U.S., born Sweden, 1882–1966

Green Mountains, 1936

Oil on canvas board, 19¹₂ x 25¹₂ in.

Kirkpatrick Foundation, Oklahoma City

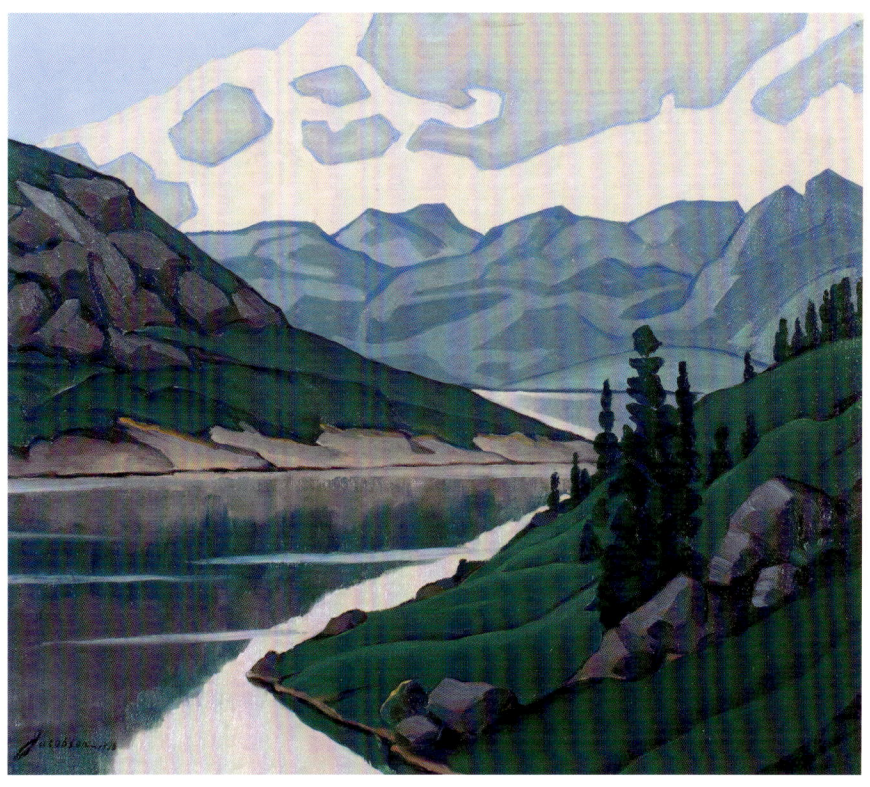

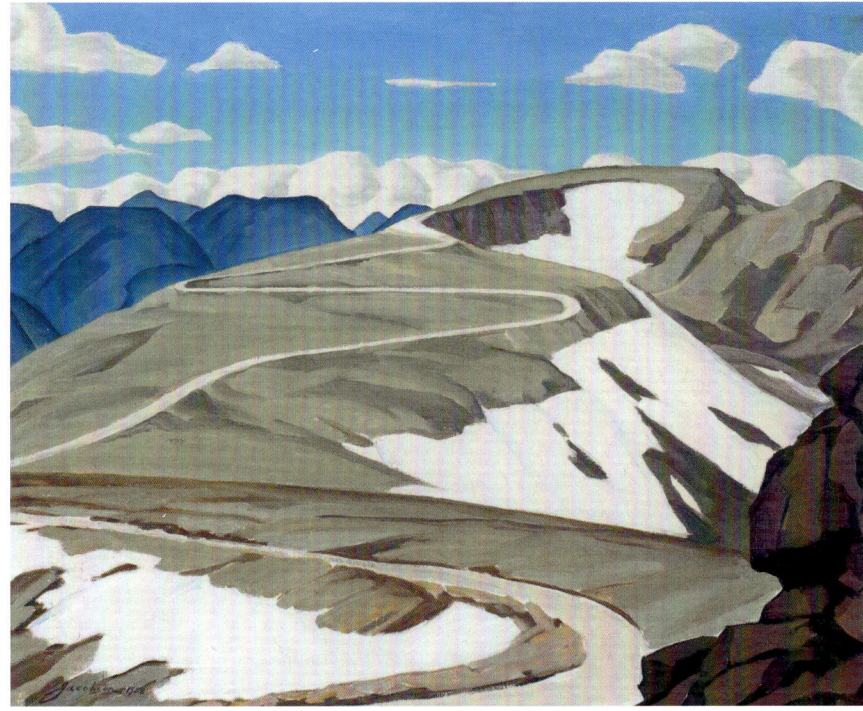

Fig. 58

Oscar Jacobson

U.S., born Sweden, 1882–1966

Trail Ridge in June, 1938

Oil on canvas, 22 x 28 in.

Collection of Peter and Grace Harris

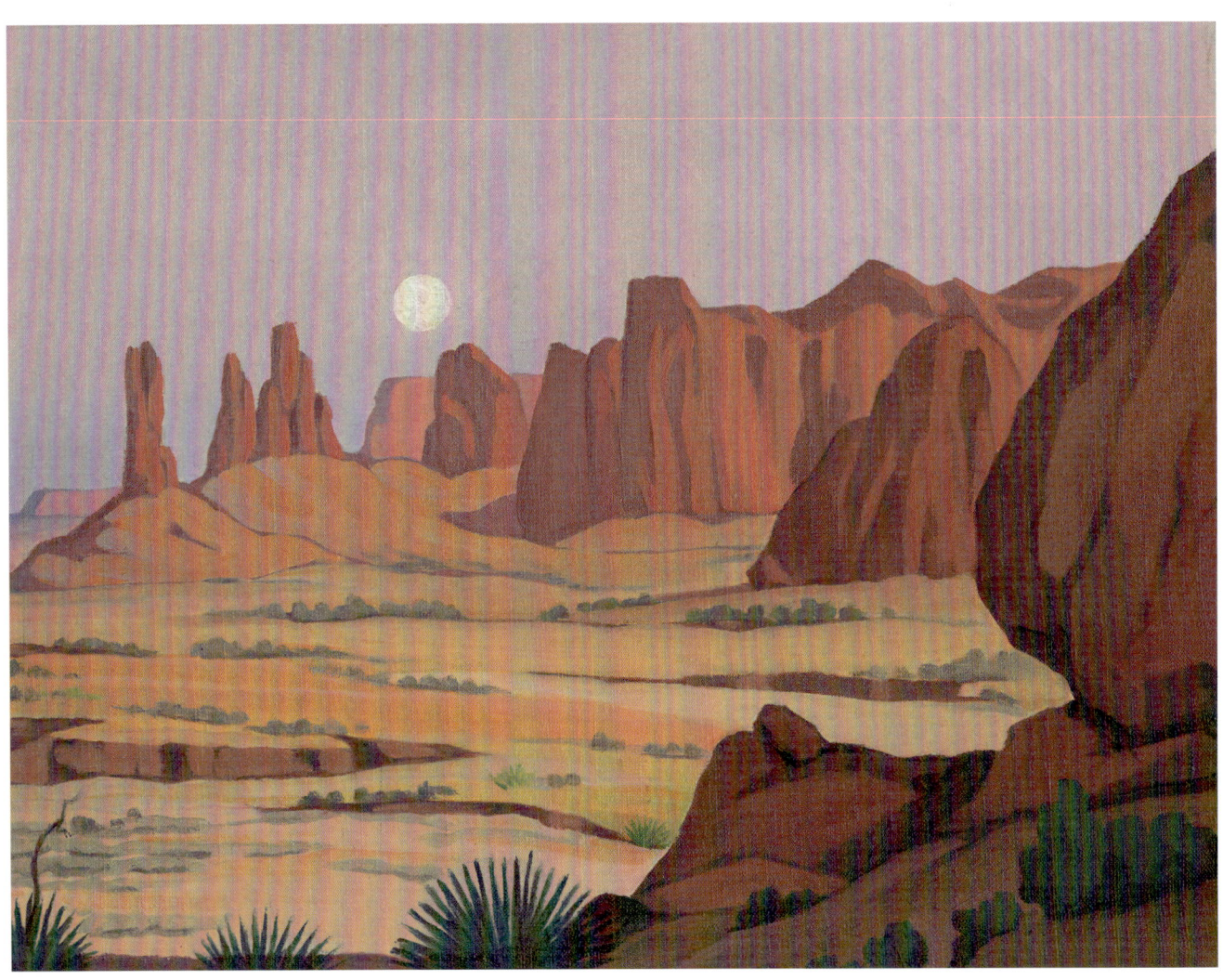

Fig. 59   Oscar Jacobson

U.S., born Sweden, 1882–1966

In the Navajo Country, 1938

Oil on canvas, 20 x 26 in.

Fred Jones Jr. Museum of Art,

The University of Oklahoma, Norman

ade in which the Works Progress Administration (WPA) touted the benefits of rural improvements. Jacobson had served as technical advisor to the Federal Art Project in Oklahoma in the 1930s and was well aware of the success of the WPA. The road had no real connection to the WPA, yet it represented a sensitive alteration of the landscape sympathetic to the concerns of conservationists. In that respect, *Trail Ridge in June* offers a subtle affirmation of Jacobson's attitude towards human alteration and habitation of the wilderness.

By the late 1930s, Jacobson had committed to the western wilderness as his primary subject and saw his paintings as a form of pictorial preservation of a world unconquered. The family frequently spent summers traveling between New Mexico and Colorado. Prior to the 1938 visit to northern Colorado, the family drove through the Navajo Reservation near Shiprock, New Mexico. The terrain brought back memories of the Sahara, and Jacobson's *In the Navajo Country* (1938; fig. 59) may be a depiction of formations in the vicinity of Shiprock.[39] The 1925–26 trip to Africa had resulted in the planar style of his mature career, so it is unsurprising that he might draw associations between the deserts of northern Africa and the American Southwest.

Jacobson seems to have been in a reflective mood in the late 1930s. He had been working professionally since 1908 and had a significant body of work. The WPA Oklahoma Art Center held a retrospective for him in 1940, and major works such as *Djedjelli, Algeria, Mountain Lake*, and *In Brown and Gray* were featured. The 1940 retrospective strengthened Jacobson's reputation as a painter of deserts and the wilderness. During the ensuing decade, the American West commanded his attention and he traveled frequently during the summers in search of subject matter, straying occasionally from his favorite sites in Colorado and New Mexico. For example, during a summer visit to the Allenspark

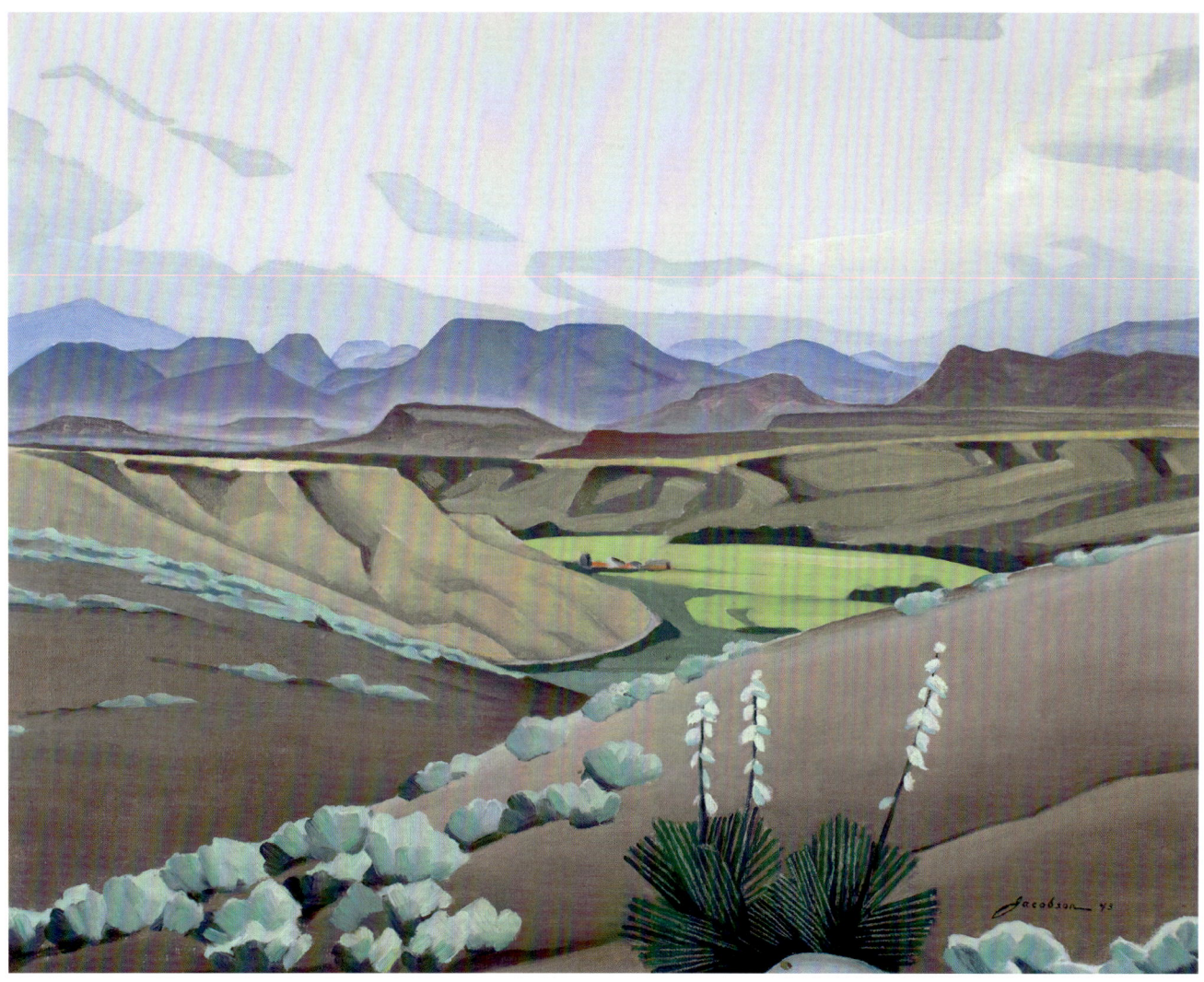

cabin in 1943, the Jacobsons visited nearby Wyoming, where he painted *Wyoming Ranch* (fig. 60). Like *Trail Ridge in June*, Jacobson minimized the impact of the ranch on the landscape, which appears insignificant next to the buttes and distant mesas of southern Wyoming. A greater simplification of natural forms is also apparent in the faceted sagebrush, stylized yuccas, and spare topography. Jacobson reduced the landscape to basic patterns, eschewed detail, and

Fig. 60

Oscar Jacobson

U.S., born Sweden, 1882–1966

Wyoming Ranch, 1943

Oil on canvas, 22 x 28 in.

Collection of Jonathan and Talitha Nichols

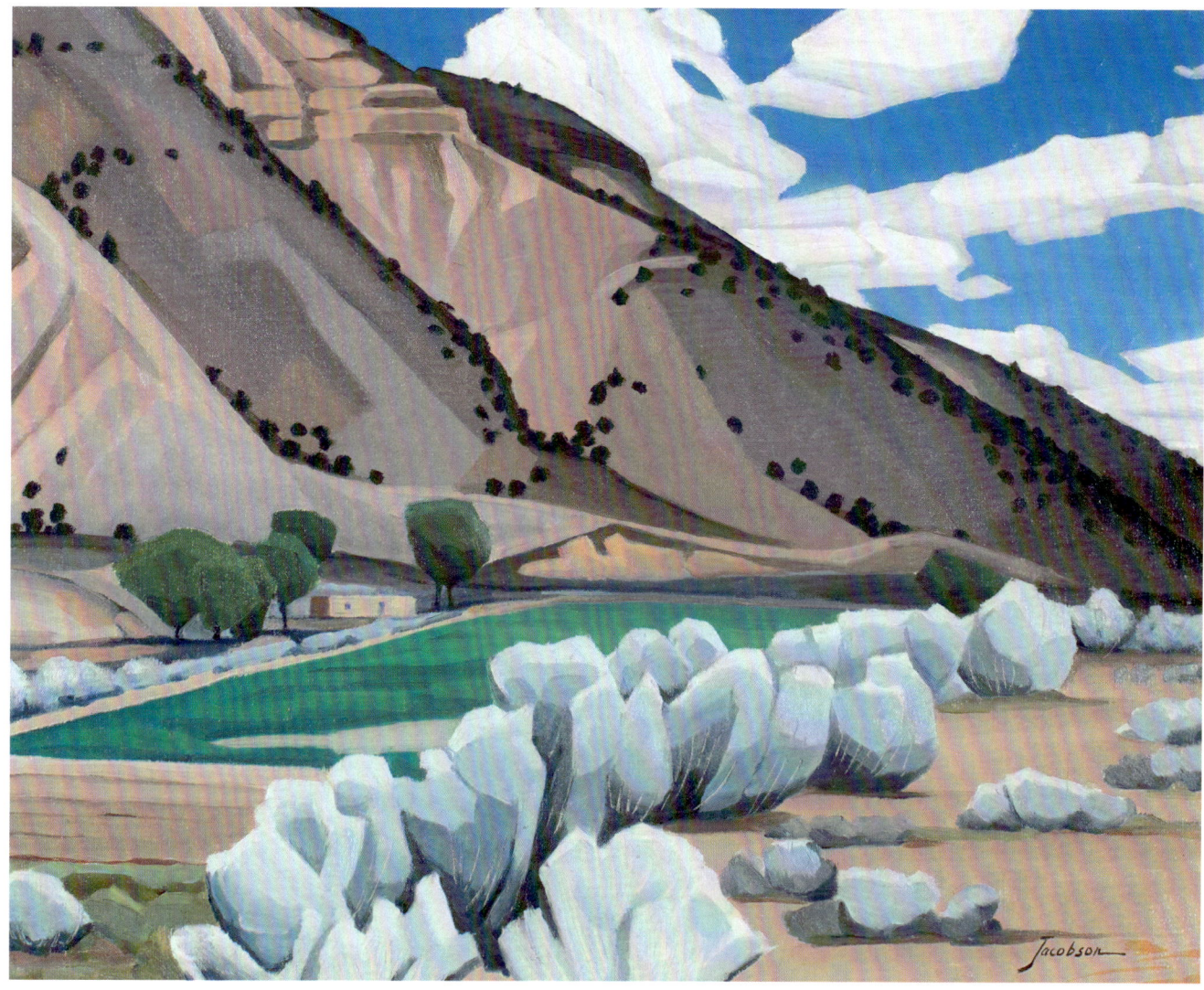

smoothed planes to emphasize essentials. This tendency is equally apparent in *Towards Questa* (1946; fig. 61). Jacobson flattened many of the forms and used color and tonal variations to suggest differentiation and volume. Clouds, sagebrush, mountains, and adobe buildings share a similar angularity.[40] The technique is also apparent in *Meeker, Long's and Martha Washington* (1950; fig. 62), which Jacobson likely composed from a site behind the Allenspark cabin. Mount

Fig. 61

Oscar Jacobson

U.S., born Sweden, 1882–1966

Towards Questa or *Road to Santa Fe*, 1946

Oil on canvas, $20\frac{1}{2}$ x $26\frac{3}{8}$ in.

Kirkpatrick Foundation, Oklahoma City

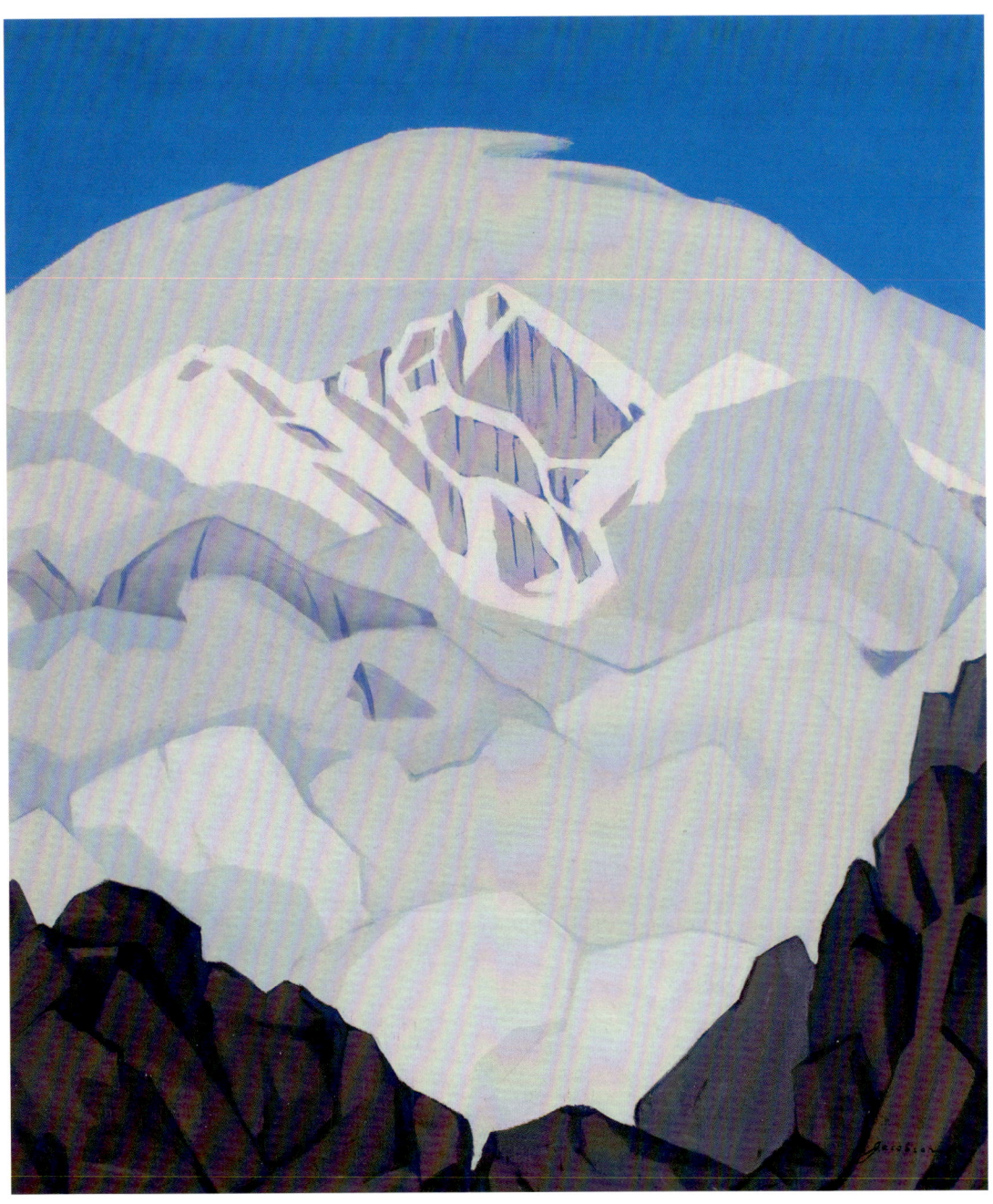

Fig. 62   Oscar Jacobson

U.S., born Sweden, 1882–1966

Meeker, Long's and Martha Washington, 1950

Oil on canvas, 34 x 30 in.

Fred Jones Jr. Museum of Art, The University of Oklahoma, Norman;

Purchase, 1970

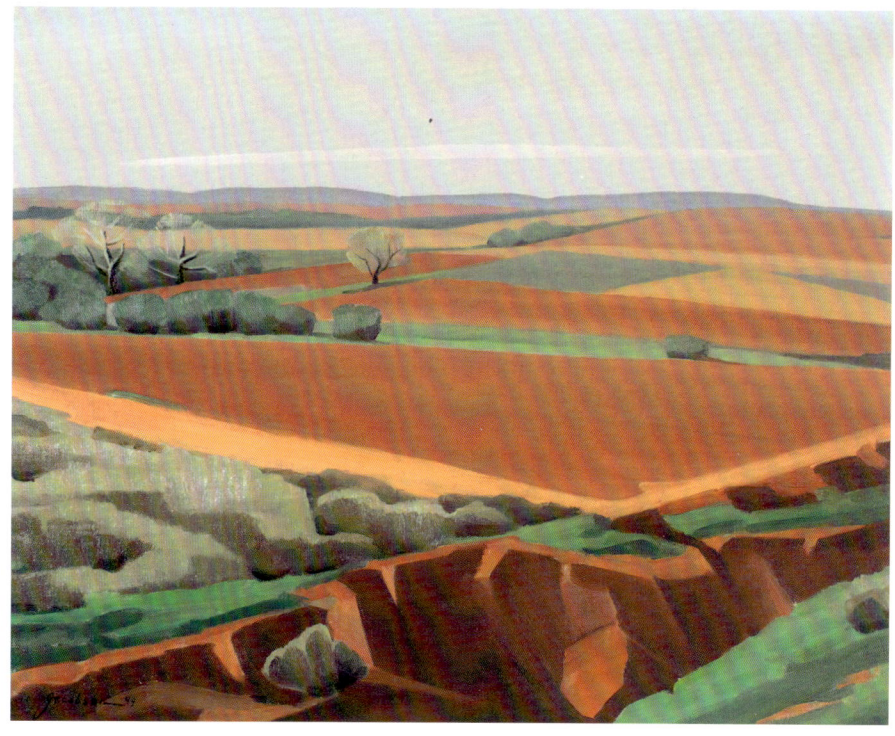

Fig. 63

Oscar Jacobson

U.S., born Sweden, 1882–1966

Light Soil, formerly *On the Road to Chickasha*, 1949

Oil on canvas, 22 x 28 in.

Oklahoma City Museum of Art.

Gift from the Kirkpatrick Foundation, 1999.036

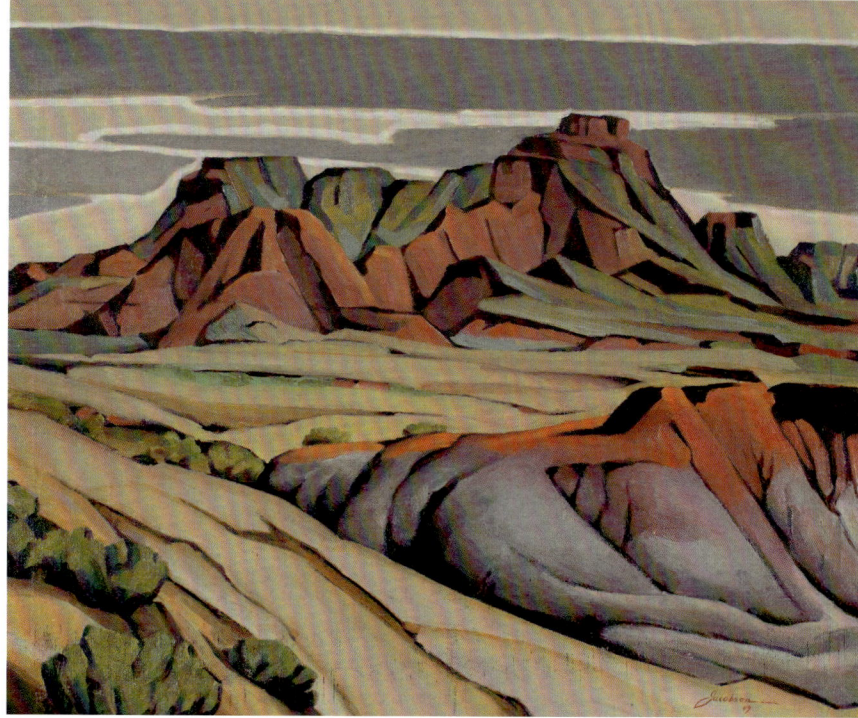

Fig. 64

Oscar Jacobson

U.S., born Sweden, 1882–1966

The Glass Mountains, 1949

Oil on canvas, 24 x 30 in.

Private collection

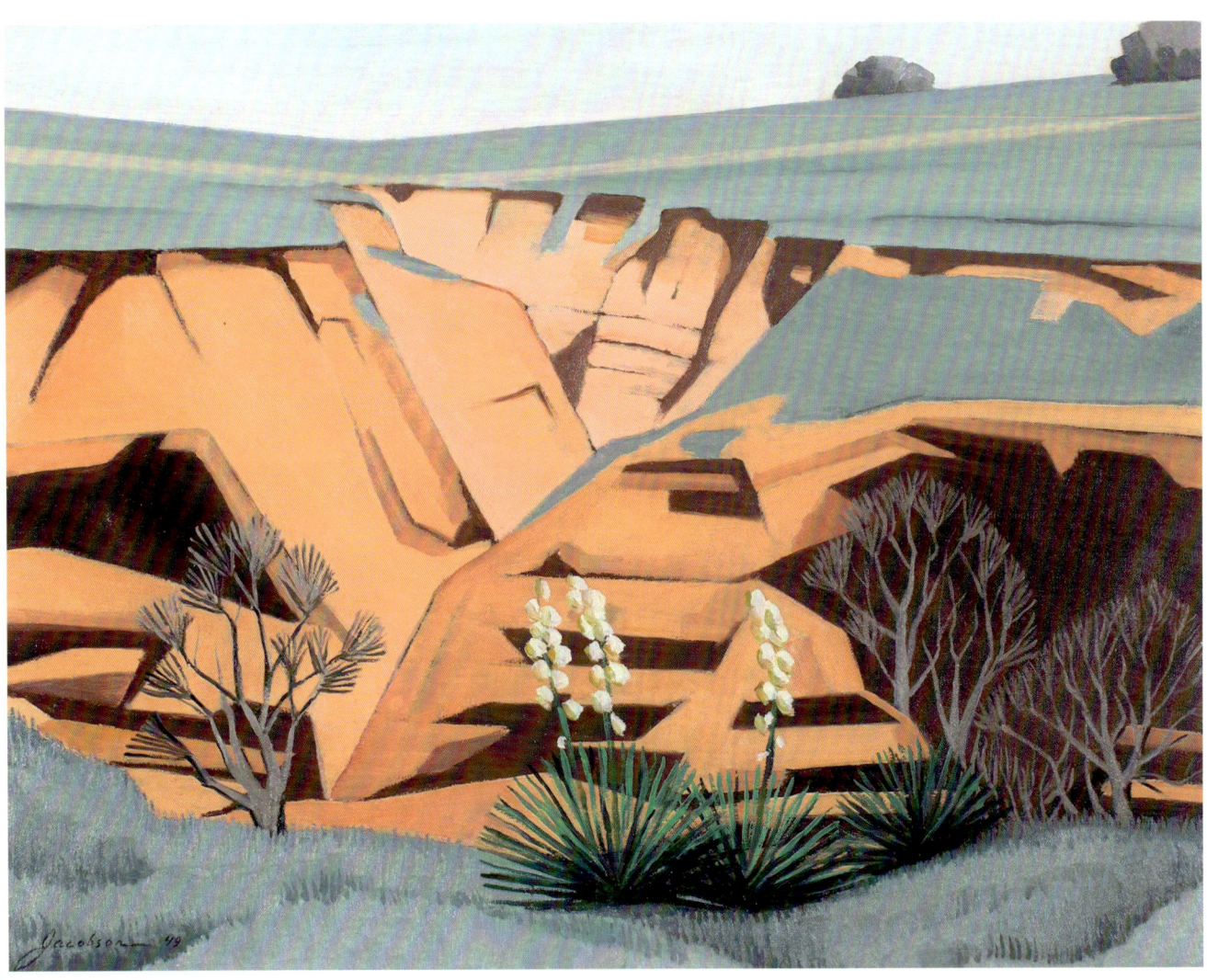

Fig. 65   Oscar Jacobson

U.S., born Sweden, 1882–1966

Horse Thief Canyon, Oklahoma, 1949

Oil on canvas, 22^1⁄$_8$ x 28^1⁄$_8$ in.

Oklahoma City Museum of Art. Gift from the Kirkpatrick Foundation, 1999.037

Meeker, Longs Peak, and Mount Lady Washington can be seen in a single view to the west of the cabin, and the artist hiked into the area frequently. He clearly hoped to evoke the sublimity he sought for much of his career in the dramatic image of the mountains framed by a sweep of clouds.

Although most summers were spent partially in Allenspark, the Jacobsons continued to travel, adding Utah and Nevada after their son-in-law Craig Sheppard accepted a position at the University of Nevada in 1947; however, their travel slowed by the end of the decade with advancing age. The artist retired from OU in 1952 at age seventy and, in the preceding years, he preferred to stay close to Oklahoma. He found inspiration in local farmland with paintings such as *Light Soil* (1949; fig. 63), clearly titled for the sandy composition of the plowed field. State landmarks and historical areas also attracted his attention. *The Glass Mountains* (1949; fig. 64) depicts the mesas and buttes near the Oklahoma panhandle that glitter subtly from an abundance of selenite. The eroded formations must have reminded Jacobson of the terrain of Arizona and New Mexico, yet he was able to reach the mountains in less than a day. Another painting from that year, *Horse Thief Canyon, Oklahoma* (1949; fig. 65), is less notable for its geological character than its largely apocryphal history. Located eight miles west of Perkins, the canyon was suspected by early settlers to be the hideout for outlaws such as the Daltons or the Doolin Gang.[41]

The year prior to *Horse Thief Canyon*, Jacobson had explained in the pamphlet for his 1948 exhibition at OU's Museum of Art his abiding interest in "the world unconquered by man, unviolated by human greed, a world untouched by misery and despair." Horse Thief Canyon, the Glass Mountains, or the farmland of *Light Soil* may not possess the desolation of the Sahara or the near inaccessibility of a Rocky Mountain summit, but each fit his image of nature unexploited. Wilderness did not necessarily mean freedom from human intervention, as even the act of protection or conservation shapes the landscapes in sometimes subtle, or not so subtle, ways.

In many respects, Jacobson's ideas on nature, expressed chiefly through his paintings, followed the conservationist ideals of Theodore Roosevelt, while also anticipating the aims behind the 1964 Wilderness Act. Signed into law by President Lyndon B. Johnson, the legislation defines the wilderness in language Jacobson surely appreciated: "A wilderness, in contrast with those areas where man and his own works dominate the landscape, is hereby recognized as an area where the earth and its community of life are untrammeled by man, where man himself is a visitor who does not remain." A letter from writer and conservationist Wallace Stegner was used to introduce the act, and his belief

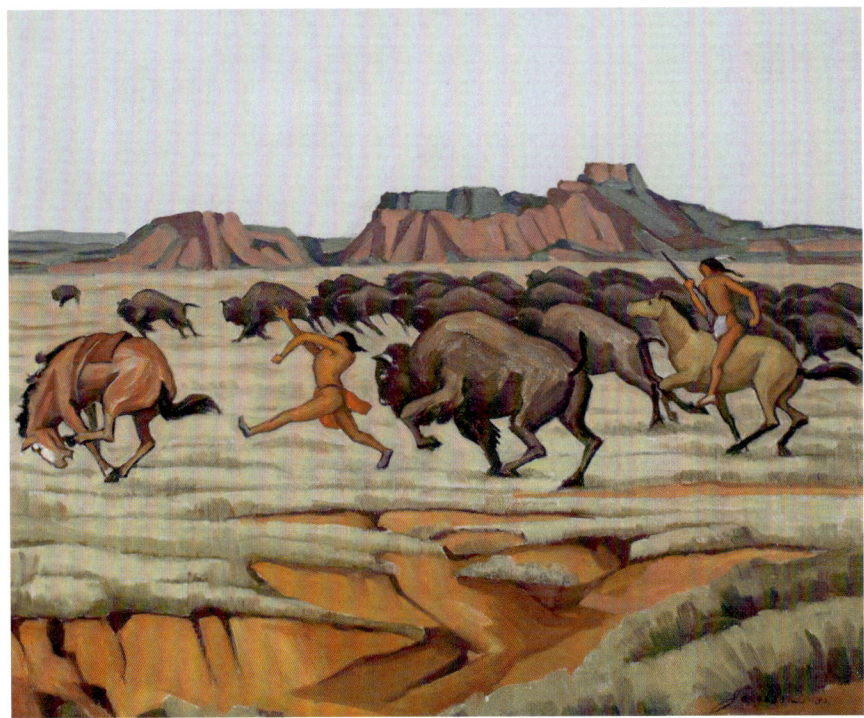

Fig. 66
Oscar Jacobson
U.S., born Sweden, 1882–1966
Buffalo Hunt in Reverse, 1952
Oil on canvas, 20 x 26 in.
Collection of Judge Robert Henry

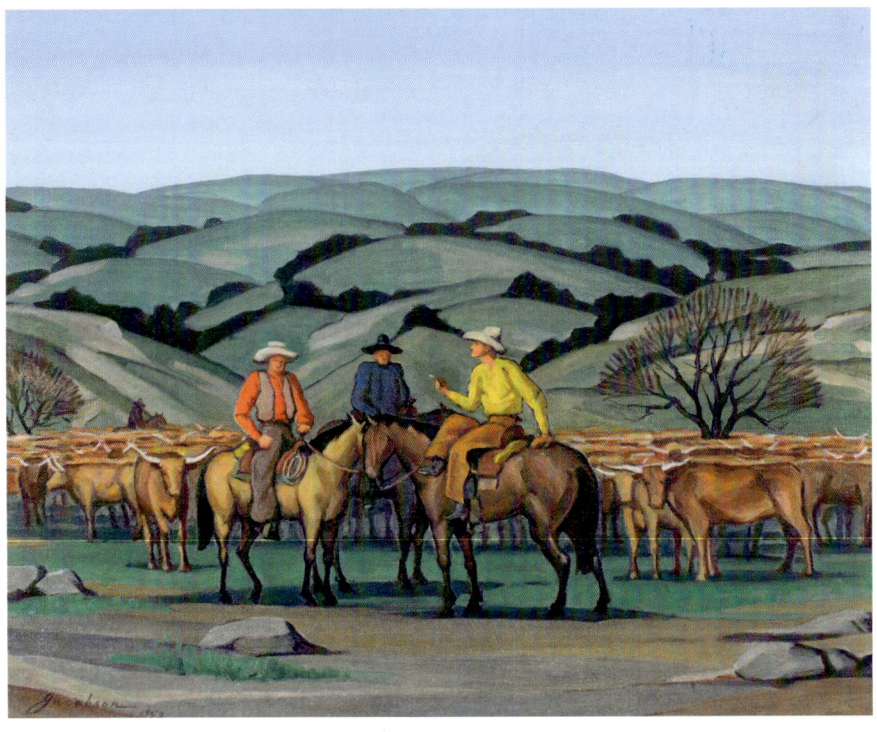

Fig. 67
Oscar Jacobson
U.S., born Sweden, 1882–1966
Resting on the Trail, 1952
Oil on canvas, 22 x 28^1⁄$_{16}$ in.
Collection of Kimball and Mary Kokles

in the wilderness as "an intangible and spiritual resource" parallels those Jacobson expressed years earlier. Stegner argued that preservation of the wilderness was "the challenge against which our character as a people was formed," and it was essential, in that respect, to the American identity. But the wilderness also promised "spiritual refreshment," removed from the things of man, and was necessary in promoting the well-being of the American people: "We simply need that wild country available to us, even if we never do more than drive to its edge and look in. For it can be a means of reassuring ourselves of our sanity as creatures, a part of the geography of hope."[42]

Jacobson's opinion on the Wilderness Act, passed two years before the artist's death, was never recorded, but it seems likely that he supported without reservation "the geography of hope." He had devoted much of his career to that notion, whether painting North Africa or the American West, and he was even inclined to meditate on the role the wilderness had played in forming the American character in the early 1950s. Despite his youthful enthusiasm for the Old West, he had largely avoided historical subject matter since his days at Yale. The pervasive popularity of Westerns in the 1950s, paired with his ideas on wilderness, impelled him to paint a series of works in 1952 on the historical American West. His *Buffalo Hunt in Reverse* (1952; fig. 66) offers a humorous take on the Plains bison hunt, in which a hapless hunter has been thrown from his horse and now scrambles for safety. By contrast, *Resting on the Trail* (1952; fig. 67) depicts three cowboys pausing on their cattle drive of Texas Longhorn. Jacobson's representation lacks the historical specificity of Charles M. Russell and his disciples, but the principal concern was not accuracy so much as recognition of the enduring mythology, recently given cinematic treatment in Howard Hawks's *Red River* (1948). Landscape in this unofficial series is largely a backdrop to the figures, a rarity in Jacobson's career, but it provides the necessary context of wilderness in which the drama of the American West unfolds.

Jacobson continued to paint into the 1960s, though he slowed considerably after surviving a brain hemorrhage in 1955. Thereafter, his paintings were based largely on familiar sites from his earlier career, especially the austere Oklahoma prairies during winter, and occasionally he reworked earlier paintings.[43] His belief in the value of wilderness, especially as an artistic subject, never wavered and persisted for the remainder of his career. He found spiritual import in nature untrammeled by human greed and expressed that, initially through an expressionist style and later through a planar style reminiscent of Cézanne that was suitable for the severity of his subject matter. Drawn to geological processes and ecological concerns, Jacobson crafted an image of the wilderness largely independent of human design. Whether painting the Rockies, the deserts of Arizona or New Mexico, or the prairies of Oklahoma, Oscar Brousse Jacobson maintained a lifelong interest in the value of a world unconquered. ❖

Notes

1   Oscar Jacobson quoted in *An Exhibition of 22 Paintings by O. B. Jacobson* (Norman: Museum of Art, University of Oklahoma, 1948). Oscar Brousse Jacobson and Jeanne d'Ucel scrapbooks, vol. 6, "1946–53," box 6, Oscar B. Jacobson Collection, Oklahoma Historical Society, Oklahoma City.

2   Jeanne d'Ucel, *Memoir and Biographical Writings*, ca. 1962, box 4, folder 1, Oscar B. Jacobson Collection, 37.

3   "Program for the Fourth," *Lindsborg News-Record*, July 2, 1902, in Jacobson and d'Ucel scrapbooks, vol. 1, "1902–11," box 1. D'Ucel records the name of the group differently in *Memoir and Biographical Writings*, p. 37.

4   Letter from Hal Johnson to Sam Olkinetzky, April 13, 1983, donor files, Fred Jones Jr. Museum of Art, University of Oklahoma, Norman. Johnson notes that the painting was given to him by Jacobson as a graduation gift in 1929 and that the artist had painted the scene prior to 1920.

5   Jacobson stated that "Modern art is not representative art—it is pure art. Just as in music one progresses from folk songs to an understanding of chamber music and symphonies, so in painting do we pass from photographic reproduction of places to a much higher form of art, that which appeals to the emotions through the medium of color." Jacobson quoted in an untitled article by an unknown author from *Christian Science Monitor*, Dec. 8, 1923, 23. In using the term "pure art," he was quoting both Maurice Denis's article on Cézanne, which was published in English in *Burlington Magazine* in 1910, and possibly Henri Matisse's "Notes of a Painter," which was published in *La Grande Revue* in 1908. "Jacobson Talks on Art Subject," *Daily Oklahoman*, Oct. 17, 1915, p. 25. The title of his lecture was "Application of Nature." There is no extant transcript of the lecture, but much of it is quoted in the article.

        D'Ucel commented, "Dad, always an ardent student of religion and philosophy, was well versed in the sacred books of Hinduism, Buddhism, etc." "Glimpses," in *Memoir and Biographical Writings*, box 4, folder 6, p. 18.

6   Theodore Roosevelt, *Outdoor Pastimes of an American Hunter* (New York: Charles Scribner's Sons, 1905), 317.

7 Theodore Roosevelt, "Our Vanishing Wild Life," *The Outlook* 103, no. 4 (Jan. 25, 1913): 161.

8 *An Exhibition of the Recent Work of Oscar Brousse Jacobson* (Norman: University of Oklahoma, 1923) in Jacobson and d'Ucel scrapbooks, vol. 3, "1918–26," box 3, Jacobson Collection. The quote is taken from a letter Roosevelt wrote to the artist Pinckney Marcius-Simons, first published in Joseph Bucklin Bishop, ed., "Roosevelt to Authors and Artists," *Scribner's Magazine* 67, no. 6 (June 1920): 641–56.

9 Jacobson began to hold regular solo exhibitions at OU most years until 1952, following his retirement.

10 d'Ucel, *Memoir and Biographical Writings*, box 4, folder 1, 76.

11 d'Ucel, "About Indians," in *Memoir and Biographical Writings*, box 4, folder 5, p. 1. D'Ucel noted, "In 1915, as we were moving from Washington State to Oklahoma, we spent the summer months in the Southwest. Dad was introducing me to the Indian side of America. We wandered through the Pueblo country; we climbed the Rock of Acoma." Jacobson's portrait is titled *The Governor of Acoma*, although Jacobson did not record the name of his sitter. It may have been Leo Garcia, who is listed as the governor in 1917. Ward Alan Minge, *Acoma: Pueblo in the Sky* (Albuquerque: University of New Mexico Press, 1976), 144.

    A Prayer for Rain (1916) was included in the first *Artists of the Southwest* exhibition and purchased by McPherson High School in McPherson, Kansas.

12 Ibid, 2.

13 John C. Van Dyke, *The Desert: Further Studies in Natural Appearances* (New York: Charles Scribner's Sons, 1901), 232.

14 J. Newton Nin, "A Fine Arts Movement in Norman, Oklahoma," *Grand Rapids News*, March 29, 1919, in Jacobson and d'Ucel scrapbooks, vol. 3, "1918–26," box 3, Jacobson Collection.

15 Harry R. Burke, "The Day's Journey," *St. Louis Times*, Jan. 15, 1924, in Jacobson and d'Ucel scrapbooks, vol. 3, "1918–26," box 3, Jacobson Collection. Jacobson considered Burke's review the finest he had ever received. Untitled article, *St. Louis Globe Democrat*, January 27, 1924, in Jacobson and d'Ucel scrapbooks, vol. 3 "1918–26," box 3, Jacobson Collection.

The early 1920s was a particularly important period in Jacobson's career, in which he exhibited and sold many of his paintings. *Navajo Going to the Snake Dance* entered the collection of Rupel J. Jones, director of the OU School of Dramatic Art, in the 1920s, although the precise date is unknown.

Photographer Richard Gordon Matzene owned *White Shadows Among the Navajos*, which Jacobson exhibited at the *Exhibition of Work by Creative Artists of the States of Missouri, Kansas and Oklahoma* and *Works by Prominent Illustrators* at the Kansas City Art Institute (KCAI), January 1923, then the *7th Annual Association of Oklahoma Artists* in March 1923, and finally at Emporia Teachers' College in January 1925.

Giant Cacti was exhibited at Central High School in Oklahoma City in March 1923, followed by a solo show at OU in October 1923 and an exhibition with fellow faculty member Gwendolyn Meux at Oklahoma College for Women (now University of Science and Arts of Oklahoma) in December 1924.

Both *The Garden of Allah* and *Painted Desert—Northern Arizona* were included in an exhibition with Meux and Edith Mahier at the Delgado Museum of Art in New Orleans in November 1923. OU faculty member Ida Z. Kirk purchased the latter painting, and the former was exhibited later at the St. Louis Public Library in January 1924, the Broadmoor Art Academy in July 1924, and the aforementioned Oklahoma College for Women exhibition.

The Needles, Colorado Desert had numerous titles before it was eventually acquired by the Oklahoma Art League in 1927–28. After its inclusion in a solo exhibition at OU in October 1923, Jacobson entered it as *The Needles (Arizona-California)* in the Delgado exhibit in November 1923. By 1924, he had altered the title to *The Needles, Arizona* for the Midwestern Artists' Exhibition at KCAI in 1924 and *Needles—Arizona* in the Oklahoma College for Women exhibit. Jacobson also selected the painting for inclusion in his retrospective exhibition at the WPA Oklahoma Art Center in 1940.

Orabai Wash was eventually owned by Jacobson's former student and future colleague at OU, Leonard Good.

16   Oscar Brousse Jacobson, "The Meaning of Modernism in Art," *The American Magazine of Art* 15, no. 1 (Jan. 1924): 699.

17   For a discussion of how the artists and writers of New Mexico responded to the Bursum Bill, see Lynn Cline, *Literary Pilgrims: The Santa Fe and Taos Writers' Colonies, 1917–1950* (Albuquerque: University of New Mexico Press, 2007) and Charles C. Eldredge, Julie Schimmel, and William H. Truettner, *Art in New Mexico, 1900–1945: Paths to Taos and Santa Fe* (New York: Abbeville Press, 1986).

18   d'Ucel, "About Indians," in *Memoir and Biographical Writings*, box 4, folder 5, p. 22.

19   d'Ucel, *Memoir and Biographical Writings*, box 4, folder 1, 97.

20   "Sooner Artist Returns from Africa with Many Canvases of Great Sahara Desert," *Daily Oklahoman*, Sept. 26, 1926, D-3.

21   *Olive Orchard in Grande Kabylie* was later owned by William Bennett Bizzell, the fifth president of OU. Jacobson included it in *Exhibition of Some Paintings of North Africa by Oscar Jacobson* at OU in March 1927 and a subsequent show at Oklahoma A&M (now Oklahoma State University) in April 1928.

22   Cézanne had a profound influence on American art in the 1910s and '20s. For further information, see Gail Stavitsky and Kathryn Rothkopf, *Cézanne and American Modernism* (New Haven, Conn.: Yale University Press, 2009).

23   Jacobson, "Fording Algeria," *University of Oklahoma Magazine* 15, no. 3 (Spring 1927): 5. He exhibited the African paintings extensively. *Sahara Desert Near Biskra, Algeria*, also titled *North of Biskra (Edge of Desert)*, was included in *An Exhibition of Some Paintings Done in Algeria and in the Northern Sahara Desert by Oscar B. Jacobson of Norman, Oklahoma*, at the MacDowell Club of Allied Arts in Oklahoma City in 1927 and then Jacobson's annual fall exhibition in 1928. He exhibited *Kairoruan, Tunis, Africa, 4th Holy City, Great Mosque* in the MacDowell Club exhibit and the March 1927 OU exhibit.

      Jacobson seems to have exhibited *Djedjelli, Algeria* more than any other painting over the course of his career, and it was featured in a string of venues: the Eva Fowler Art League in Sherman, Texas, in January 1927; the Harbour-Longmire Co. in Oklahoma City in November 1927; *Exhibition of Some Paintings of North Africa by Oscar Jacobson* at OU in March 1927; a show of the North African paintings at the Madison Art Association at the State Historical Museum in Wisconsin in May 1927; the Society of Independent Artists in New York City in April 1928; the Ainslie Galleries in New York City in November 1928; the Dallas Women's Club, an exhibit organized by the Dallas Art Association, in February 1929; Kroch's Bookstore in Chicago in June 1929; the University of Tulsa in January 1932; an *Exhibition of American Paintings* at Harrisburg Art Association Art Gallery in Pennsylvania in March 1931; a faculty exhibition at the OU Memorial Union in February 1938, and another faculty exhibition in September 1949.

24 William Cunningham, "The Art of Oscar Brousse Jacobson," *Haldeman-Julius Quarterly* 1, no. 1 (Jan. 1927): 28.

25 Demma Ray Oldham, "The Oasis," *Daily Oklahoman*, Aug. 12, 1928, 8-C.

26 Rogers largely based his comment on that of Mark Twain, who quipped, "If you don't like the weather in New England, just wait a few minutes." The original source of Rogers's adaptation is unclear.

        Jacobson's *Purple Waters* was formerly owned by Emil Krayttli, secretary to the Board of Regents, in the late 1920s. A notation on the verso indicates that it was loaned to the office of the OU President but is unclear as to which president and when.

27 *The Quartz Mountains* was formerly owned by John and Grace Lee Frank, owners of Frankoma Pottery. John had been the ceramics instructor at OU from 1927 to 1936. Both *Oklahoma Mosaic* and *The Red Tank*, titled *Indian Pool* in his record books, were exhibited in solo shows at OU in 1937 and 1940, respectively.

28 For further information on *Medicine Park*, see Linda Paulson Branson, "The Evolution of a Resort Community: Medicine Park, Oklahoma," (master of arts thesis, University of Oklahoma, 1992).

29 Paul B. Sears, *Deserts on the March*, 2nd ed. (Norman: University of Oklahoma Press, 1947), 145, 130.

30 Jacobson not only exhibited *In Brown and Grey* at the Coronado Quatro Centennial Exhibition, but also at his solo show at OU that same year. He also considered the painting important enough to feature in his retrospectives in 1941 and 1961 at OU's Museum of Art (now the FJJMA).

31 d'Ucel, *Memoir and Biographical Writings*, box 4, folder 2, p. 189. Jacobson originally listed the date of *Below Raton* as 1929 in his record books, but he could have been in error. The painting was included in exhibitions after 1934, most notably *An Exhibition of Recent Paintings by Oscar Brousse Jacobson* at OU in October 1936 and *An Exhibition of Most Recent Paintings by O. B. Jacobson* at OU in November 1940. He also included the painting in his 1941 retrospective and another exhibit at Benedictine Heights College in Tulsa in October 1958.

32   "Artists of Five States Bow Before Oklahoma's Painters," unidentified press clipping, in Jacobson and d'Ucel scrapbooks, vol. 4, "1926–32," box 4, Jacobson Collection. *Mountain Lake* is dated 1926 in Jacobson's record books, although that is likely an error. The painting was exhibited nearly as much as *Djedjelli, Algeria*, and in many of the same exhibits: Harbour-Longmire Co., Ainslie Galleries, the Dallas Women's Club, and Kroch's Bookstore (see n. 23). *Mountain Lake* was also included in Jacobson's 1928 exhibition at OU, a University of Tulsa exhibit in January 1932, and the 1940 and 1961 retrospectives.

33   *Emerald Lake, No. 1* was included in his 1936 annual fall show at OU, *An Exhibition of Recent Paintings by Oscar Brousse Jacobson.*

34   http://www.utepasshistoricalsociety.org/ute-pass-history/, accessed August 29, 2014.

35   Harvey L .Carter, *The Pikes Peak Region: A Sesquicentennial History* (Colorado Springs: The Dentan Printing Company, 1956), 32. *Green Mountains* was included in Jacobson's annual exhibition at OU in 1936 and his 1941 retrospective.

36   James McTighe, *Roadside History of Colorado* (Boulder, Colo.: Johnson Books, 1984), 121.

37   Jacobson seems to have painted *en plein* air rarely. He often sketched with colored pencil and developed paintings from the sketches. D'Ucel recalled that on a drive into the Rockies in the late 1930s, Jacobson was interested in the view from a peak, with clouds below, but had no supplies with him: "On pieces of paper bags, with an ordinary pencil, he hurriedly made sketches; he could only list the colors. His visual memory keen; besides, he set to work as soon as we returned; so he was able to express the majesty of the scene in his paintings." D'Ucel, *Memoir and Biographical Writings*, box 4, folder 2, p. 215.

38   Prior to the World's Fair, the painting was included in Jacobson's 1938 OU show. He then sent it to the Nebraska Art Association Semi-Centennial Annual Exhibition of Painting in 1940. It was featured in *The Six States Exhibit: Colorado, Iowa, Kansas, Missouri, Nebraska, South Dakota*, organized by the Society of Liberal Arts at the Joslyn Art Museum in Omaha in 1946. Jacobson also included it in his 1961 retrospective.

39   d'Ucel, *Memoir and Biographical Writings*, box 4, folder 2, 219–20.

40   *Wyoming Ranch* was once owned by Oklahoma artist Alice Fleming. *Towards Questa* was included in *Exhibition of Twenty-one Paintings by Jacobson of Colorado, Utah, Oklahoma, Wyoming and New Mexico* at OU in October 1946. Jacobson titled the painting *Towards Questa* in his photographic record books, but the painting is inscribed *Road to Santa Fe* on the verso. The titles would seem to be inconsistent, and it is unclear which is accurate."

41   Jacobson held an exhibition of work painted during summer 1949 that included *Horse Thief Canyon, Oklahoma, Light Soil*, and *The Glass Mountains. Light Soil* entered the collection of Joseph Benton, a former opera singer and an instructor of voice at OU. The title *On the Road to Chickasha* is inscribed on the back, but in a hand that does not seem to be Jacobson's. In his photographic record book, the painting is titled *Light Soil* and the title of *On the Road to Chickasha* is associated with a different painting.
      The Glass Mountains was owned by the Franks and included in Jacobson's 1961 retrospective.

42   From http://wilderness.org/bios/former-council-members/wallace-stegner/, accessed on April 19, 2013.

43   For example, sometime after 1953 Jacobson made substantial changes to his painting *90 Miles to O'Brien's Bar (Southern New Mexico)* (1923, altered later; Fred Jones Jr. Museum of Art). Originally titled *89 Miles to O'Brien* in volume one of Jacobson's photographic record books, the painting was enlarged by almost an inch in every direction using extra canvas after restretching, and Jacobson added a large wash in the foreground of the composition. Other paintings seem to have been retouched by Jacobson in the 1950s and '60s, although the subject requires further research.

Detail (facing page), see Fig. 64, page 87
Oscar Jacobson
U.S., born Sweden, 1882–1966
The Glass Mountains, 1949

Detail (pages 102–103), see Fig. 56, page 81
Oscar Jacobson
U.S., born Sweden, 1882–1966
Trail Ridge in June, 1938

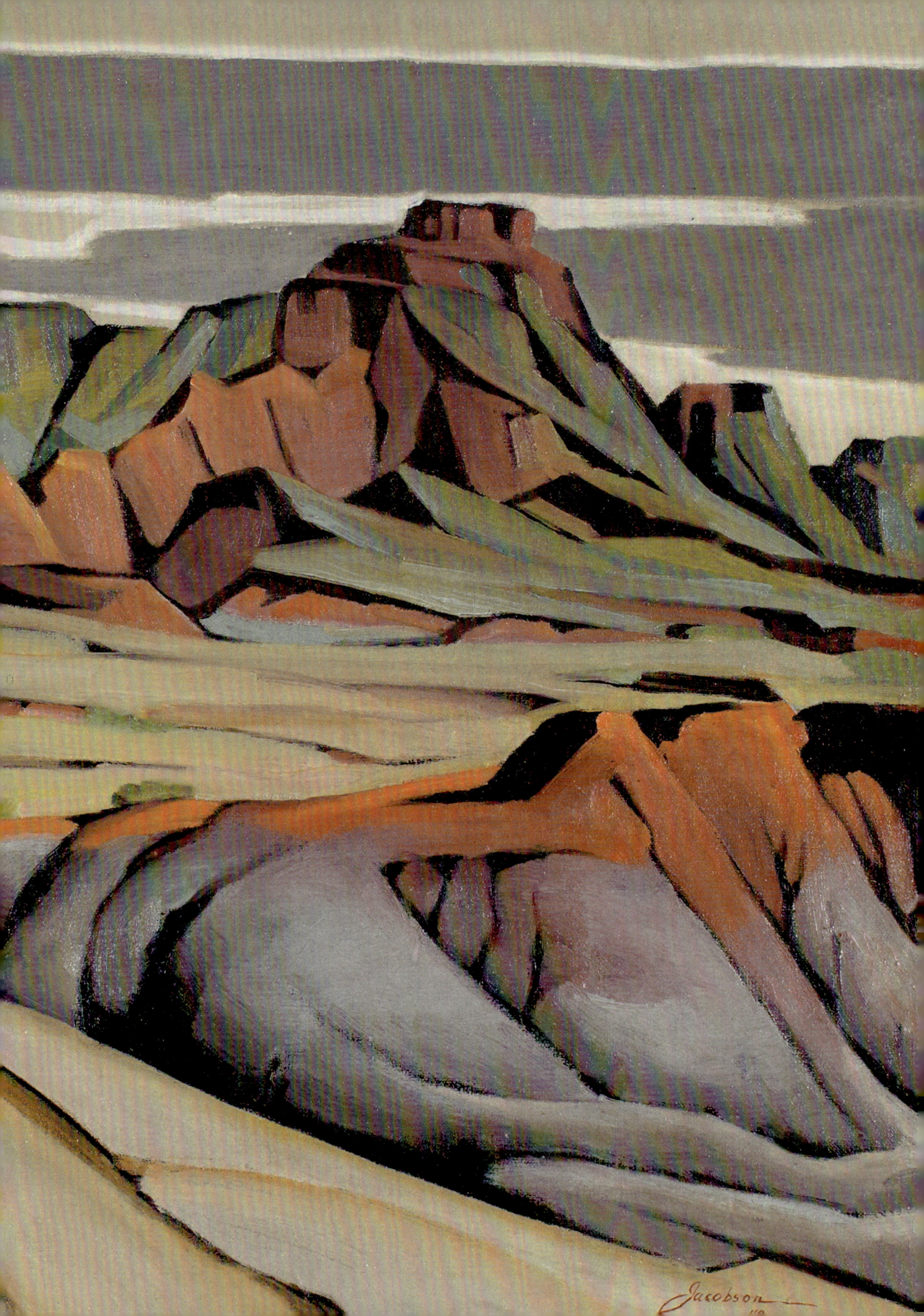

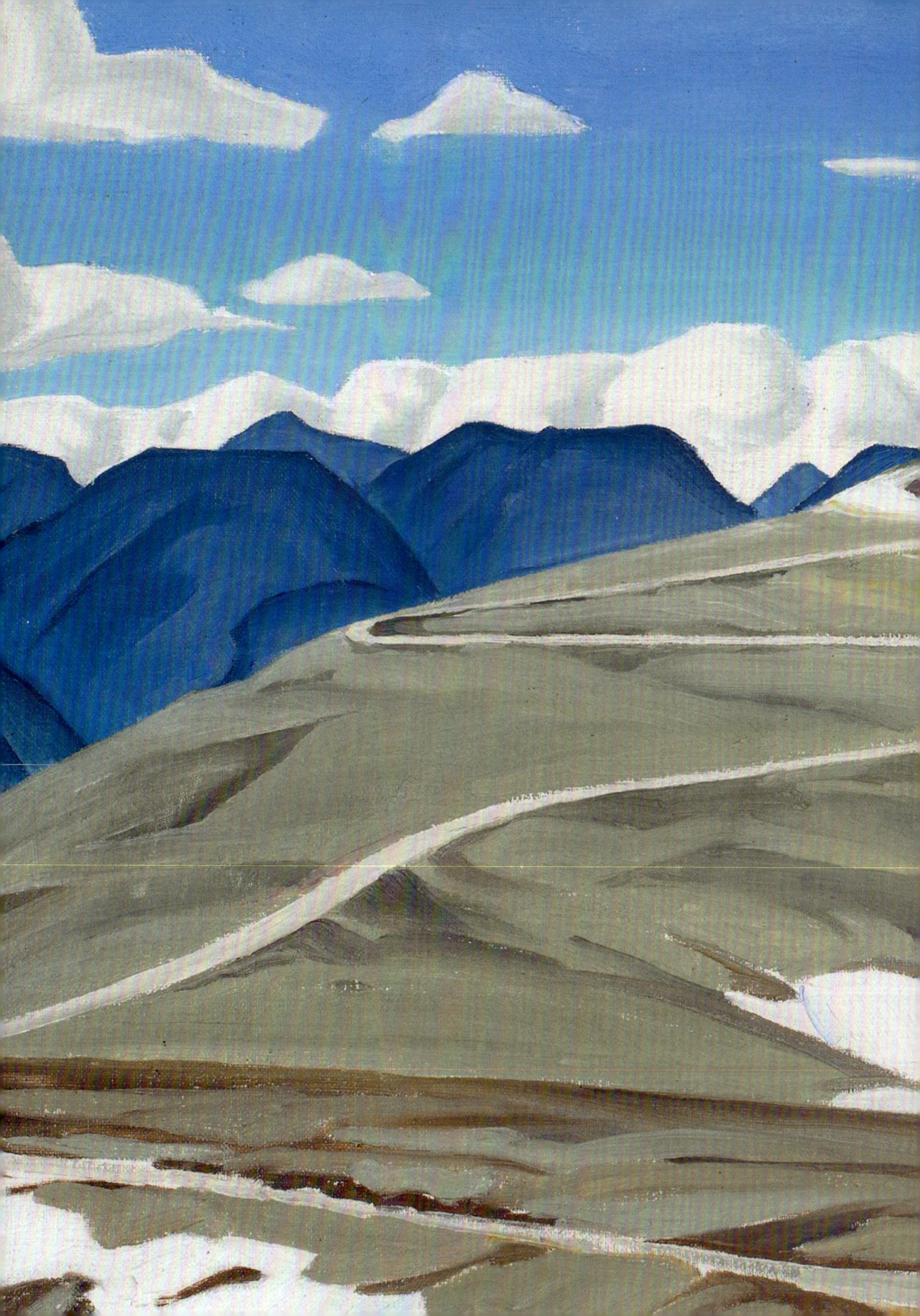

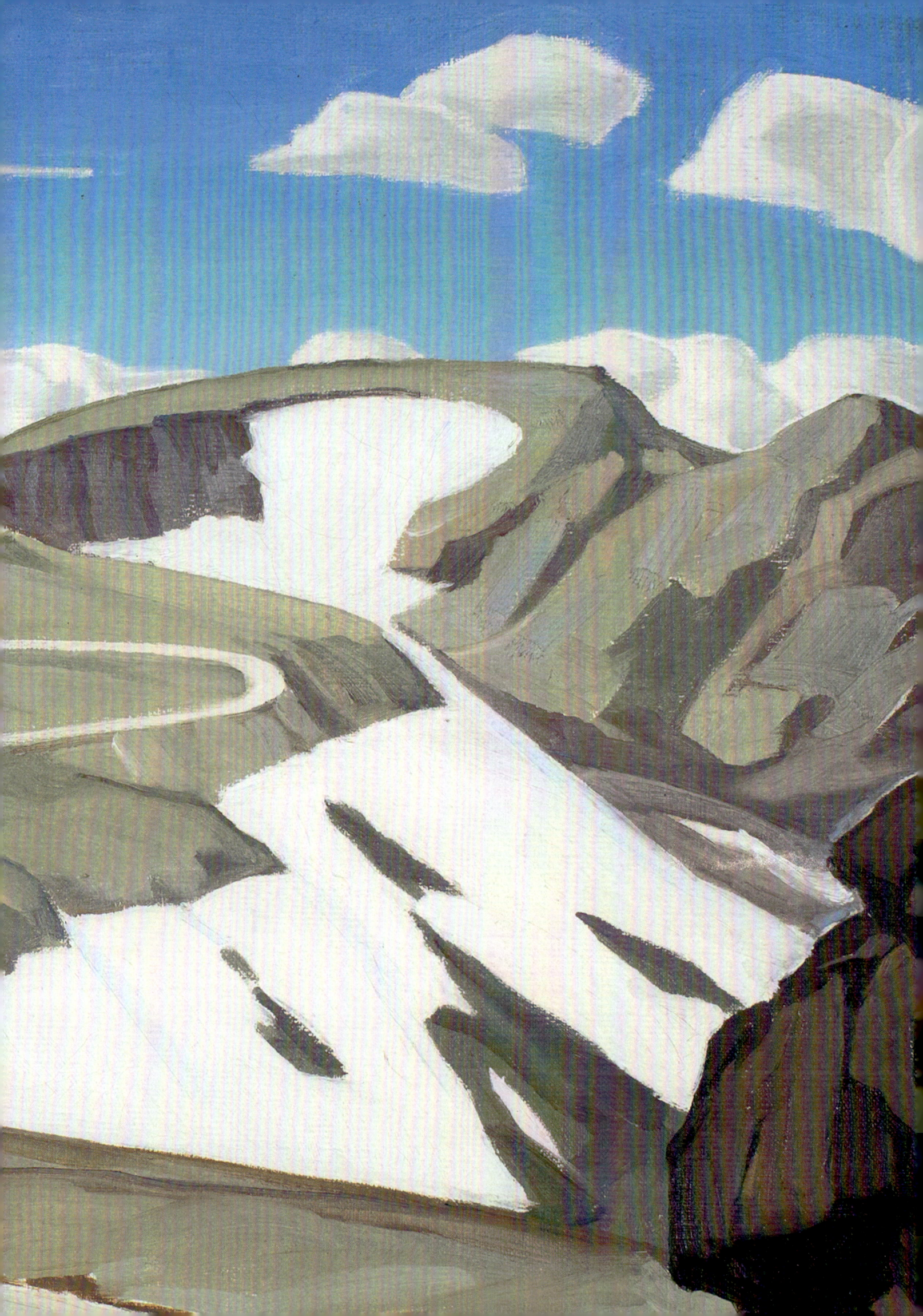

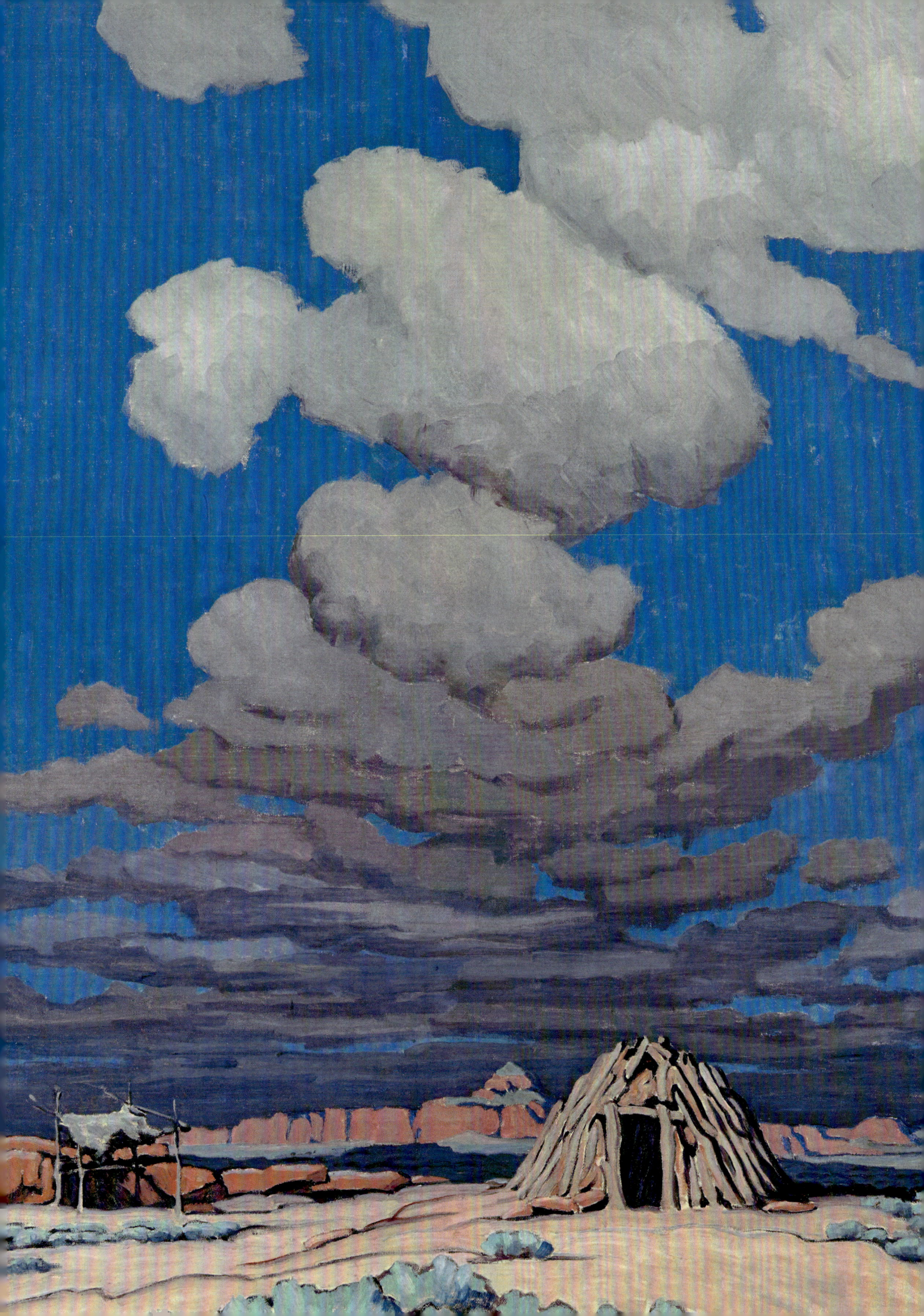

From Indigenous America to North Africa

The Cosmopolitan World of Oscar Jacobson and Jeanne d'Ucel

Janet Catherine Berlo

In 1906, the New Haven Saturday Chronicle published an article titled "Unique 'Kawraw Kiote's Den': Tales of True Frontier Life as Shown in Rooms of Four Yale Men." It describes the sitting room of four students from western states, one of whom was Oscar Jacobson of Kansas:

> The rooms of these quondam ranchers is a veritable museum, and are said to contain the largest private collection of Indian relics east of the Mississippi. Among these curios is to be found a genuine Sioux chief's war bonnet. This striking piece of headwear is made of selected eagle feathers and is worth a little fortune in itself. Other articles are Navajo blankets, beaded leggins [*sic*], moccasins, arrows, strings of wampum, war clubs, etc. A special object of pride is a peace pipe direct from "the great red pipestone quarry," mentioned in Longfellow's Hiawatha.[1]

Referring to Jacobson, the article mentions that one of these "cowboy students" is an artist whose paintings also adorn the room. The accompanying photo shows an artful arrangement worthy of a department store window (fig. 68). Behind the requisite Oriental carpet and overstuffed sofa of an early twentieth century collegiate room are numerous paintings of western scenes, the aforementioned headdress, leggings, and textiles, as well as cowboy hats and a panoply of other objects. But this was no static display; other photos published in New Haven periodicals show Jacobson wearing his headdress, moccasins, and leggings as he played a Pawnee chief in the play *Sunset,* written by one of his roommates and performed in theatres around Connecticut in 1906 and 1907.[2]

Detail, see Fig. 27, page 52

Oscar Jacobson

U.S., born Sweden, 1882–1966

White Shadows—Among the Navajos, 1922

Unique "Kawraw Kiotes' Den"

Tales of True Frontier Life as Shown in Rooms of Four Yale Men.

One of the most unique students' rooms at Yale is the "Den" of the suite occupied by four Westerners. It is familiarly known as the "Kawraw Kiotes' Den." The "Kiotes," who desired their names withheld, but were at last persuaded to give them, are born and bred in the West, and hail severally from Kansas, New Mexico, Colorado and South Dakota. They are Mr. Carl Ostrum, Mr. Oskar Jakobson, Mr. Oscar Freeburg and Mr. Harry Larson. Their boyhood experiences were those of "busting" bronchos, and "punching" cattle. But their ambition for books, which was born in the public schools, soon brought them together at a leading Western college located in Kansas. From there they were attracted to Yale, for this university is said to be very popular in the west.

While at this school the "Kiotes" were allowed to renew their ranch life every summer, but upon coming East, they couldn't bear to leave it all behind, so, as one of them expressed it, they "took all the clothes along," but since they can't wear them here, they had to "hang them up on the walls." It is,

perhaps, necessary to explain that a Westerner considers a cartridge belt and a healthy Colt an essential part of his clothing.

The rooms of these quondam ranchers is a veritable museum, and are said to contain the largest private collection of Indian relics east of the Mississippi. Among these curios is to be found a genuine Sioux chief's war bonnet. This striking piece of headwear is made of selected eagle feathers and is worth a little fortune in itself. Other articles are Navajo blankets, beaded leggins, moccasins, arrows, strings of wampum, war clubs, etc. A special object of pride is a peace pipe direct from "the great red pipestone quarry," mentioned in Longfellow's Hiawatha. Besides these things, the "Kiotes" have several original Indian photographs procured personally from such characters as Geronimo, Handsome Elk, etc., and, in a place of honor, a real little "Silver Heels" from the Ponca tribe in Indian Territory. Two other photographs must also be mentioned. One is Bessie Hill, the noted cowboy girl of Chamberlain, South Dakota, and the other is Lucille Mulhall, the champion lady roper of the world, who appeared last year at the Horse Show in New York.

The young arsenal already alluded to includes several cap-and-ball revolvers that did service during

pioneer days beyond the Mississippi; some of these have notches in the handle, and any question as to the wherefore of these marks is invariably followed by an ominous silence.

A favorite whim of the cowboy was to utilize the brim of his "sombrero" for a daily journal. And the following entries were taken at random from one of these hats: "Plugged Attorney 'Red Jacket's' silk hat;" "Met Borax Bill with his twenty-nine mule team;" "Poor Jack—bit by a rattlesnake." The "Kiotes" are great on notices and original posters, which express some such sentiment as "Don't stare at us—Nature made us this way;" "We are not responsible for accidents on this ranch;" or "Don't be polite—we are not used to it," etc.

What most impresses the visitor to this den is the genuineness of everything exhibited. There is the smell of powder about the guns, and the freshness of the plains is exhaled from the atmosphere of these rooms. And every article, whether handcuffs, rattlesnake skins, buffalo horns, coyote skin, or Mexican bullfighter's costume, has its own little story and it takes the "Kiotes" to tell it.

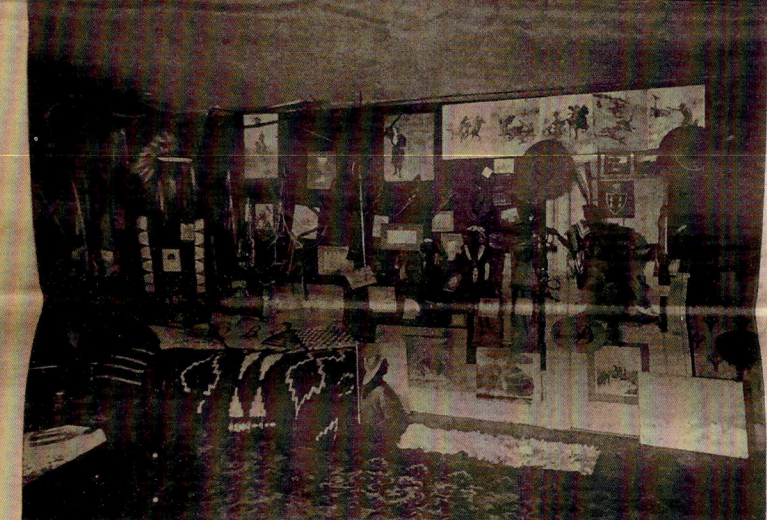

CORNER IN THE DEN, SHOWING THE COLLECTION OF WESTERN ARTICLES.

These interesting rooms have lately been the scene of many teas, and some of the best society of New Haven has inspected the curios of these cowboy students. One of them is an artist, and many of his original paintings adorn the rooms. He has had no little success as an illustrator, one of his best attempts being a cowboy girl for a poem of which a quotation runs as follows:

> O, the wooly wild is callin'
> And it's there that I should be
> Where my lovin' lass is livin'
> Waitin' patiently for me,
> On the road to Santa Fe
> Where the merry breezes play
> In the sand amid the sage brush
> And the sun shines all the day.
> O, the road to Santa Fe,
> Where the sun shines all the day,
> Where my lovin' lass is livin'
> Let me go, and stick and stay.

The "Kiotes" are fast becoming acclimated to the East, however, and they say they are learning to like the "Tenderfoots" because of their culture, pleasantness, and general air of tolerance. But it is a far cry from a pair of "chaps" to a dress suit, or from the never absent "bandanna" to a white cravat, and, we doubt not, that the "Kiotes" return many a time from some social function, and, throwing off their

confining coats, look with longing eyes at their favorite "clothes" on the wall.

During the summer our friends will occupy a cottage on the road to Woodmont, and there is genuine western hospitality in their words when they say "Our latch string always hangs out."

FINAL HORSE SHOW PLANS

Long List or Entries Received for Society's First Exhibition.

The final plans for the horse show, to be held next Monday and Tuesday, are now completed, and the entry list is a much longer and far better one than was at first expected. All horse owners are greatly interested in the show, and a pleasing feature is the number of high-class draught horses which have been entered by a number of business firms, as it was not at first expected that this class would be as popular. It will also be a large society event, and nearly all owners in the society set have one or more entries. Although the first show ever held in New Haven, it is bound to be a complete success, and will certainly not be the last. All of the boxes have been sold and nearly all of the parking spaces. There is to be a refreshment tent for the holders of boxes, reserved seats and parking privileges.

In many classes there has been a large number of entries, thus making the contests more interesting. Three prizes are offered in each class, the first one in every case having been offered by someone interested in the show. Many owners have a number of horses entered, some being represented in every class. Some of the owners represented are Mr. Louis E. Stoddard, Mr. Hayes Q. Trowbridge, Mr. Walter L. Goodwin, Mr. Howard Phipps, Mr. R. G. Keeney, Mr. Hugh Legare, Mr. J. C. Rathbone, Mr. I. Watson Webb, Mr. Jackson Dykeman, Mr. Richard F. Ely, Mr. Frank S. Butterworth, Miss Eleanor F. Nesbit, Miss Barbara Brewster, Mr. Elijah J. Ball, Judge Livingston W. Cleaveland, Mr. D. W. Armstrong, Mr. E. E. Garrison, Mr. Charles H. Wolfe, General Phelps Montgomery, General George H. Ford, Mrs. Frank L. Stiles, Mrs. Dwight N. Moore, Mr. J. A. Gillies, Mr. William R. Tyler, Dr. Willis H. Crowe, Mr. Charles Waterhouse, Jr., Mr. G. W. H. Hughes, Mr. John Moran, Mr. Julius G. Day, Dr. W. J. Sheehan, Mr. B. S. Bradley, Mr. Charles H. Downs, Dr. E. C. Ross, Mr. W. H. Unmack, Mr. Edward O'Neil, Mr. I. G. Richey, Mr. Olin L. Dibble, Mr. Edward Malley, Mr. Louis Linder, Mr. Pierrepont B. Foster, Mrs. Henry S. Parmelee, Mr. William R. Shaffer, Mr. C. E. Fairchild, Mr. Henry L. Hotchkiss, Mr. H. C. Warren, Mr. I. H. King, Colonel Rutherford Trowbridge, Mr. H. L. Lewis, Mrs. Morris F. Tyler, Miss Mildred Wilson, Mr. William Brewster, Mr. Rudolph Steinert, Miss Mazie Cotter, Mr. Julius G. Day, Mr. A. A. Eisele, Mr. A. M. Young, Peck & Bishop, Sperry & Barnes Co., Atwood Remedy Co., E. J. Duggan, Abner Hendee, D. M. Welch & Son, Stoddard, Gilbert & Co., Mr. Harry Peters, Mr. R. L. Bishop, Police department, Judge A. Heaton Robertson, Mr. George L. Clark, Mr. E. H. Burgess, and Mr. N. W. Hubinger.

No Smoke for Him.

There is a clever young physician in Philadelphia who has never been able to smoke a cigar. "Just one poisons me," says the youthful doctor.

Recently the doctor was invited to a large dinner party given by a New York friend. At the conclusion of the repast, when the women had left the table, cigars were accepted by all the men except the physician from Philadelpia. Seeing his friend refuse the cigar, the host in astonishment exclaimed:

"What, not smoking? Why, my dear fellow, you lose half your dinner!"

"Yes, I know I do," meekly replied the doctor, "but if I smoked, I would lose the whole of it."

Fig. 68

"Indian Corner" in Oscar Brousse Jacobson's suite of rooms at Yale, 1906, as published in *Saturday Chronicle*, June 2, 1906, from Oscar Brousse Jacobson and Jeanne d'Ucel scrapbooks, volume 1, "1902–11."

Jacobson's devotion to contemporary American Indian painting of his era is well-known to scholars of Native art, for he provided Oklahoma Native artists with opportunities for education, income, and exhibition across the United States and Europe, and published portfolios of reproductions of Native art that were sought after by collectors. With his French-born wife, Jeanne d'Ucel (fig. 69), Jacobson mentored and championed Native artists, tirelessly working to ensure that their work received international acclaim, exhibition in major museums and galleries, and publication.[3] The Jacobsons also traveled across North Africa during a sabbatical year in the 1920s, amassing a collection of Berber arts that they gave to the University of Oklahoma. In addition to publishing with her husband on Native art and writing articles for Oklahoma magazines on local arts and events, d'Ucel wrote a book on Berber arts and lectured on North African music. In the decades before 1950, this worldly couple brought a wide-ranging cosmopolitan point of view to students at OU and citizens of Oklahoma.

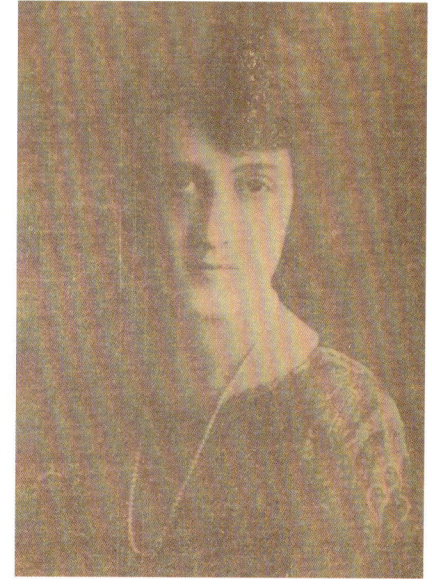

Under the direction of Jacobson, the OU Museum of Art acquired more than three hundred works of Native American art (with a strong focus on twentieth century paintings) and eighty-six works of North African art (principally textiles, ceramics, and metalwork). This essay charts the couple's interest in these two fields of non-European arts, and the legacy of their collecting, mentorship, and scholarship.

The roots of Oscar Brousse Jacobson's interest in Native art began in his childhood as a Swedish emigrant to rural Kansas.[4] As evidenced in the anecdotes about his Yale rooms and his amateur theatrical career, such interests were already well developed by the time he studied painting as a post-graduate at Yale University. As they traveled in the West, and befriended Kiowa artists in Oklahoma, the world of Native art became central to Jacobson and to his wife as well, for she shared many of his interests, both personally and professionally.

For this catalogue honoring Jacobson's work, I have examined museum holdings and records, as well as previously unpublished and underutilized sources on the Jacobsons (including their own unpublished writings), in order to provide a fuller picture of the contributions to art and art history made by this indomitable couple. The fields of Native American art and, to a lesser extent, North African art, were greatly enriched by their dedication and talent, as was the institution that would become the Fred Jones Jr. Museum of Art at the University of Oklahoma.

Fig. 69
Photograph of Jeanne d'Ucel, from *Daily Oklahoman*, November 11, 1928, p. C-1.

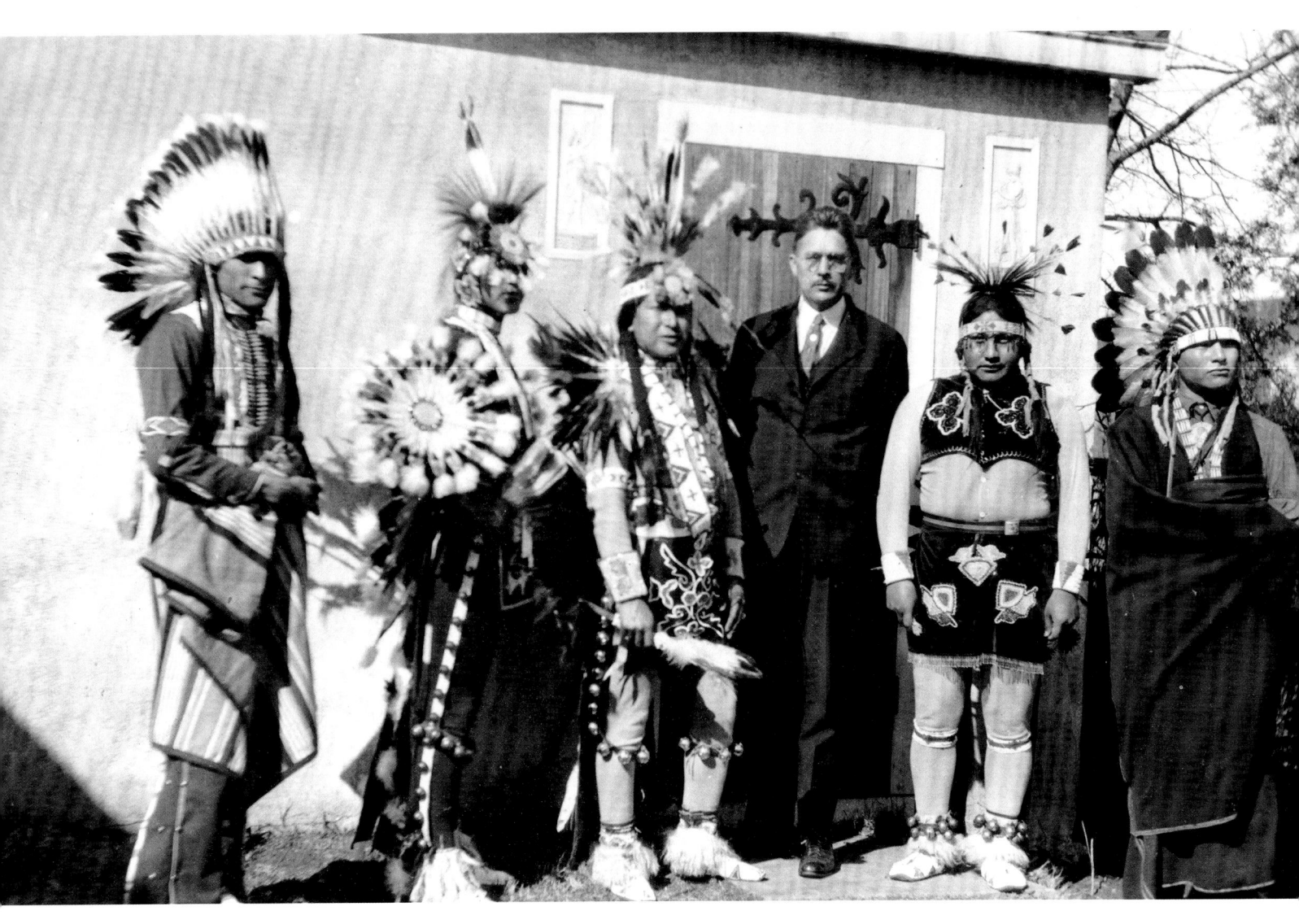

Fig. 70   Oscar Jacobson and members of the Kiowa Five, 1929 *(left to right)*:

Monroe Tsatoke, Jack Hokeah, Stephen Mopope, Jacobson, Spencer Asah,

and James Auchiah.

Native American Art at the University of Oklahoma and Beyond

Outside of Norman, Oklahoma, Oscar Jacobson is today best known for his mentoring of the Kiowa artists who came to the university in 1926–27, and who were catapulted to international recognition through his efforts (fig. 70). Four male students (Spencer Asah, c. 1905–1955; Jack Hokeah, 1902–1969; Steven Mopope, 1898–1974; and Monroe Tsatoke, 1904–1937) arrived at the University of Oklahoma in the early spring of 1927, stayed some months, and returned in January 1928, joined by Bou-ge-tah (Lois) Smokey (1907–1981). They had experimented with painting while attending St. Patrick's Mission School in Anadarko. An Indian agent named J. A. Butin brought the budding artists to Jacobson's attention, hoping that their efforts might be further encouraged.[5]

Yet Jacobson was neither their only mentor at the university, nor their first. Jacobson was in Chicago when the Kiowa students arrived in Norman. According to contemporaneous accounts—and according to Jacobson and d'Ucel themselves—it was art department faculty member Edith Mahier who received and mentored them.[6] Mahier welcomed the four young men (along with two wives and a baby) into her home, found them places to live, offered friendship and encouragement, and received them into her studio for gentle critique and direction as they drew and painted.[7]

The Jacobsons' championing of these worthy artists had an economic incentive as well as an artistic one, for the artists needed to support themselves while in Norman. In manuscripts apparently written for the Jacobsons' children, d'Ucel recounted:

> We helped them directly by buying many of their works; and Dad buttonholed his friends to make sales. He also arranged for the Indians to give dance performances and he booked them in many cities in Oklahoma and outside the state. All this, however, was insufficient. Dad was able to interest the kind oilman, Lew Wentz, who agreed to finance the students and Dad promised to make them famous. Only, fearing that unearned money might have an undesirable effect, Dad persuaded Mr. Wentz to buy paintings instead of giving the funds outright. This proved a good incentive and, as Lew Wentz donated many of the paintings he bought to the Art Museum at the university, it formed the nucleus of a fine collection there.[8]

The Kiowa artists' style of painting was in tune with Art Deco and other early twentieth century modern trends. Collectors and exhibit audiences admired the flat, decorative patterning, the strong bright palette, the controlled use of gouache, and the insight into Native dance, ceremonial dress, and other customs that these works provided. In the undated *Chief and Two Indian Women* (fig. 71), Mopope depicts a man of rank dressed for a public occasion in beaded leggings, moccasins, and dance apron, his hair bedecked with honoring feathers. He is flanked by identically dressed women wearing long skirts, striped shawls, and soft, high deerskin moccasins.

According to anthropologist Lydia Wyckoff, within a year of their arrival at the university, so many works by the Kiowa artists were sold that the collection had to be "replenished and increased" before the exhibition schedule could continue.[9] Having spent time in Santa Fe, surely Jacobson was familiar with the Pueblo watercolor movement that had gained recognition starting in 1919; this would have been a good model for his own efforts with the young Kiowa artists.

Prominent artists such as Marsden Hartley and John Sloan were championing the work of contemporary Pueblo painters, ensuring that it was seen, purchased, and talked about. The first exhibits of Pueblo paintings took place at the Museum of Fine Arts in Santa Fe in 1919, followed by exhibitions at the Arts Club in Chicago in 1920, and the Society of Independent Artists in New York City in 1920, 1921, and 1922. Sloan was so enthusiastic about the work that he proclaimed it "the only 100% American art produced in this country," and it was featured in many popular magazines.[10] In 1922, Amelia Elizabeth White (a prominent player in the Santa Fe scene) opened the first Indian art gallery in New York City and worked tirelessly to promote Native art and artists, exhibiting her collections in Europe and in New York City from 1929 to 1931. Jacobson collected many of these works and marketed the Kiowa artworks in similar fashion, taking gouache paintings with him when he attended a meeting of the American Federation of Arts in the late 1920s, for example, and sending them to the International Congress for Art Education in Prague, Czechoslovakia, in 1928. In her unpublished essay about Indian art, Jeanne d'Ucel recalled that a visitor to the Prague exhibit had mentioned that "she could not get near the Kiowa room, so packed it was with onlookers," and that:

Fig. 71 (facing page)

Stephen Mopope (Qued Koi)

U.S., Kiowa, 1898–1974

Chief and Two Indian Women, n.d.

Tempera on paper, 15 x 12 in.

Fred Jones Jr. Museum of Art, The University of Oklahoma, Norman

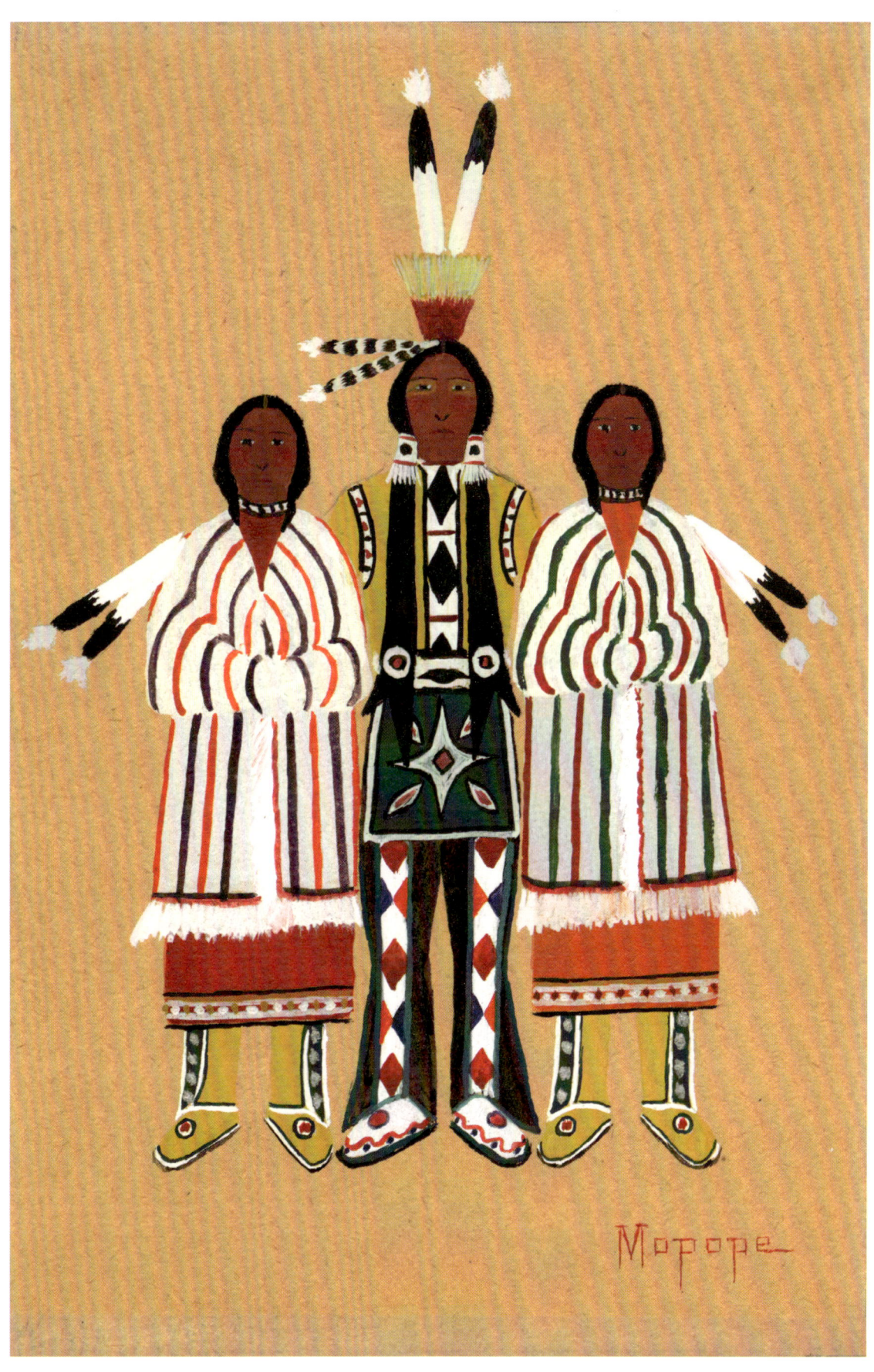

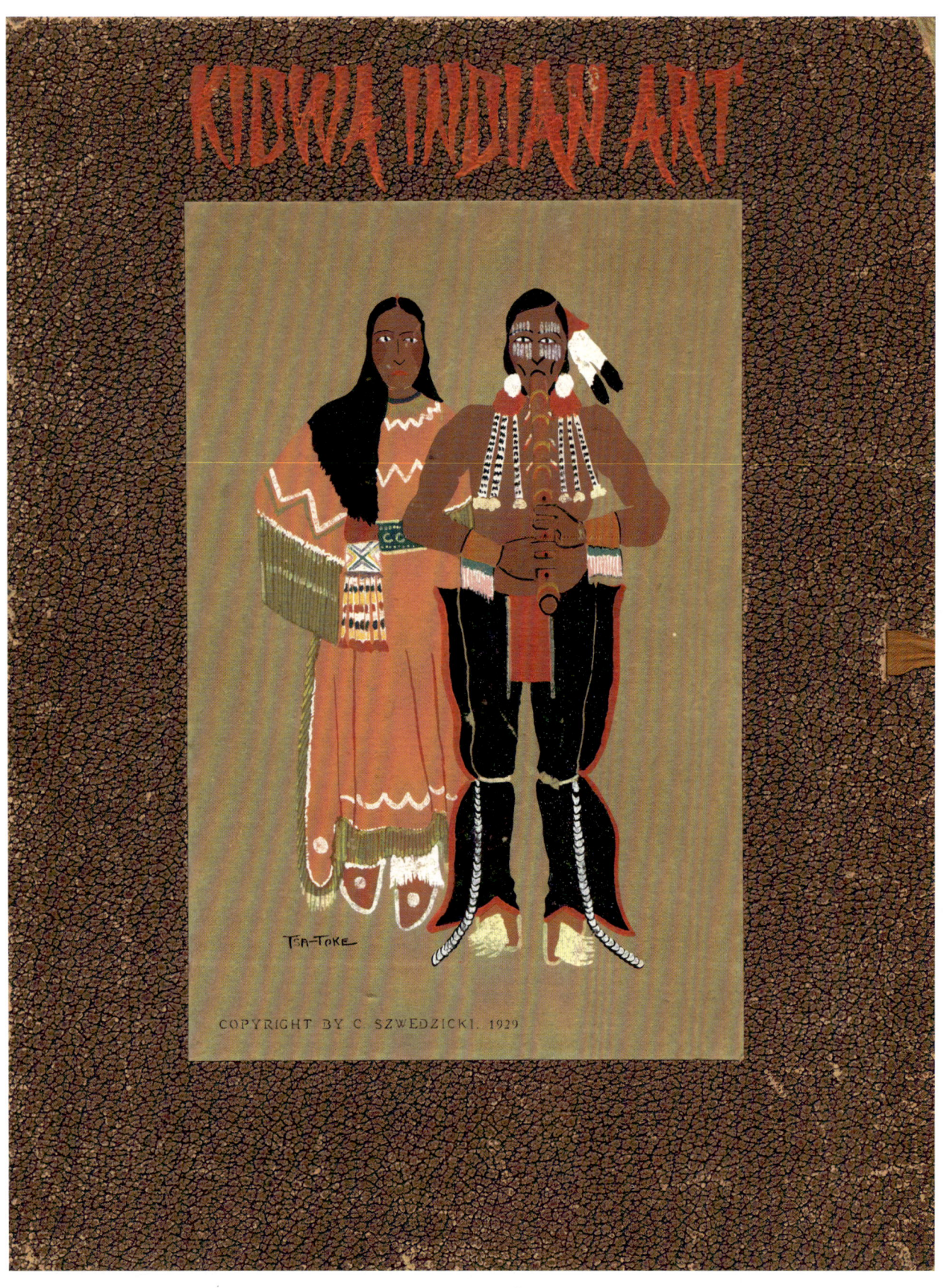

KIOWA INDIAN ART

TSA-TOKE

COPYRIGHT BY C. SZWEDZICKI. 1929

Art critics everywhere became lyrical about the strange watercolors. Art magazines, even such as the haughty *Apollo* of London, usually so stingy of its space, devoted several pages, with full spreads in color, and great praise. This boomeranged, and the big American metropolitan newspapers also gave full page reproductions of the Indians' works: the *Chicago Tribune, Philadelphia Ledger, New York Times,* and many others. The *American Magazine of Art* had a whole number [issue] about this:[11]

Indeed, Jacobson's extensive scrapbooks, in which he obsessively chronicled his life's achievements, include many clippings from such magazines, as well as from local Oklahoma papers that proudly reported the successes of the Kiowa artists both at home and abroad.[12]

In 1929, *Kiowa Indian Art*, the most elegant, meticulous publication on American Indian art ever offered for sale up to that time, was issued, and advertised widely in American art magazines (fig. 72). This portfolio of thirty high-quality reproductions of the contemporary Kiowa paintings being made at the University of Oklahoma was printed in both French and English, with an introduction by Jacobson. All of the works were from Jacobson's own collection and were sent to France for reproduction by C. Szwedzicki, a small fine-arts printer in Nice. Issued in an edition of seven hundred and fifty copies, and sold for the astronomical price of thirty-five dollars—an amount that equaled the weekly salary of a college-educated professional of the day—it was highly sought-after by collectors and institutional libraries.[13] In her unpublished writings, d'Ucel solves the mystery about how this acclaimed portfolio came to be published abroad, writing that the publisher had seen the paintings on exhibit in Prague in 1928 and solicited them for his publishing house.[14]

The portfolio's cover, bearing a painting of a man and woman entitled *The Love Call* by Monroe Tsatoke, exemplifies the style of painting presented within: opaque watercolor thickly applied to the paper with little modeling. Detail is expressed through line and dot, to great decorative effect. Tsatoke's other works in the portfolio depict dancers and warriors. Steven Mopope focused on portraits of families, warriors, and peyoteists, among other subjects. He and Jack Hokeah were both competitive dancers, and they depicted dancers with great eloquence. Spencer Asah is represented by a self-portrait, dancing. Lois Smokey's one work, *Kiowa Family*, evinces great interest in women's beadworking traditions. The men featured here came to be known as "The Kiowa Five," with the addition of James Auchiah (1906–1974), who did not arrive at

Fig. 72 (facing page)
Cover of *Kiowa Indian Art*, 1929
15 x 11½ in.
Fred Jones Jr. Museum of Art,
The University of Oklahoma, Norman

the University of Oklahoma until a few months after the others—too late for inclusion in the portfolio.[15]

The paintings were reproduced by the labor-intensive process known as *pochoir*. Similar to a silkscreen or serigraph, pochoir is a process that requires exactingly-trained craftspeople to execute the stencil-cutting and hand-coloring of images. Its height of popularity and expertise was in early twentieth century France, where pochoir workshops translated original artists' works into limited-edition prints, often for books or portfolios.[16] Pochoir was an excellent choice for reproducing the Kiowa paintings, in which flat, unmodulated areas of color, with no shading, were prevalent. Because of its painstaking process, and the fact that each color uses a separate stencil, pochoir requires that each sheet of paper be handled, and paint applied to a stencil, numerous times. Though the thirty-five dollar price tag was extraordinarily high in the year of the American stock market crash, *Kiowa Indian Art* was produced using the finest possible method to approximate looking at the hand-painted gouache (opaque watercolor) originals. Pochoir mimicked the look of the original gouache closely, for in both the paint lays thickly on the surface of the paper. Jacobson had the publisher stamp the back of each print with the words "*l'Edition d'Art C. Szwedzicki*," so that they would not be mistaken for, or misrepresented as, original works of art. By disseminating the work of Kiowa artists in a French-made portfolio of pochoir prints, Jacobson was aligning the work of these artists with other well-known modern art movements, such as Art Deco, and placing them before the same audience that appreciated the Art Moderne on display at the *Exposition Internationale des Arts Décoratifs et Industriels Modernes* held in Paris in 1925, which the Jacobsons saw on their way to a year-long stay in Algeria.[17]

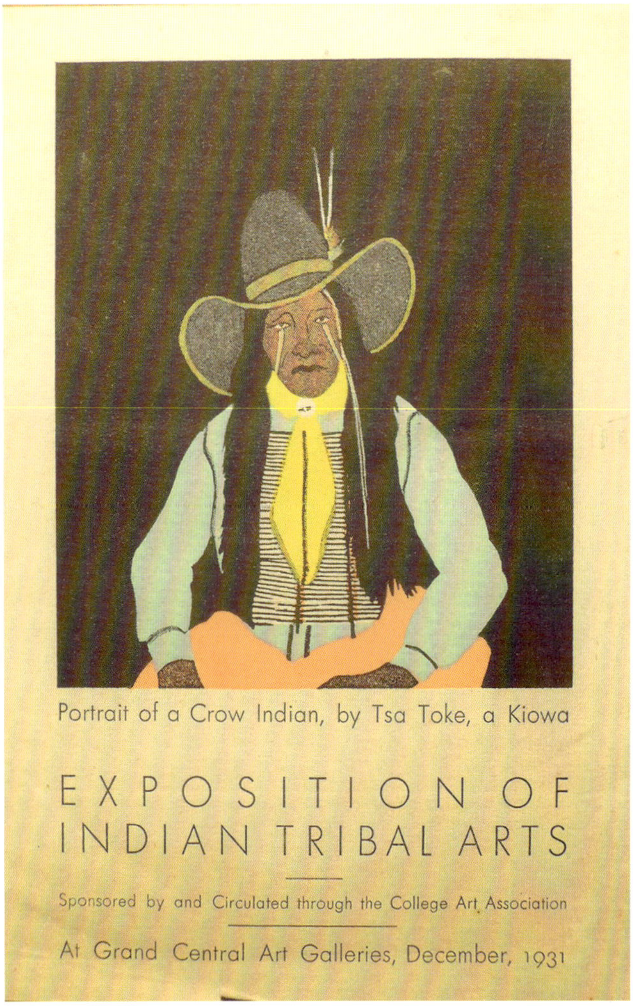

The publication of *Kiowa Indian Art* came at a time when American Indian art of the West and Southwest had been prominent in the public imagination for nearly a decade. Jacobson's high profile in advocating for these artists caused others to take note of his skills. Though Amelia Elizabeth White and John Sloan were the chief organizers of the ground-breaking *Exposition of Indian Tribal Arts* in New York in 1931, d'Ucel recounts that at a dinner party in Santa

Portrait of a Crow Indian, by Tsa Toke, a Kiowa

EXPOSITION OF INDIAN TRIBAL ARTS

Sponsored by and Circulated through the College Art Association

At Grand Central Art Galleries, December, 1931

Fig. 73

Cover of prospectus for *Exposition of Indian Tribal Arts*, Grand Central Galleries, New York, December 1931, featuring *Portrait of Crow Indian* by Monroe Tsatoke. Oscar Jacobson Collection, Western History Collection, University of Oklahoma Libraries

Fe the preceding summer, White and others had tried to persuade Jacobson to assume the chairmanship of this huge curatorial project. But "a serious and lengthy illness made it impossible for him to shoulder the heavy burden of work it entailed; he could only serve as consultant from afar."[18]

Works by the Kiowa Five were exhibited at the New York 1931 exposition, which subsequently toured both American and European cities. Monroe Tsatoke's portrait of a Crow man graced the cover of a flyer for the event (fig. 73). This powerful miniature portrait is arresting in its graphic simplicity, and it seems to anticipate by more than forty years the bold portraiture of T. C. Cannon and Fritz Scholder. D'Ucel wrote a manuscript to be included in the catalogue of the exhibit, for in Jacobson's files is a letter asking for its return; it concerned the Kiowa painters, whose work does not have its own essay in the catalogue, but only a brief mention in a short essay on American Indian painting.[19] By this time, d'Ucel had written several essays on Kiowa art for local and regional magazines.[20]

Scholars sometimes mistakenly think of the *Kiowa Indian Art* portfolio simply as the means for introducing the world to this artistic experiment hatched in Oklahoma. But it was, in fact, the result of an intense interest worldwide in new American Indian paintings. As Jacobson wrote in the introduction, "Collections of their paintings have been exhibited in many of the art museums of the country, and a large number of the paintings have found homes among art collectors." Of the five portfolios produced by the publishing house C. Szwedzicki in France over a twenty-five year period, three were to be arranged and authored by Oscar Jacobson.

Jacobson collected a great deal of Native art, both for himself and for the museum in the 1930s and '40s, including many more works by the six original Kiowa artists who had studied at OU, and emerging artists such as Blackbear Bosin, Ernest Spybuck, and numerous others. He amassed a significant collection of works by Pueblo artists who came to fame in the 1920s and early '30s, such as Awa Tsireh, Tonita Peña, and Fred Kabotie, as well as the Pueblo artists and others who studied with Dorothy Dunn and Gerónima Cruz Montoya at the Studio School, established in 1932 at the Santa Fe Indian School. Jacobson collected many objects of ethnographic interest that were later transferred to the Stovall Museum of Anthropology on the OU campus. A few Native works that were not paintings remained at the OU Museum of Art, however, including several Navajo textiles of fine quality (fig. 83).

During the years of the Great Depression, Jacobson was not only head of the OU School of Art, teaching, painting, and keeping up a robust exhibition and lecture schedule, but he also took on another administrative task, serving as the director of a New Deal Arts program for the state of Oklahoma—the Public Works of Art Project (PWAP).[21] Again, his wife, d'Ucel, narrates this family history best:

> The P.W.A.P. consisted almost entirely of frescoes for public buildings, libraries, schools, courthouses, etc. It required much traveling to inspect the various projects to see that they were up to standards. This meant Dad had to contribute not only his own time and effort; usually he made the trip in his own car, at his own expense. He also had to make reports to HQs [headquarters]. His concern for the plight of Indian artists who had not been included at first brought him an additional load. For, when he called the attention of Washington to this, they simply asked him to take on that phase also.[22]

Jacobson contracted well-known Native artists to be part of this initiative, and its successor, the Treasury Relief Art Project (TRAP). Tsatoke and Asah painted murals of Oklahoma Indians in the State Historical Society building in Oklahoma City. Auchiah and Mopope were awarded commissions for the Federal Building in Muskogee. Mopope did murals on the walls of the post office in Anadarko, while Acee Blue Eagle (1907–1959), Dick West (1912–1996), and Woody Crumbo (1912–1989) painted works in other regional post offices.[23]

In 1945, Jacobson resigned the directorship of the School of Art, a position he had held since his arrival in 1915. But his work with Native art and artists continued unabated. In 1948, he and the Sioux painter Oscar Howe (1915–1983), who was in Norman working with Jacobson on another Native art portfolio, served as jurors for the *Third Annual American Indian Painting Exhibition* at the Philbrook Art Center in Tulsa (fig. 74). Begun in 1946, the Philbrook's annual exhibition was a significant national venue for Native painters for more than thirty years. Howe was living in Norman at the time and had won First Prize in the 1947 Philbrook competition. From mid-1947 to mid-1948, he worked for Jacobson on a big project: the publisher C. Szedzwicki wanted to publish more portfolios on American Indian topics, and for one of them Jacobson was planning an ambitious historical overview of Native clothing to be depicted in original paintings commissioned from Howe.

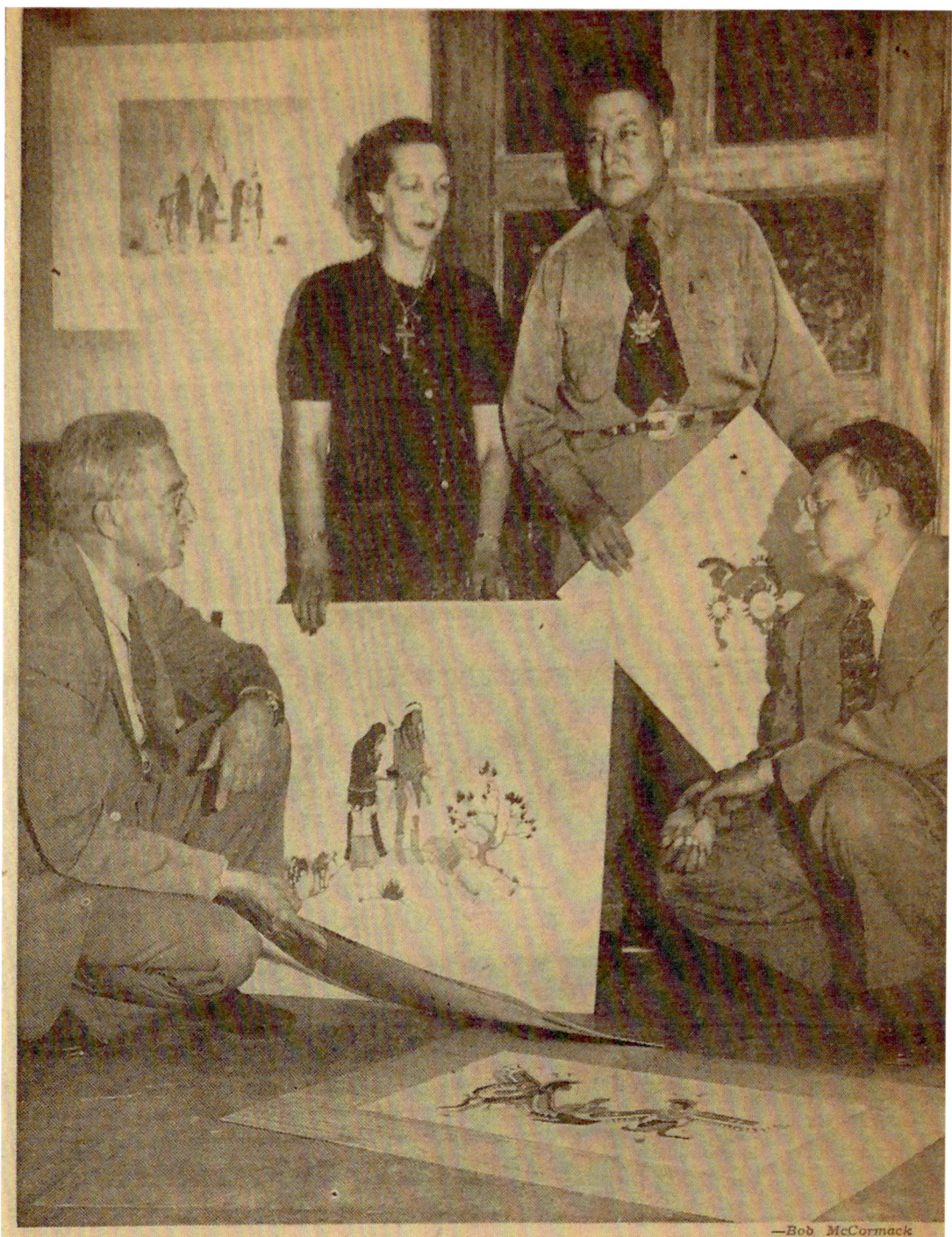

—Bob McCormack

THEY CHOSE THE WINNERS—Indian artists from all over the nation and Alaska must wait until May 4 to learn the verdict of this jury which last week chose the winners in Philbrook Art Center's third national competition for Indian painting. In the foreground are Dr. Oscar B. Jacobson and Oscar Howe, from the University of Oklahoma. Standing is Tulsa's Wolf Robe Hunt, third jury member, and Miss Dorothy Field, curator of Indian art at Philbrook, who managed the competition. Total entries this year numbered 164. Of these 96 were accepted for exhibition, representing the work of 55 Indian artists. Ten prizes will be awarded, totalling $1,250.

Fig. 74   "They Chose the Winners," from *The Tulsa World*, April 25, 1948, sec. 5, p. 5. Jury
            for the *Third Annual American Indian Painting Exhibition*, 1948. The Philbrook Art
            Center, Tulsa. *Left to right:* Oscar Jacobson, Dorothy Field (curator of Indian Art
            at the Philbrook), and Native artists Wolf Robe Hunt and Oscar Howe.

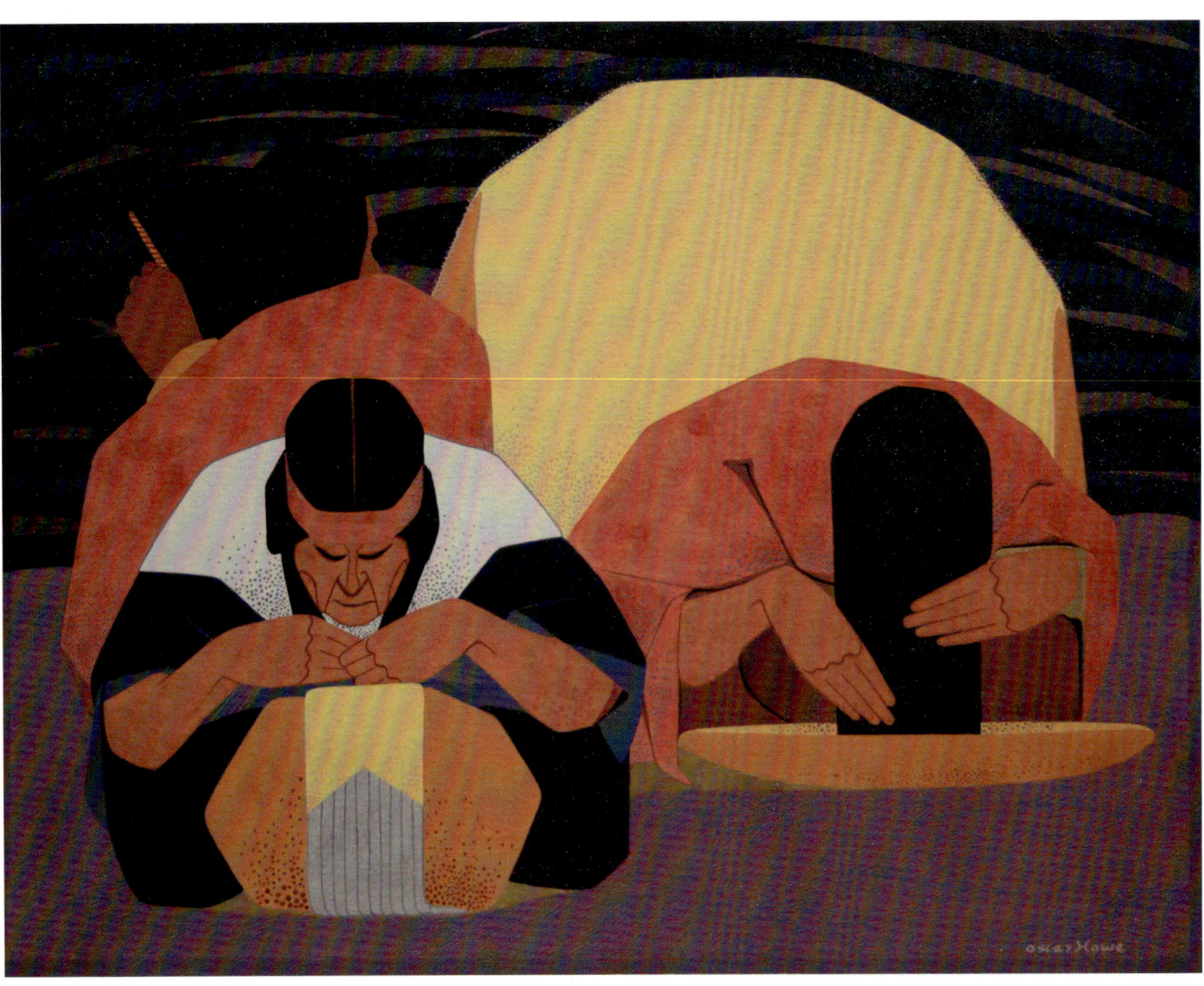

Fig. 75   Oscar Howe (Mazuha Hokshina)

U.S., Yanktonai Nakota, 1915–1983

Three Women, ca. 1953

Tempera on paper, 18 x 24 in.

Fred Jones Jr. Museum of Art, The University of Oklahoma, Norman;

MFA Thesis selection, School of Art, 1953

Jacobson had purchased two of Howe's tempera paintings for the museum in the 1930s.[24] The talented painter had studied at the Studio School in Santa Fe in the mid-1930s, produced murals for the WPA in South Dakota in the late 1930s, and studied fresco painting under Olle Nordmark at the Indian Art Center at Fort Sill, Oklahoma, in 1940, before serving in World War II. To my knowledge, no correspondence survives between Jacobson and Howe that reveals how Oscar Howe came to be involved in the Indian costume portfolio. D'Ucel recalled that the project required that she and Jacobson conduct prodigious research to provide the necessary historical details to ensure accurate depictions of the clothing in Howe's pictures: "Assembling the material for this study involved a surprising amount of labor. Absolute accuracy was required. To secure it, we read all sorts of things, letters, diaries, reports, etc. to garner sometimes only an infinitesimal bit of information."[25]

Though Howe worked with the Jacobsons on this project in 1947–48, *North American Indian Costumes (1564–1950)* was not issued until 1952; it was the final title in the series of five Szwedzicki portfolios.[26] During his stay in Norman, Howe painted some sixty examples of Native clothing from across North America, fifty of which were chosen for the portfolio. Notably, Jacobson sought to bring the inventory of Native dress up to contemporary times. Some plates depict modern Natives of the Southern Plains and Southwest, wearing some clothing in common with other Americans of that era—dresses, cowboy boots, and blue jeans.[27]

The task for Howe was to present the figures with visual clarity, so the images of their clothing would be easy to read. His own paintings were far more complex; at the time of this commission, Howe was on his way to becoming one of the best-known contemporary Native American painters. He went on to earn his MFA at OU in 1954, with a thesis exhibit of tempera paintings. These works predicted the innovative modernist works that would follow, and Jacobson collected work from that exhibit, too. In *Three Women* from 1953 (fig. 75), Howe has radically simplified the planes of the figures so that they are block-like and monumental in feeling. His subsequent figures of Sioux dancers, riders, and a tableaux from mythic narratives would become fractured into numerous facets on the picture plane. Their neo-Cubistic abstraction was a harbinger of what was to follow for some contemporary Native painters.[28]

But Jacobson and d'Ucel were looking firmly at the styles of the past when they collaborated on another portfolio for Szwedzicki: the two volume *American Indian Painters*, issued in 1950.[29] Volume I contains thirty-six plates, while volume II has forty-one, all reproducing works made between 1920 and 1948. Jacobson and d'Ucel traveled during the summers of the 1940s, garnering biographical details for the lengthy captions on each artist. D'Ucel wrote of their teamwork, "To save his time, I did research on the historical background and I helped him assemble the necessary biographical information."[30]

For this portfolio, Jacobson and d'Ucel wrote a substantial introduction to the topic of American Indian painting, as well as lengthy personal notes in the captions to the plates.[31] By the late 1940s, Jacobson was perhaps feeling the need to set down his recollections of more than twenty years of associating with some of these artists, and their text offers personal anecdotes along with some biographical information not published elsewhere. The United States—and the role of Native people in it—had changed considerably by 1950. In the portfolio captions are the Jacobsons' remarks about Bachelor's degrees, experiences in the Second World War, and even a Guggenheim fellowship for Fred Kabotie. A fiction of self-taught Indian painters untouched by modern life or Western modes of artistic representation could no longer be maintained.

Among the artists in *American Indian Painting* whose works are in the University of Oklahoma's Fred Jones Jr. Museum of Art collection are Acee Blue Eagle (1909–1959) and Walter Richard (Dick) West (1912–1996), artists with whom Jacobson had worked in his capacity as director of the Oklahoma PWAP. In the works chosen for this portfolio (plates 4 and 5), Blue Eagle mirrors the simplicity of some of the works in the 1929 *Kiowa Indian Art* portfolio (1939; fig. 76, *The Prophet*). Dick West provides a self-portrait in portfolio plate 36, *Dick Dancing*. In his caption, Jacobson observes, "It is thoroughly Indian in technique and execution, but his mastery of anatomy and movement reveals years of artistic training." That training was at the University of Oklahoma, where, under the tutelage of Jacobson and others, West earned a BFA (1941) and an MFA (1950). When this portfolio was produced, Dick West was the head of the Art Department at Bacone College in Muskogee, Oklahoma, a job he held from 1947 to 1970.[32]

Volume II includes many of the well-known Pueblo painters of the first half of the twentieth century, among them Awa Tsireh (1898–1955), Velino Herrera (1902–1973), Tonita Peña (1893–1949), Pablita Velarde (1918–2006) and Fred Kabotie (c. 1900–1986). In the caption to *Prayer for Rain* (1917-1919; fig. 77; plate 44 of the portfolio), Jacobson pronounces Kabotie "Dean of living Pueblo painters." The work is an ambitious scene with some twenty dancers arrayed in a range of poses. In the late 1910s and 1920s, Kabotie painted the Hopi Snake Dance on many occasions, as well as the dances of other Pueblos. Some paintings, such as this one, omit any sense of place and focus on the ceremonial performers. Velino Herrera's *Pueblo Pottery Makers* (1941; fig. 78, plate 41 of

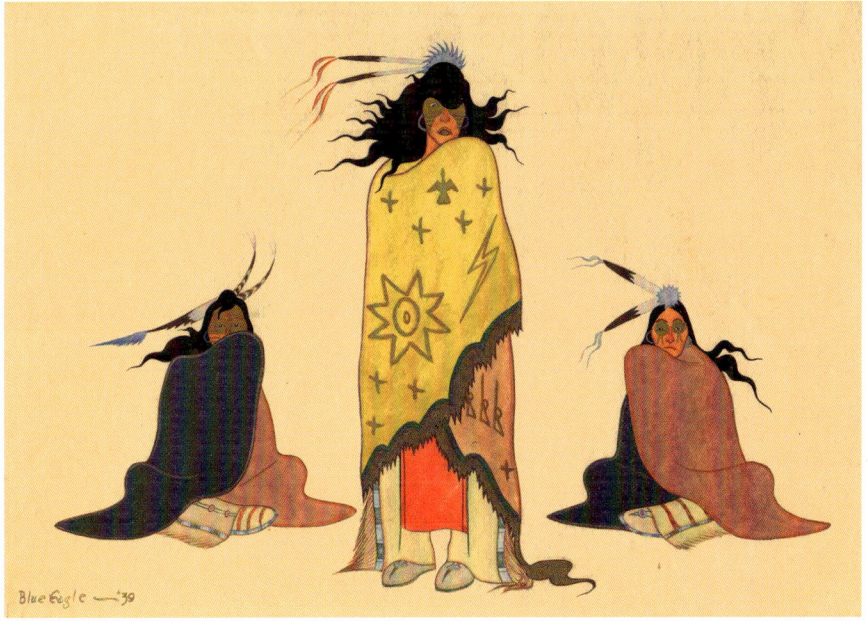

Fig. 76

Acee Blue Eagle

U.S., Muscogee (Creek) and Pawnee, 1907–1959

The Prophet, 1939

Tempera on paper, 14 x 19 in.

Fred Jones Jr. Museum of Art, The University of Oklahoma, Norman;
Museum purchase, 1940

Fig. 77

Fred Kabotie (Naqavoy'ma)

U.S., Hopi, 1900–1986

Prayer for Rain—Ceremonial Dance, 1917–1919

Tempera on paper, 14 x 23 in.

Fred Jones Jr. Museum of Art, The University of Oklahoma, Norman;
Museum purchase, 1934

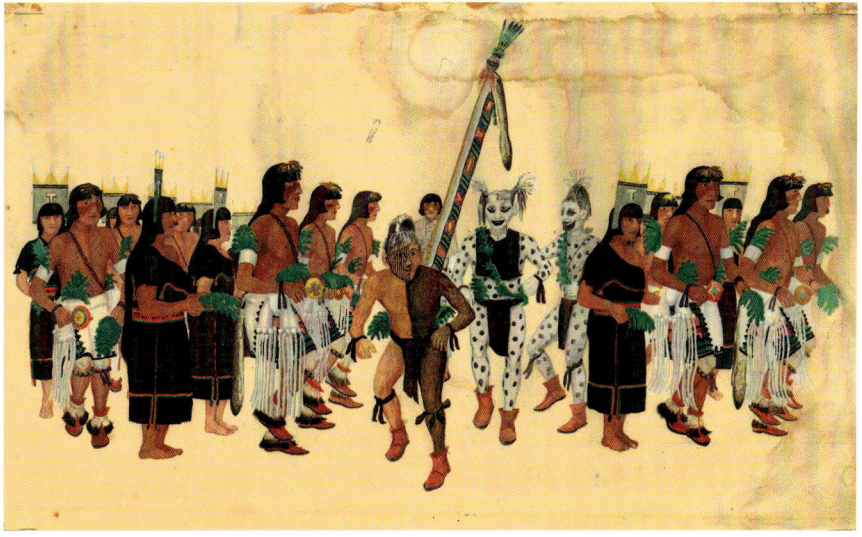

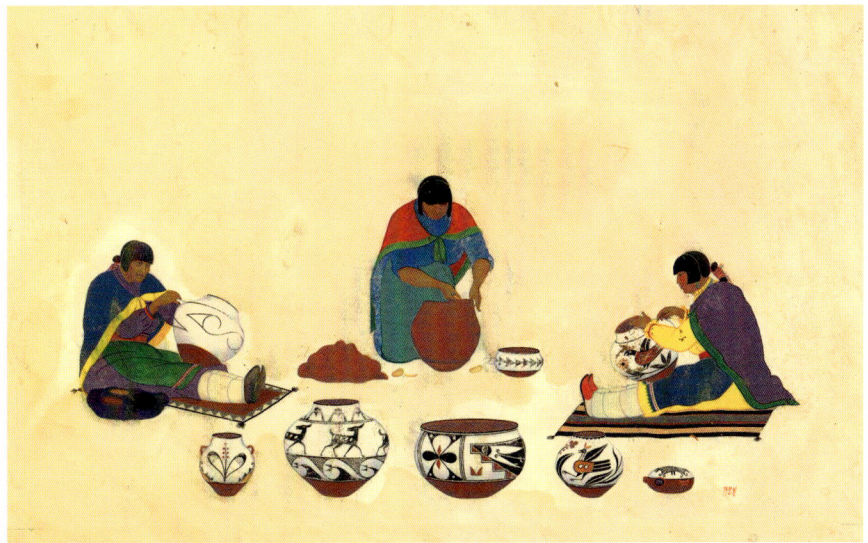

Fig. 78

Velino Shije Herrera (Ma Pe Wi)

U.S., Zia, 1902–1973

Pueblo Pottery Makers, 1941

Tempera on paper, 14¹⁄₂ x 23 in.

Fred Jones Jr. Museum of Art, The University of Oklahoma, Norman;
WPA Collection, 1942

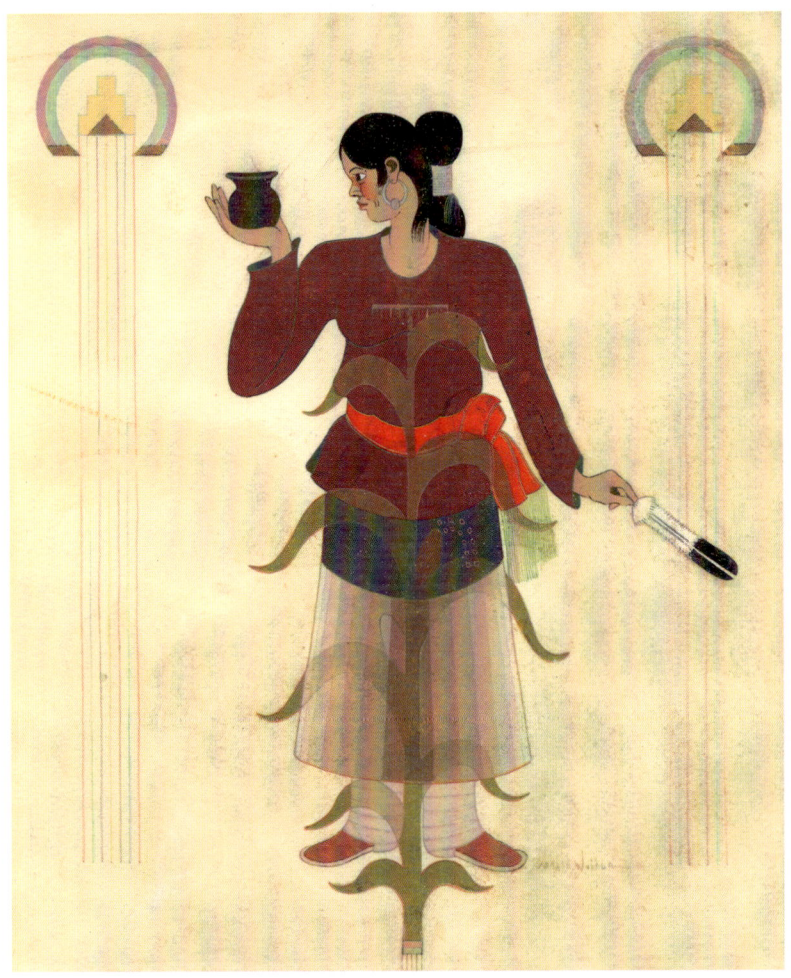

Fig. 79

Gerald Nailor (Toh Yah)

U.S., Navajo, 1917–1952

Female Rain and Corn, n.d.

Tempera on paper, 14 x 12 in.

Fred Jones Jr. Museum of Art, The University of Oklahoma, Norman;
Museum purchase, 1940s

Fig. 80

Allan C. Houser (Haozous)

U.S., Chiricahua Apache, 1914–1994

Navajo Squaw Dance Chorus, n.d.

Tempera on paper, 14^{1}2 x 15^{7}8 in.

Fred Jones Jr. Museum of Art, The University of Oklahoma, Norman;
Museum purchase, 1942

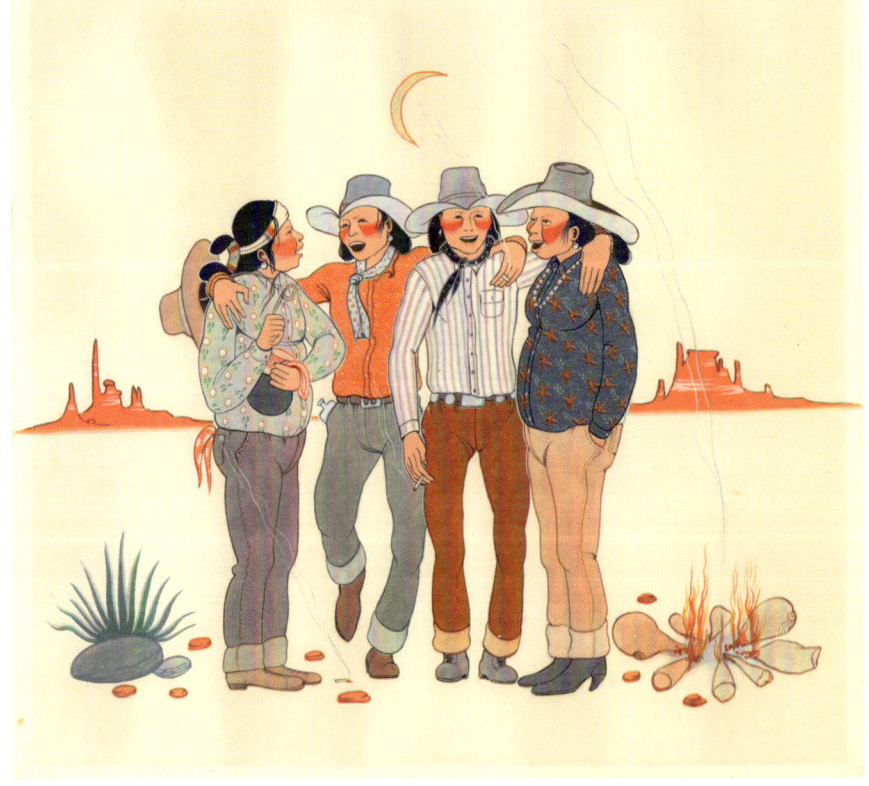

the portfolio) is a beautiful study of the stages of making Pueblo pottery, from shaping the clay to painting the imagery on the pots. Five Pueblo pots with various profiles grace the foreground.

Eleven Navajo and Apache artists are included in the 1950 portfolio, and Jacobson collected many works by such artists for the museum, including paintings by Narciso Platero Abeyta (1918–1998), Harrison Begay (1917–2012), Gerald Nailor (1917–1952), and Allan Houser (1914–1994). Nailor's undated *Female Rain and Corn* (fig. 79; plate 71 in the portfolio) is a single figure composition, in which a stalk of growing corn is superimposed over the standing Navajo woman. Houser, best known today for his modernist works of sculpture, is represented in the portfolio by *Resting Cowboys*, a vignette depicting twentieth-century cigarette-smoking, boot-wearing Indian cowboys (portfolio plate 68). One undated work by Houser in the OU collection, *Navajo Squaw Dance Chorus*, also depicts Indian cowboys (fig. 80). Many of Houser's early paintings depict traditional scenes of Apache or Navajo dancers, or Apache warriors on horseback. From 1937 to 1950, Jacobson collected six works by Houser, who went on to become one of the most highly regarded Native American artists of the second half of the twentieth century, principally for his large-scale sculptural works.[33]

Shortly after publication, a reviewer wrote of *American Indian Painting*: "This work created an artistic sensation in Europe and America. It was snatched up by museums, libraries, and by discriminating collectors, so that it is now out of print."[34] Some of the works from Jacobson's personal collection that appear in this portfolio are now in the National Museum of the American Indian; others are in the collection of the Fred Jones Jr. Museum of Art.

'*Half a Ton of Native Art': The Jacobsons in North Africa*
While Native North America was the main focus of the Jacobsons' interest in other cultures over many decades, a year-long sojourn to North Africa from August 1925 to August 1926 provided much intellectual and artistic nourishment, as well as "native art" of a different sort for the ever-growing museum collection. At the beginning of the fall semester of 1926, The *Daily Oklahoman* published an article with the headline, "Sooner Artist Returns from Africa with Many Canvases of Great Sahara Desert." It begins, "Oscar B. Jacobson, head of the school of painting and design at the University of Oklahoma, has fifty-four canvases, half a ton of native art, a healthy coat of tan and hundreds of Kodak pictures to testify to an interesting twelve months."[35]

During a sabbatical year, the Jacobsons and their three children sailed to France, bought a Ford touring car, and took a boat across the Mediterranean to Algeria. Of the collection of pottery, jewelry, textiles, and metalwork that they collected while there, the article went on to say that "it is perhaps the largest of its kind ever brought to this country." Just a month after announcing the Jacobsons' return, The *Daily Oklahoman* advertised that these artifacts, as well as one hundred photographs, would soon be exhibited at the museum, with the artists' own paintings to be exhibited at a later date.[36]

In Jacobson's own words for publication in *Oklahoma Magazine*, the artist compared the vermilion soil of North Africa to that of Oklahoma, and the mountains of Africa to the Colorado Rockies, but "somewhat finer." While many of the published articles written by others about this trip focused solely on him, Jacobson describes the journey into "the formidable mountain vastness of Grande Kabylie" in the first person plural, saying that his mission was "to paint pictures and to trail to its lair the strange and beautiful peasant crafts that I suspect still exist among these primitive mountain folk, and [for] Mrs. Jacobson to search out their social customs, songs, legends, and religious practices."[37] In a woman's magazine, d'Ucel wrote a lighthearted article about their life there. She describes shopping for the garments "necessary for self-respecting people in the desert": her husband's embroidered white gown, the white drapery to cover his head, "and the forty feet or so of camel's hair cord with which an Arab gentleman fastens this drapery," as well as her own "bloomer-like garment that requires seventeen yards of cloth, the face veil, and the haik or cloak—headdress and veil all in one—of creamy wool, soft as silk" (fig. 81).[38] The accompanied photographs, credited to Oscar Jacobson, show d'Ucel in the burnouse she describes purchasing in the article, as well as in western dress bargaining for vegetables in the town of Touggourt in northeast Algeria.

Both Jacobson and d'Ucel lectured widely about their travels in North Africa, and wrote many popular articles. One, in The *Daily Oklahoman*, includes

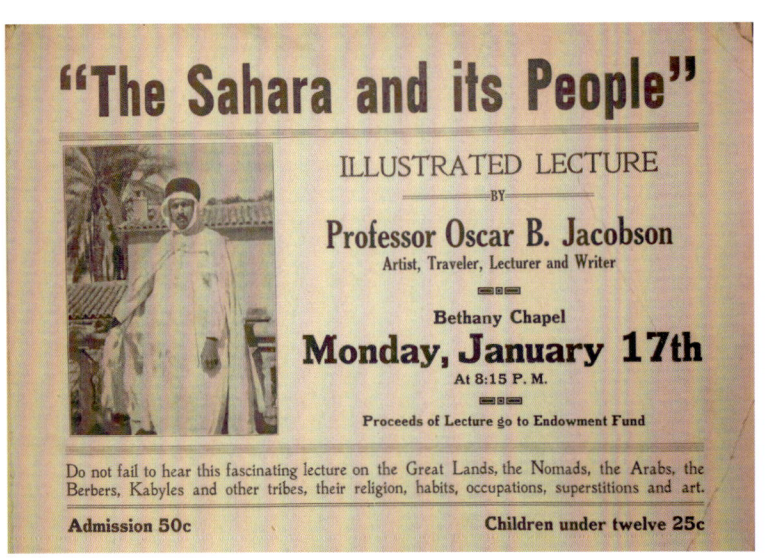

"**The Sahara and its People**"

ILLUSTRATED LECTURE
BY
Professor Oscar B. Jacobson
Artist, Traveler, Lecturer and Writer

Bethany Chapel
Monday, January 17th
At 8:15 P. M.

Proceeds of Lecture go to Endowment Fund

Do not fail to hear this fascinating lecture on the Great Lands, the Nomads, the Arabs, the Berbers, Kabyles and other tribes, their religion, habits, occupations, superstitions and art.

Admission 50c   Children under twelve 25c

Fig. 81

"The Sahara and its People," ca. 1926

a photo of d'Ucel veiled and bejeweled like a Berber woman, only her eyes and a wisp of hair showing.[39] But d'Ucel also wrote a substantial book, *Berber Art*, published by the University of Oklahoma Press in 1932 (fig. 82). The cover illustration was drawn by her husband, as were the endpaper maps and the headbands for the opening of each chapter. Described on the flyleaf as "the first introduction to Berber art," it is a serious study that considers the history and the language of Berber people as well as their art.[40] Both pottery and metalwork are discussed, as are the *kilim* (flat weave) traditions of the Berbers. With eyes accustomed to Navajo weaving traditions of the American Southwest (fig. 83), the Jacobsons could appreciate both the technical complexity and the magnificent geometry of Berber textiles (fig. 84 and 85). D'Ucel writes knowledgeably about the different regional styles and traditions in all of the arts that she considers. Of the weaving of a rug under the direction of the *reggam*, or professional male weaver, she writes:

> The making of a rug is a joyous undertaking on which neither effort nor time is spared. It is often, in fact, the occasion for a *touizah* or weaving bee, when the neighborhood women share in the work which lasts several weeks, and which fills the winter days with a sociable activity. The wool having been sheared in the spring, had to be washed, carded, spun, and dyed, and this took most of the summer. Now the upright loom is brought to the center of the house and the warp of white wool is stretched between the rollers.[41]

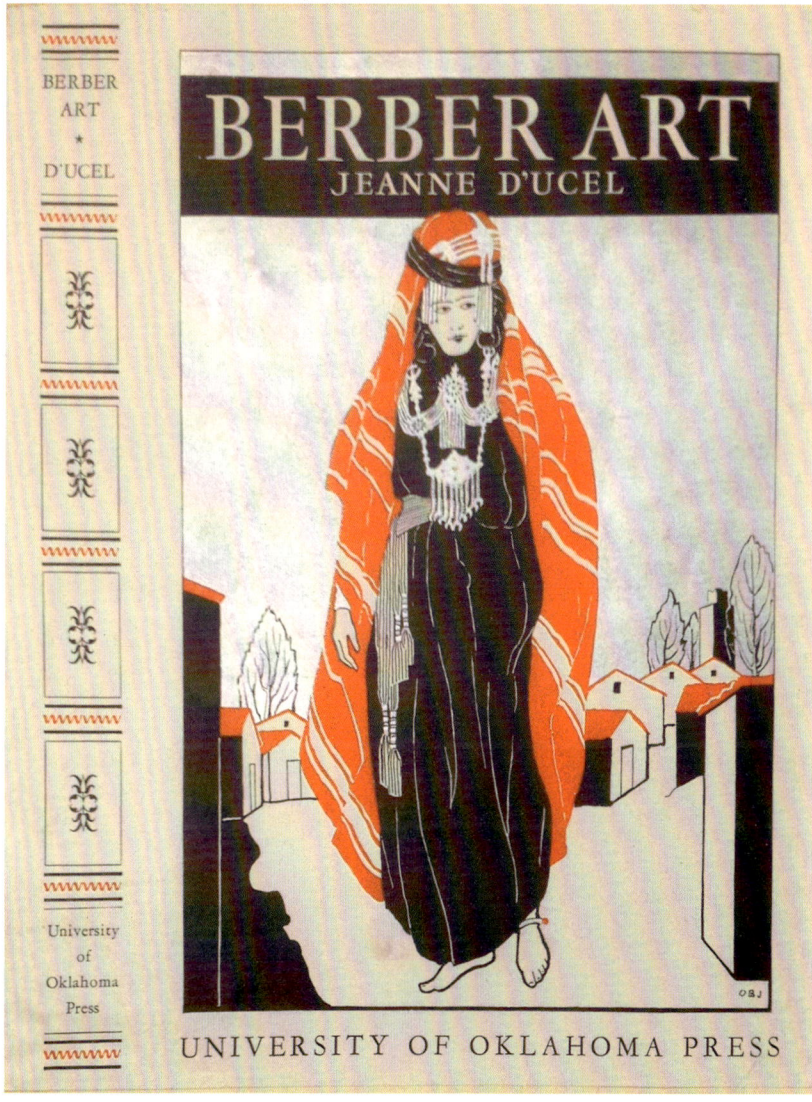

Fig. 82

Jeanne d'Ucel, *Berber Art*, 1932, cover illustration by Oscar Brousse Jacobson.

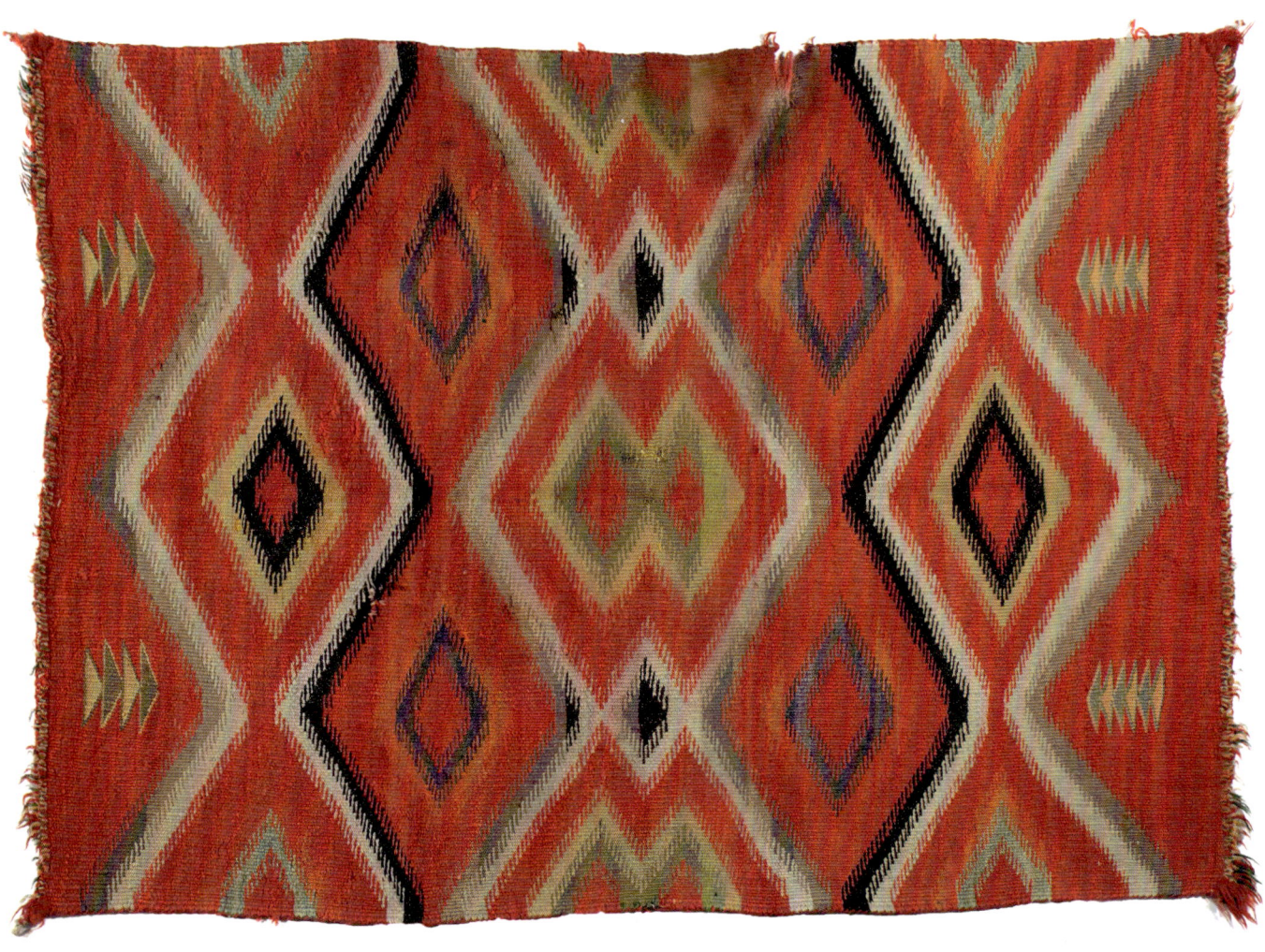

Fig. 83

Unknown artist

U.S., Navajo

Eyedazzler Blanket, ca. 1885

Wool, 50 x 33¹⁄4 in.

Fred Jones Jr. Museum of Art, The University of Oklahoma, Norman; Museum purchase, 1941

Facing page:

Fig. 84 (above)

Unknown artist

North Africa, likely Algeria

Rug, n.d.

Wool, 80¹⁄2 x 50 in.

Fred Jones Jr. Museum of Art, The University of Oklahoma, Norman;
O. B. Jacobson Collection of North African Art

Fig. 85 (below)

Unknown artist

Algeria, Kabylie region (Leqbayel), Imazighen (Berber)

Rug, n.d.

Wool, 64 x 44 in.

Fred Jones Jr. Museum of Art, The University of Oklahoma, Norman;
O. B. Jacobson Collection of North African Art

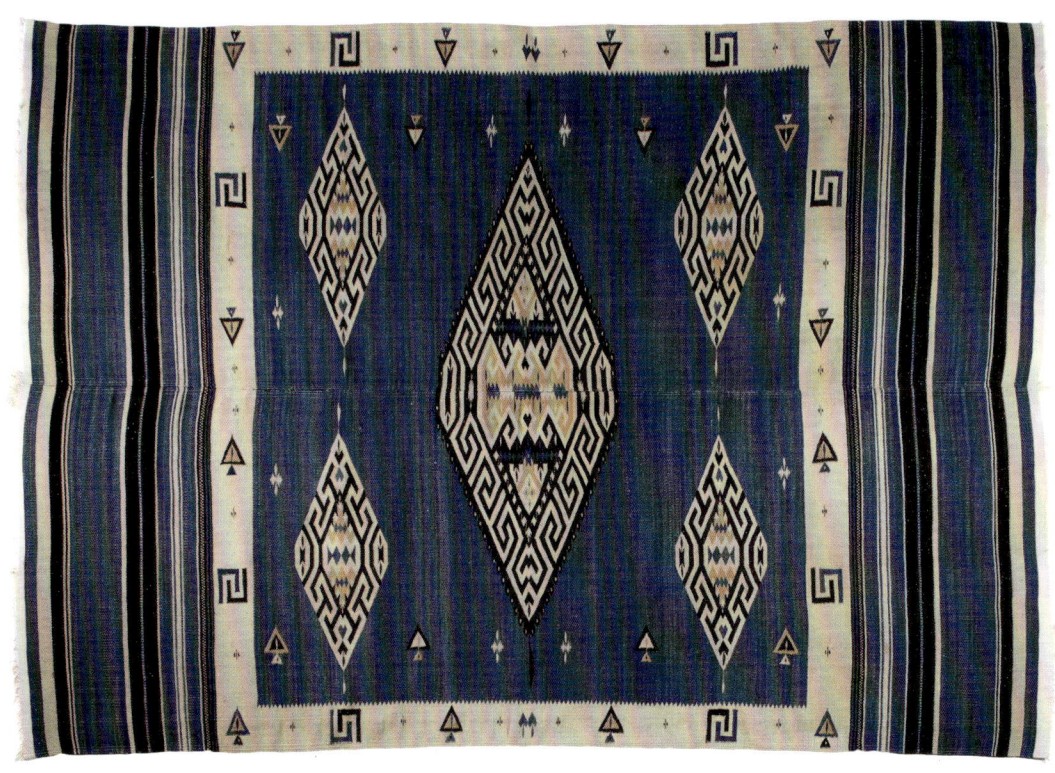

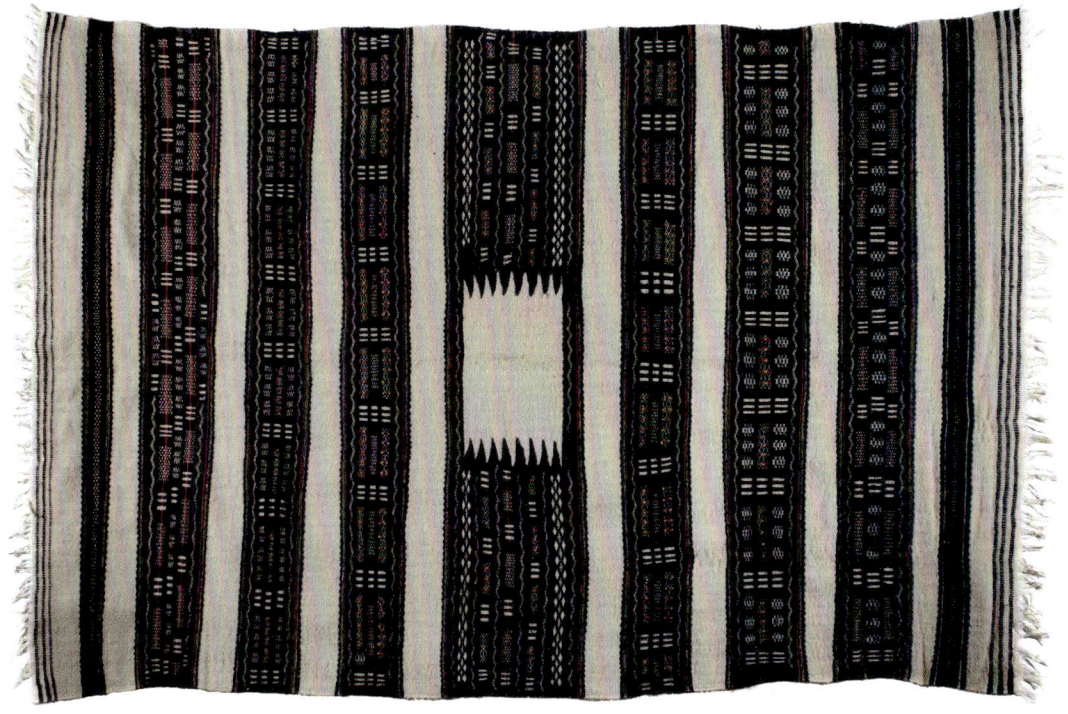

While many of the accompanying illustrations are of objects either in the Jacobson Collection or that of the Museum of Art, others were provided by the Government of Algeria. One leather bag described as "very old" exemplifies the dyed leather "embroidery" of Tuareg women (fig. 86; plate 42 in the book). Occasionally a Native American simile emerges, as when d'Ucel likens the design of a Berber saddlebag to an Indian parfleche.[42]

Fig. 86
Unknown artist
Algeria, Imazighen (Berber), Kel Ahaggar
Man's Leather Bag, n.d.
Leather, $20^3/_4$ x $7^1/_4$ x $^5/_8$ in.
Fred Jones Jr. Museum of Art, The University of Oklahoma, Norman;
O. B. Jacobson Collection of North African Art

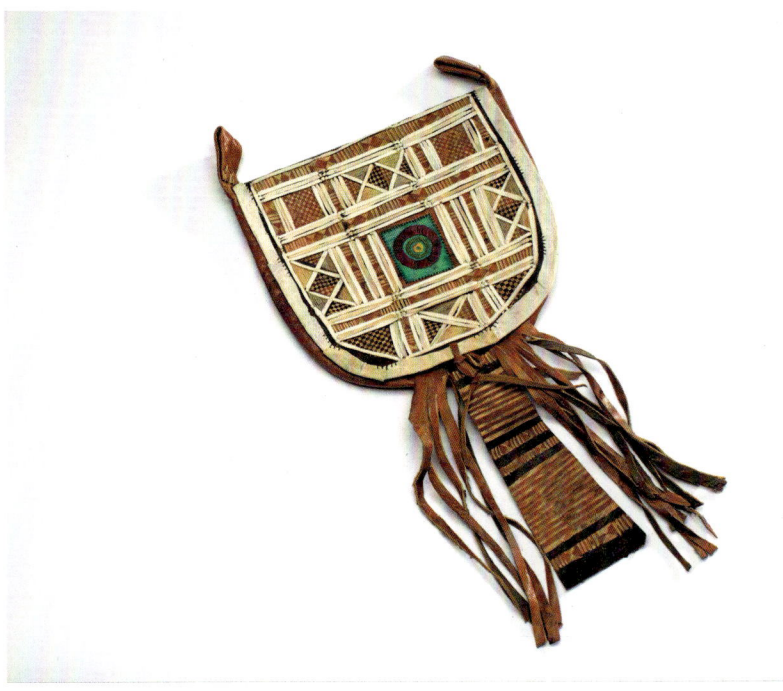

Little attention has been paid to Jeanne d'Ucel in scholarly literature that has focused on Oscar Jacobson's achievements alone, it is worth remembering that of the two, only she wrote a full-length academic book, as well as "helping" her husband, sometimes with work for which only he received the credit. D'Ucel even noted in her family memoir that when Oscar was ill or out of town, she taught his art history classes at the university.[43] Within days of meeting Oscar Jacobson at a September student advising fair, when both were teaching at Washington State College in 1911, the two became daily companions. By New Year's Day of 1912 they were engaged. In 1915, they traveled cross-country to Norman, Oklahoma, where they would find their life's work. She described their meeting, in her native French, as "*le coup de foudre*"—love at first sight. It was a love that lasted for more than five decades (fig. 87), nourished by art, travel, Native American and North African cultures, and a dedication to family, community, and the life of the mind. ❀

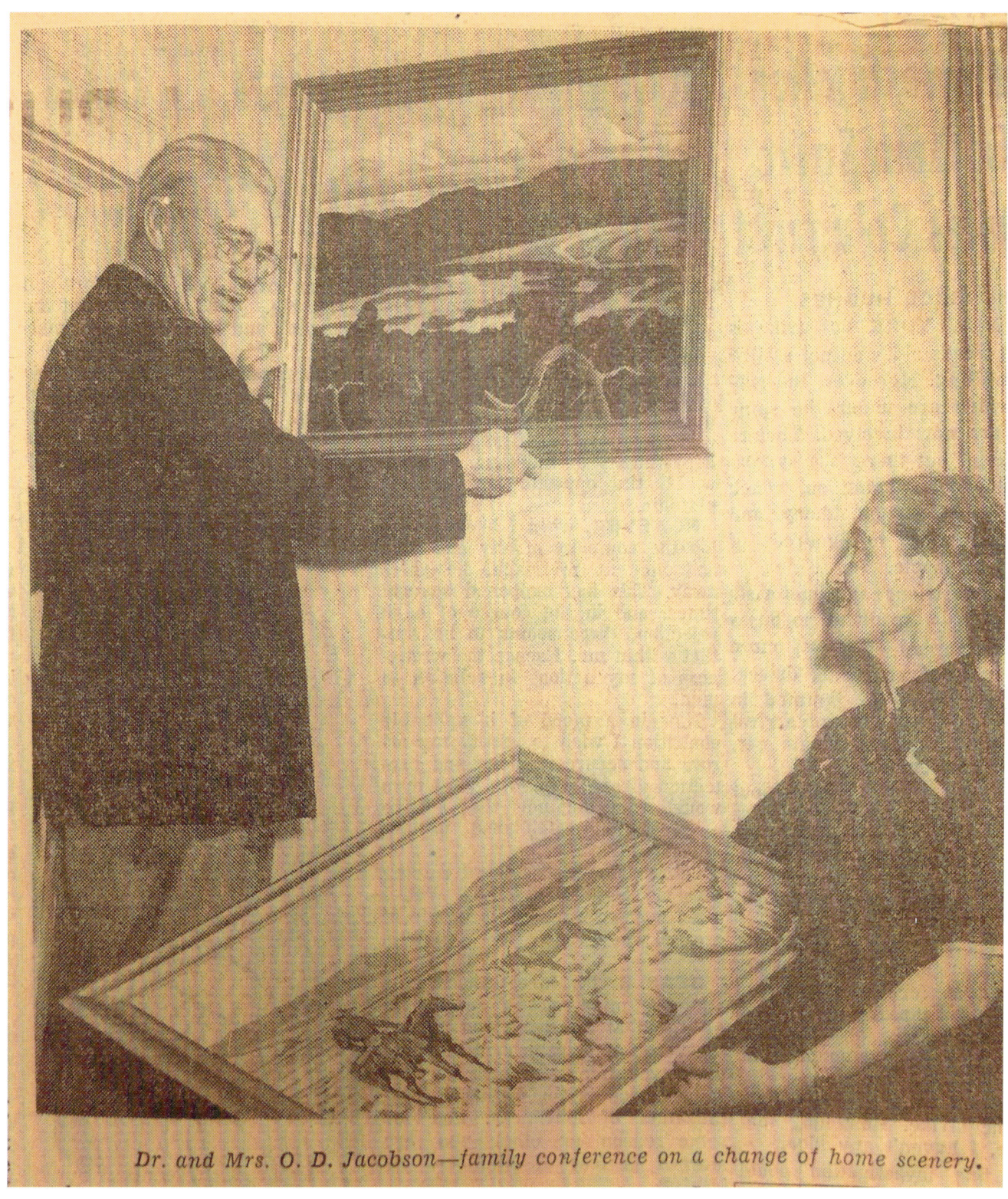

Dr. and Mrs. O. D. Jacobson—*family conference on a change of home scenery.*

Fig. 87   Dr. and Mrs. O. D. [*sic*] Jacobson—family conference on a change of
            home scenery," from *Daily Oklahoman*, January 19, 1953

Acknowledgements

I am grateful to Mark White, heather ahtone, and Emily Ballew Neff for facilitating my participation in this project and providing me with information and access to objects during my research trip to Norman in the summer of 2014. I owe special thanks to Mark White for his generosity in sharing his own research materials, publications, and insights with me, and for his careful critique of my manuscript.

Notes

1   "Unique 'Kawraw Kiote's Den: Tales of True Frontier Life as Shown in Rooms of Four Yale Men," *Saturday Chronicle*, June 2, 1906, n.p., in Oscar Brousse Jacobson and Jeanne d'Ucel scrapbooks, vol. 1, "1902–11," box 1, Oscar B. Jacobson Collection, Oklahoma Historical Society, Oklahoma City.

2   "Amateurs Do Well: 'Sunset' is Given at the Foy Auditorium," *New Haven Union*, December 21, 1907, and "Yale Men in a Western Play," *Saturday Chronicle*, Dec. 14, 1907, in Jacobson and d'Ucel scrapbooks, vol. 1, box 1.

3   D'Ucel's given name was Sophie Jeanne Brousse (1892–1967), but she published under the name of her mother, who died when she was a child. Significantly, upon their marriage, Oscar Jacobson adopted her birth patronym, "Brousse," as his middle name. As was common during most of the twentieth century, in private life d'Ucel was known as "Mrs. Oscar Jacobson." See, for example, photo and caption, "Mrs. Oscar B. Jacobson of Norman had charge of an interesting lesson on oriental rugs at the meeting of the Oklahoma Art League Monday afternoon . . . ," *Daily Oklahoman*, Nov. 13, 1928, 6.

4   See Anne Allbright's and Mark Andrew White's essay in this catalogue for further information.

5   d'Ucel, "About Indians," in *Memoir and Biographical Writings*, ca. 1962, box 1, folder 5, Oscar B. Jacobson Collection, p. 56. Published sources credit field matron Susie Peters who worked with the Kiowa, but d'Ucel is adamant about placing the credit elsewhere. See typescript pages 5, 25–26.

6   See d'Ucel, "Eli—Artist and Teacher," *The Sooner Magazine* 1, no. 8 (May 1929):
    256–58; Isabel Campbell, "With Southwestern Artists—All Indians Have Six
    Fingers," *Southwest Review* 14, no. 3 (1929): 360–69. Of Mahier, Jacobson wrote,
    "She deserves considerable credit for the renaissance of Indian art. I put the
    first Kiowa artists in her charge. It was entirely a labor of love; Ely gave most
    generously of her time to instruct them." Edith Mahier, unpublished typescript
    written after 1950, Oscar Jacobson papers, box J-13, Western History Collec-
    tion, University of Oklahoma.

7   Campbell, "With Southwestern Artists," 360. The artists did not participate
    in formal university classes, for it was thought that this would "ruin" their in-
    digenous style of painting.

8   d'Ucel, "About Indians," 7.

9   Lydia Wyckoff, ed., *Visions and Voices: Native American Paintings from the Philbrook Mu-
    seum of Art* (Tulsa, Okla.: Philbrook Museum of Art, 1996), 25.

10 J. J. Brody, *Pueblo Indian Painting: Tradition and Modernism in New Mexico, 1900–1930*
    (Santa Fe, New Mex.: School of American Research Press, 1997) provides the
    best history of this movement. See also Walter Pach, "Notes on the Indian
    Water-Colours," *The Dial* 68, no. 3 (1920): 343–45; Edgar Lee Hewett, "Native
    American Artists," *Art and Archaeology* 13, no. 3 (1922): 103–12; and Marsden
    Hartley, "Red Man Ceremonials: An American Plea for American Aesthet-
    ics," *Art and Archaeology* 9 (Jan. 1920): 7–14.

11 d'Ucel, "About Indians," 10. The reference to the British art magazine *Apollo*,
    refers to a review of the 1929 *Kiowa Indian Art* portfolio in the Nov. 1929 issue of
    the magazine. See also "American Notes," *The Connoisseur* (Sept. 1931): 209–10
    for an article on the upcoming Exposition of Indian Tribal Art in New York,
    and "The Editors Page," in *International Studio* (Aug. 1931): 6, for an article on
    the upcoming exposition that illustrates *Indian Prayers* by Jack Hokeah, from the
    Jacobson Collection, and proclaims that after the exposition, "there will be no
    reason for anyone not becoming fully aware of the beauty and importance of
    Indian art, and living Indian art at that." Clippings preserved in Jacobson and
    d'Ucel scrapbooks, vol. 4, "1926–1932," box 4.

12 See, for example, "State Indians' Art to Be Shown Nationally," *Daily Oklahoman*,
    Aug. 7, 1927, A-11; "A Kiowa Art Exhibit," *My Oklahoma* (summer 1927), and
    other clippings in Jacobson and d'Ucel scrapbooks, vol. 4, box 4.

13 In 1931, according to the *Chicago Tribune*, a college-educated businesswoman earned about thirty-two dollars a week. See "Business Woman Earns Average Salary of $1,500," *Chicago Daily Tribune*, Mar. 1, 1931, G4.

14 d'Ucel, "About Indians," 10. In a previous publication, I surmised that Jacobson, with his many international contacts, and his knowledge of the latest trends in fine reproduction of art works, had reached out to a French publisher. See Janet Catherine Berlo, "The Szwedzicki Portfolios of American Indian Art, 1929–1952, Part I," *American Indian Art Magazine* 34, no. 2 (Feb. 2009): 39.

15 Some scholars refer to "The Kiowa Six," in order to include the work of Smokey, but her participation was much more short-lived than that of the others.

16 Works by Marc Chagall, Paul Cézanne, William Blake, Leon Bakst, and others were widely disseminated through pochoir prints. Moreover, pochoir plates were often featured in French fashion magazines, and in portfolios illustrating the latest in industrial design and architecture. See Burr Wallen, *Pochoir: Flowering of the Hand-Color Process in Prints and Illustrated Books, 1916–1935* (Santa Barbara: University of California–Santa Barbara Art Museum, 1978) and Jean Saudé, *Traité d'enluminiere d'art au pochoir* (Paris: Editions de l'Ibis, 1925). I explain the technique of *pochoir* more fully in Berlo, "The Szwedzicki Portfolios, Part I," 38–39.

17 Jacobson and his family left Norman in August 1925 and, after visiting *L'Exposition internationale des arts décoratifs et industriels modernes* in Paris, they bought a Ford touring car and motored through southern France to the Mediterranean. "Sooner Artist Returns from Africa with Many Canvases of Great Sahara Desert," *Daily Oklahoman*, Sept. 26, 1926, D-3. On the Industrial Exposition, see *Encyclopédie des Arts Décoratifs et Industriels Modernes du XXième Siècle*, 12 vols. (Paris: Office Central d'Editions et de Librairie, Imprimerie Nationale, 1925) and Tag Gronberg, *Designs on Modernity: Exhibiting the City in 1920s Paris* (Manchester, Eng.: Manchester University Press, 1998).

18 d'Ucel, "About Indians," 17. See also Gregor Stark and E. Catherine Rayne, *El Delirio: The Santa Fe World of Elizabeth White* (Santa Fe, New Mex.: School of American Research Press, 1998), especially chapter 4.

19 John Sloan and Oliver LaFarge, *Introduction to American Indian Art*, 2 vols. (New York: Indian Tribal Arts Inc., 1931). Volume 2 contains "Modern Indian Painting," an essay by Alice Corbin Henderson (pp. 3–11), which includes one illustration of Spencer Asah's *Eagle Dancer*, from Jacobson's collection, and six illustrations of Pueblo watercolors. D'Ucel's manuscript, "Indian Painters of Oklahoma" (11 pp. typescript), is housed in the Oscar B. Jacobson Collection, Oklahoma Historical Society, Oklahoma City.

20 See, for example, d'Ucel, "American Indian Painting," *The Western Art Magazine* (May 1929): 7–8, and "An International Sensation—Kiowa Indians' Art in New Conquest," *Sooner Magazine* 2, no. 4 (Jan. 1930): 127–28.

21 This was separate from, but related to, the better-known Works Progress Administration (WPA), a federal arts project of the New Deal.

22 d'Ucel, *Memoir and Biographical Writings*, box 1, folder 3, p. 189.

23 For the participation of Oklahoma Native artists in WPA mural projects, see also Jennifer McLerran, *A New Deal for Native Art: Indian Arts and Federal Policy 1933–1943* (Tucson: University of Arizona Press, 2009), 166–77 and 184–93. See also John Anson Warner, "Native American Painting in Oklahoma: Continuity and Change," *The Journal of Intercultural Studies* 23 (1996): 14–129.

24 The undated *Sioux Horses*, museum purchase in 1937, accession #1002, and *Sioux Horse Chase* (1936), museum purchase in 1938, accession #1015.

25 d'Ucel, "About Indians," 39. The research survives in the collection of the FJJMA in the form of tracings on onionskin paper of important paintings and prints from art history. The Jacobsons used the work of artists such as George Catlin and Karl Bodmer as models for their research. The tracings seem to be in Jacobson's hand and not Howe's.

26 Oscar Broussse Jacobson, *North American Indian Costumes (1564–1950)*, illus. by Oscar Howe, 2 vols. (Nice, France: l'Edition d'Art C. Szwedzicki, 1950). Each portfolio contained twenty-five plates, and the two-volume set cost eighty dollars. Only two hundred and fifty copies were issued and it was published only in English. Jacobson gave all of the original works of art to the Museum of the American Indian (now the National Museum of the American Indian, in Washington D.C.). He donated one hundred paintings in all, including some

from the 1950 portfolio, all from the 1952 portfolio, plus ten more by Howe that clearly were part of that project but not included in the published portfolio. See David Fawcett and Lee Callander, *Native American Painting: Selections from the Museum of the American Indian* (New York: Museum of the American Indian, Heye Foundation, 1982): 91–93.

27   See, for example, Jacobson, *North American Indian Costumes*, plates 46, 47, 49, 50.

28   For examples, see Frederick J. Dockstader, ed., *Oscar Howe: A Retrospective Exhibition, Catalogue Raisonne*, plates 32, 41, 42, 45, 52; Mark A. White, "A Modernist Moment: Native Art and Surrealism at the University of Oklahoma," *Journal of Surrealism and the Americas* 7, no. 1 (2013): 52–70, and Mark A. White, "Oscar Howe and the Transformation of Native American Art," *American Indian Art Magazine*, 23, no. 1 (Winter 1997): 36–43, and Bill Anthes, *Native Moderns: American Indian Painting, 1940–1960* (Durham, N.C.: Duke University Press, 2006).

29   Jacobson and d'Ucel, *American Indian Painters*, 2 vols. (Nice, France: l'Edition d'Art C. Szwedzicki, 1950). Its price was one hundred dollars. Most of the works illustrated in Volume I not owned by Jacobson were already in the OU collections. All of the artists in the 1929 Kiowa portfolio are represented here, as well as James Auchiah, the other member of the Kiowa Five. See Janet C. Berlo, "The Szwedzicki Portfolios of American Indian Art, 1929–1952, Part II," *American Indian Art Magazine* 34, no. 3 (May 2009): 58–67.

30   d'Ucel, "About Indians," 31.

31   Longer biographies of many Native artists exist in both handwritten and typescript form in the Oscar Jacobson papers, box J-13, Western History Collection, University of Oklahoma.

32   Ruthe Blalock Jones, "Bacone College and the Philbrook Indian Annuals," in Wyckoff, *Visions and Voices*, 55.

33   See W. Jackson Rushing III, *Allan Houser, An American Master* (New York: Harry N. Abrams, Inc., 2004).

34 J. Craig Sheppard, in a review of the subsequent portfolio, "American Indian Costumes," *Books Abroad* 30 (Summer 1956): 286–87, quote p. 286.

35 "Sooner Artist Returns from Africa with Many Canvases of Great Sahara Desert," *Daily Oklahoman*, Sept. 26, 1926, D-3.

36 "African Exhibit for University," *Oklahoma Daily*, 1926. The clipping is dated Oct. 26 in Jacobson's scrapbook, vol. 4, but the article in question does not appear in that issue of the newspaper. His own paintings were exhibited the following spring. *Exhibition of Some Paintings of North Africa by Oscar Jacobson,* March 1927, in Jacobson and d'Ucel scrapbooks, vol. 4, box 4.

37 Oscar Jacobson, "Fording Algeria," *University of Oklahoma Magazine* 15, no. 3 (March 1927): 5. The title refers to the fact that a Ford touring car took them on this desert journey.

38 d'Ucel, "Shopping in the Sahara," *The Household Magazine* (May 1929): 18. Clipping preserved in Jacobson and d'Ucel scrapbooks, vol. 4, box 4.

39 "Oklahoma Writers," *Daily Oklahoman*, April 2, 1929, in Jacobson and d'Ucel scrapbooks, vol. 4, box 4.

40 Today, many Berber and Tuareg people of North Africa prefer the term Imazighen or Amazigh to "Berber," a word that finds its root in the outsider's term "barbarian." Imazighen means simply "the free people." See Cynthia Becker, "Matriarchal Nomads and Freedom Fighters: Transnational Amazigh Consciousness and Moroccan, Algerian, and Nigerien Artists," *Critical Interventions* 5 (Fall 2009): 70–101, and Lisa Bernasek, *Artistry of the Everyday: Beauty and Craftsmanship in Berber Art* (Cambridge, Mass: Peabody Museum Press, Harvard University, 2008).

41 d'Ucel, *Berber Art* (Norman: University of Oklahoma Press, 1932), 179.

42 d'Ucel, *Berber Art*, 172.

43 d'Ucel, *Memoir and Biographical Writings*, box 1, folder 3, 184.

Detail (pages 136–137), see Fig. 29, page 53
Oscar Jacobson
U.S., born Sweden, 1882–1966
Apache Night or *Arizona Night*, 1923

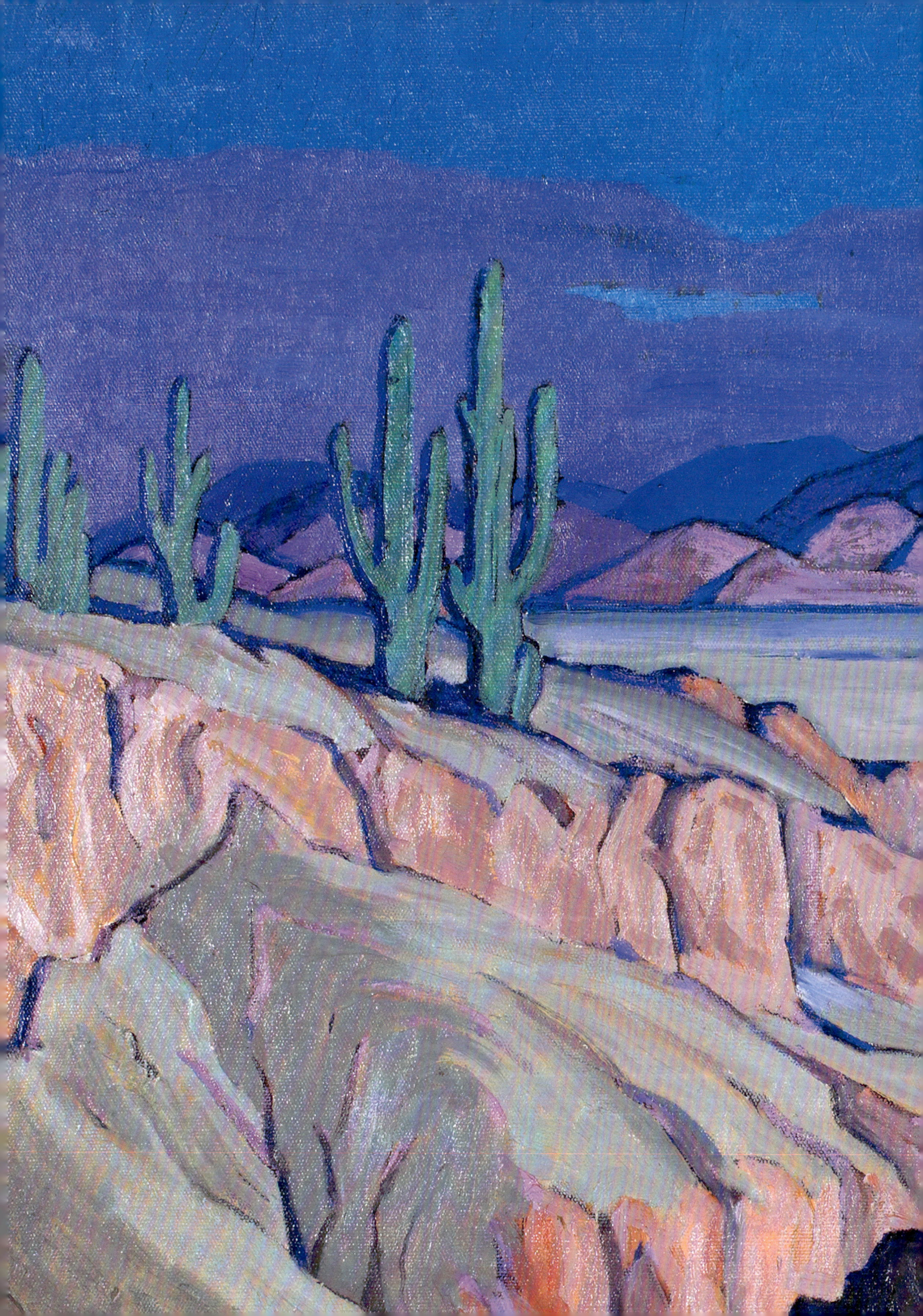

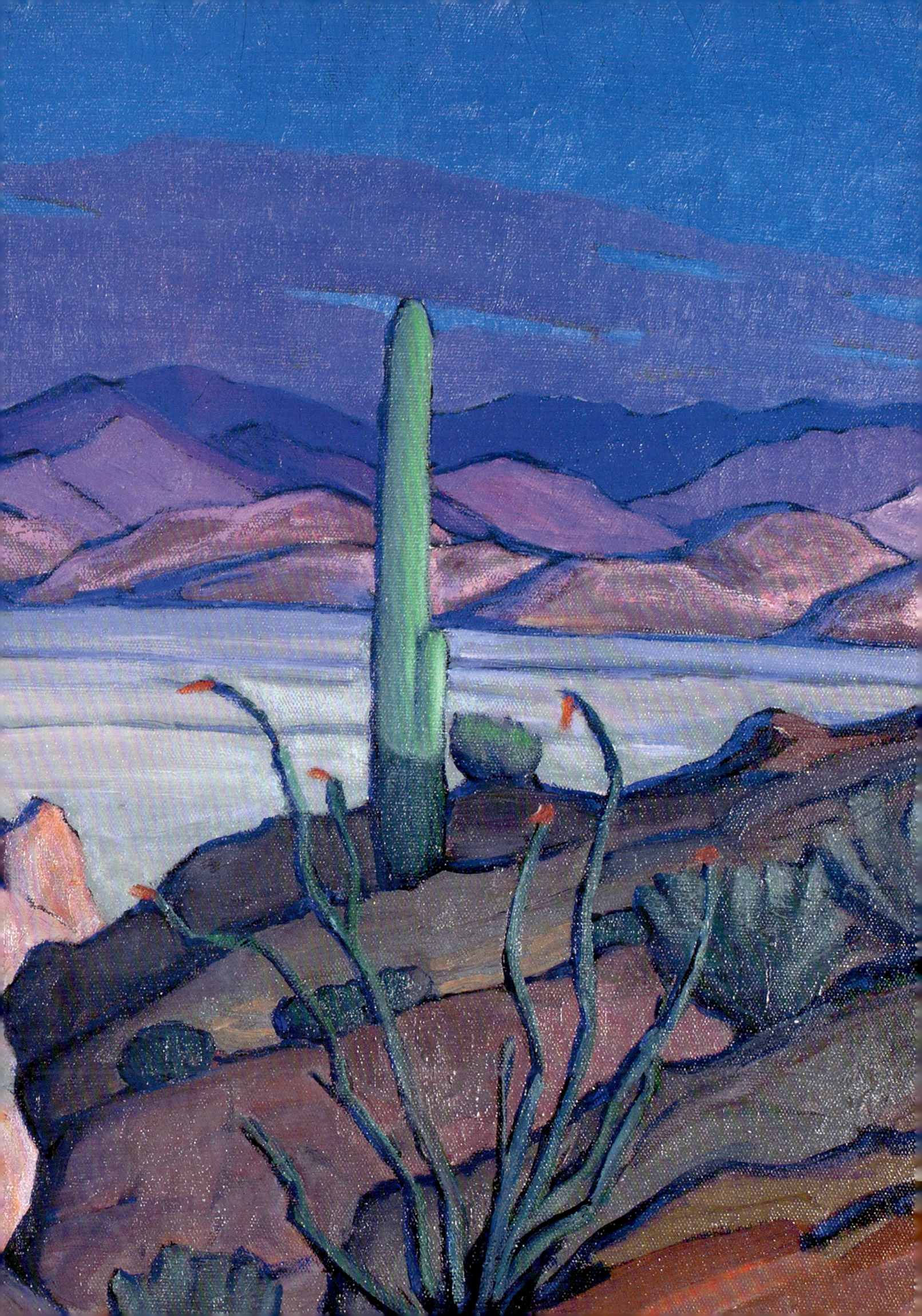

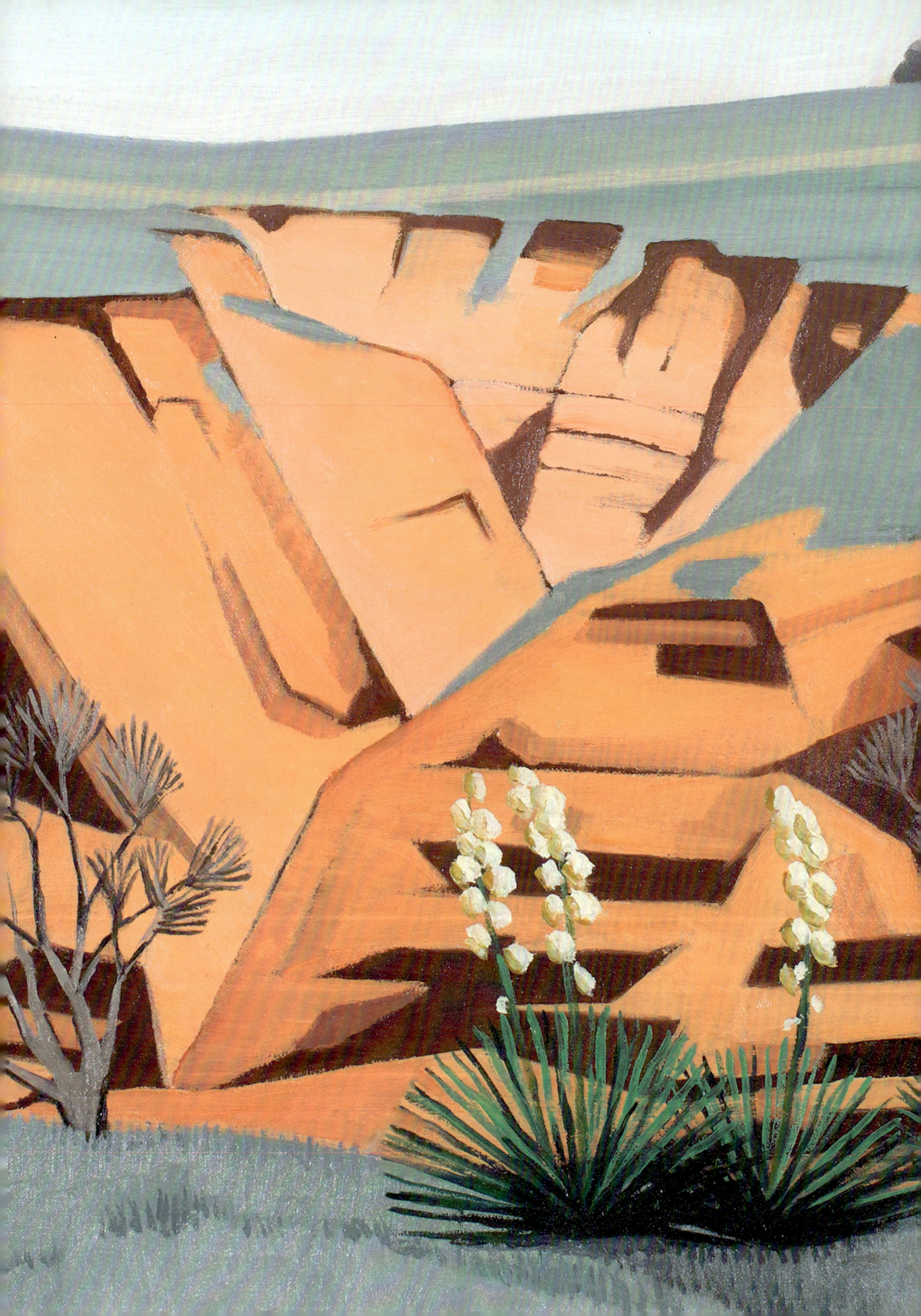

Chronology

Compiled by Melynda Seaton

1882   Anders Oskar Jakobson is born on May 16 possibly on the island Västra Eknö, in Västervik, Kalmar län, Sweden.

1890   The Jakobson family relocates to Lindsborg, Kansas.

1895   Jakobson enrolls in drawing and painting classes at Bethany College. His studies will continue into the 1903–04 year. His name is often Anglicized in the college register. Sophie Brousse (Jeanne d'Ucel) is born in Aubenas, France.

1902   Jakobson and his equestrian group, called both Jakobson's Rough Riders and the Crazy Ridge Wild West Riders, performs at the Fourth of July parade in Lindsborg.

1903   Jakobson leaves Bethany for St. Louis, where he is appointed a member of the Jefferson Guards for the Louisiana Purchase Exposition.

1904   Jakobson serves as an attaché for the Royal Swedish Commission in St. Louis. In March, he resigns from the Jefferson Guards to serve as Custodian of the Fine Arts Building at the Louisiana Purchase Exposition. The Anglicized spelling "Jacobson" begins to appear in press.

1905   Jacobson enrolls at Yale University.

Detail, see Fig. 65, page 88
Oscar Jacobson
U.S., born Sweden, 1882–1966
Horse Thief Canyon, Oklahoma, 1949

1906   Jacobson wins the Henry F. English scholarship.

1907   Jacobson exhibits *The Quarter Breed* in the Seventh Annual Paint and Clay Club
exhibition at Yale. He and his classmates, dubbed the Kawraw Kiotes, perform
a western melodrama titled *Sunset.*

1908   Jacobson receives his Bachelor of Painting from Bethany College. In July, he
accepts a position as the chair of the new art department at Minnesota College
in Minneapolis.

1910   Jacobson begins lecturing on a number of art historical subjects, including
"The Beauty of Nature and the Impressionists," "Impressionism in Art," and
"Contemporary Artists of Sweden."

1911   Jacobson resigns from Minnesota College for a position as the head of painting
and drawing at Washington State College in Pullman, Washington.

1912   Jacobson marries Sophie Jeanne Brousse d'Ucel in August and adopts Brousse
as his middle name. In September, he files for American citizenship.

1914   Jacobson studies informally at the Louvre and visits Sweden and Denmark.

1915   In July, Jacobson accepts a position as the head of the art department at the
University of Oklahoma. On the trip to Norman, the Jacobsons visit the Pan-
ama-California Exposition in San Diego, which prompts them to travel through
Arizona and New Mexico. They take a special interest in Acoma Pueblo.

1916   In March, Jacobson is elected secretary of the newly-formed Association of
Oklahoma Artists. He is recognized in June with an honorary BFA degree
from the School of Fine Arts at Yale University; a distinguished honor because
the award is one of six of its kind handed out by Yale in the previous fifty years.
In October, Jacobson exhibits thirty-nine paintings at OU and, in November, the group exhibition *Artists of the Southwest* includes his painting, *The Prayer
for Rain*, which is purchased for the permanent collection at McPherson High
School in Kansas.

1917   In January, OU hosts the *Second Annual Art Exhibition of Oklahoma*, which includes artists from Oklahoma, as well as Missouri, Kansas, and Texas. In April, Jacobson is promoted to Associate Professor at OU. In June, the Jacobsons' daughter, Yvonne Françoise Brousse Jacobson, is born. Jacobson exhibits forty-one paintings at OU in October, which is his third solo exhibition at the university since his arrival.

1918   In February, Jacobson is included in the *Third Annual Exhibition of Art of the Southwest*. In March, he organizes an exhibit of American photography for OU. The Jacobsons finish building their home at 609 Chautauqua.

1919   In January, OU hosts the *Fourth Annual Southwest Art Exhibition*, which Jacobson helps to organize. In May, Jacobson gives the lecture "East and the West" at the Tenth Annual Convention of the American Federation of Arts at the Metropolitan Museum of Art, New York. The essay is later published in the *American Magazine of Art* in November 1920. The Jacobsons' son, Oscar Andre Jacobson, Jr., is born in December.

1920   In April, Jacobson exhibits in the *Ninth Exhibition by Swedish-American Artists* at the Swedish Club in Chicago. In October, Jacobson announces that enrollment has grown in the School of Art from 23 students in 1915 to 225 in 1920. In November, Jacobson is included in *American Painters of Swedish Descent* at the Art Institute of Chicago.

1921   In January, Jacobson announces his hope to establish a museum at OU, starting with the acquisition of Japanese military uniforms from World War I. The Jacobsons' daughter, Yolande Helene Brousse Jacobson, is born in May.

1922   Jacobson serves as one of three jurors for an exhibition at the Kansas City Art Institute. Later in the year, he leads a tour group to France, Italy, Switzerland, Holland, Bavaria, Belgium, and England.

1923   In January, *White Shadows Among the Navajos* is included in the *Exhibition of Work by Creative Artists of the States of Missouri, Kansas and Oklahoma* and *Works by Prominent Illustrators* at the Kansas City Art Institute. In March, Jacobson is awarded a second prize for the photograph, *In the Artist's Garden*, by *American Photography Magazine.* In May, Jacobson presents "The Meaning of Modernism in Art" at the Fourteenth Annual American Federation of Arts convention in St. Louis, Missouri. Jacobson exhibits his artworks created in the previous two years under the title *Exhibition of Recent Work by Oscar Brousse Jacobson* in the reading rooms at OU Library. In November, a *Special Exhibition of Painting by O. B. Jacobson; Gwendolyn Meux; Edith Mahier* opens at the Delgado Museum of Art in New Orleans.

1924   In January, Jacobson participates in two exhibits, one at the St. Louis Public Library and another one at the Kansas City Art Institute, and he also publishes the article, "The Meaning of Modernism in Art," in the *American Magazine of Art.* During the summer, he serves as director of the Broadmoor Art Academy in Colorado Springs.

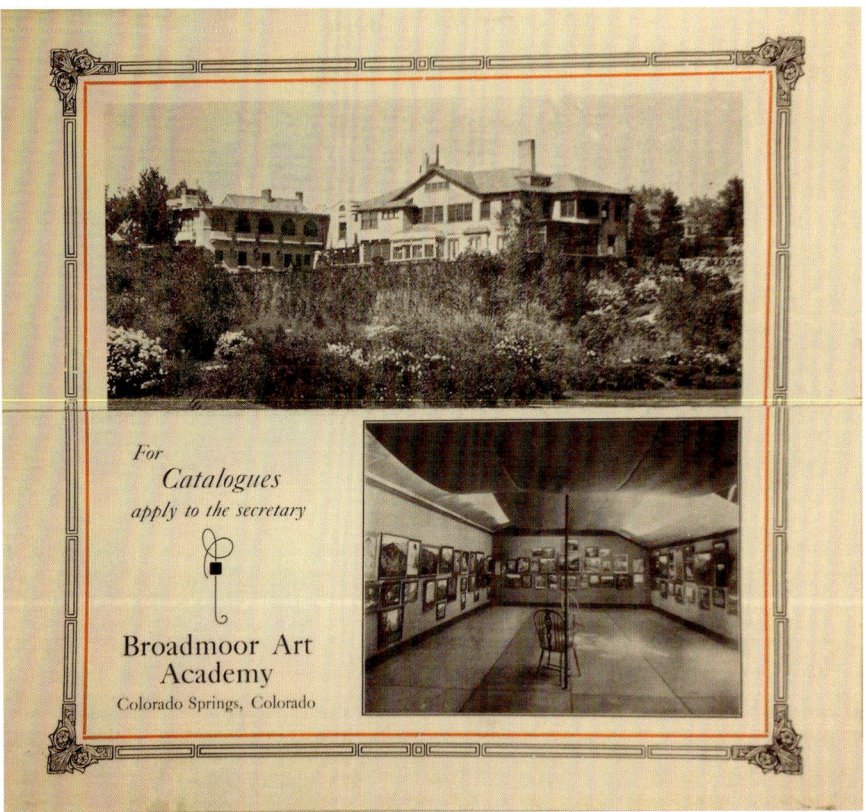

Fig. 88

Flier for the Broadmoor Art Academy, ca. 1924

Fig. 89 (facing page)

Reproduction of Jacobson's photograph

In the Artist's Garden, ca. 1923

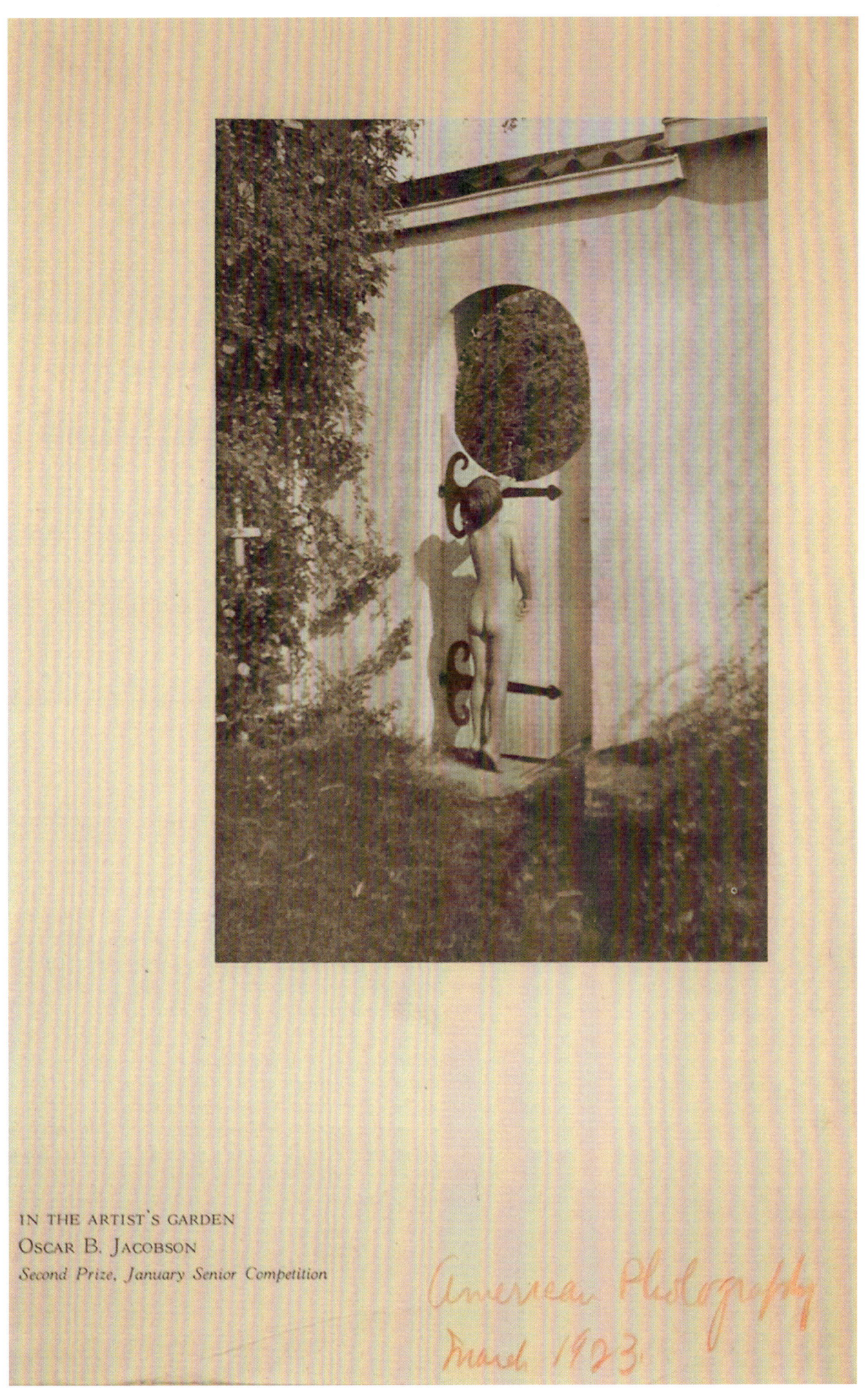

IN THE ARTIST'S GARDEN
OSCAR B. JACOBSON
Second Prize, January Senior Competition

American Photography
March 1923.

1925   Jacobson exhibits his personal collection of Asian art at OU in February. In August, he begins a yearlong sabbatical, and the Jacobsons travel to France with their ultimate destination being northern Africa, especially Morocco, Algeria, and Tunisia. They collect numerous examples of art and crafts during their travels.

1926   Upon returning from northern Africa, Jacobson lectures repeatedly about his travels. Jacobson exhibits the material they collected at OU in October and includes several paintings from the trip in the Association of Oklahoma Artists exhibition in November at the Harbour-Longmire Co., a gallery and frame shop.

1927   In January, "The Art of Oscar Brousse Jacobson" by William Cunningham appears in *Haldeman-Julius Quarterly*. In March, *Exhibition of Some Paintings of North Africa by Oscar Jacobson* features twenty-eight new paintings on view at OU. Jacobson follows with an exhibition of twenty-two works depicting North Africa at the Madison Art Association in Madison, Wisconsin, hosted by the State Historical Museum in May. In the spring semester, four Kiowa artists, Spencer Asah, Jack Hokeah, Steven Mopope, and Monroe Tsatoke, begin taking nonaccredited courses working in the studio of fellow art professor, Edith Mahier. In September, Jacobson exhibits his personal collection of artwork from northern Africa at OU. In November, Jacobson gives a lecture at the opening reception for an exhibition of his paintings at the salon of Harbour-Longmire Co. That same month, Jacobson exhibits at the annual meeting of the American Federation of Arts at University of Nebraska and serves on the panel discussion "Modern Trends in Art" with Birger Sandzén and Ernest L. Blumenschein.

1928   Lois Bou-ge-tah Smokey joins the group of four Kiowa men at OU in January, but only stays for a semester. Bou-ge-tah Lois Smokey takes her place in the fall. Jacobson begins campaigning for a proper facility to house OU's growing art collection. In April, *Djedjelli, Algeria* is included in the Society of Independents exhibition in New York. Jacobson has an exhibition at the Ainslie Galleries in New York City in November. In July, Jacobson is named honorary chief of the Kiowa tribe in a ceremony near Anadarko and is described as the "second white man to be taken into the tribe." That summer, the paintings of the Kiowa artists are also shown at the 6th International Congress for Art Education in Prague. In November, Jacobson organizes an exhibition of works by the Kiowa artists for the Joplin Art League and then the Portland Museum of Art in December. That same month, announcements appear for *Kiowa Indian Art*, published by C. Szwedzicki in Nice, France.

1929 In June, Jacobson exhibits at Kroch's Bookstore in Chicago, Illinois. In November, he is hospitalized for an infected gallbladder.

1930 In February, the new Fine Arts building at OU opens. An exhibition of artwork by Asah, Hokeah, Mopope, and Tsatoke, which Jacobson helped to organize, opens at the Minneapolis Institute of Art.

1931 *Mountain Lake* receives a gold medal at the *Midwestern Artist Exhibition* at the Kansas City Art Institute. In December, Jacobson exhibits twenty-eight paintings at OU.

1932 The Jacobsons begin building a cabin in Allenspark, Colorado, completing it sometime in 1933. The cabin will become the family's second home, and they spend most summers there after 1933.

1934 Jacobson serves as technical advisor in charge of the Public Works of Art Projects in Oklahoma, a role that continues into 1935. In October, *An Exhibition of the Recent Paintings by Mr. O. B. Jacobson* is held at the School of Art galleries at OU.

1935 In February, Jacobson serves as a member of the jury for the *Midwestern Artist Exhibition* at Kansas City Art Institute.

1936 Jacobson serves as technical advisor on the Treasury Relief Art Project, beginning in 1936 and continuing through 1937. In April, OU receives a gift of Asian material from oilman Lew Wentz and photographer R. Gordon Matzene that leads to the creation of the OU Museum of Art. Jacobson is named director. In October, *An Exhibition of Recent Paintings by Oscar Brousse Jacobson* is on view at OU.

1937   *Mountain Lake* is included in the *Second National Exhibition of American Art*, organized by the Municipal Art Committee, City of New York at the American Fine Arts Society Galleries in New York City. In October, *An Exhibition of Recent Paintings Never Before Publically Exhibited by Oscar B. Jacobson* opens at OU.

1938   In March, Jacobson exhibits thirty-five paintings at W.P.A. Oklahoma Art Center in the Municipal Auditorium. In October, OU hosts *An Exhibition of Recent Paintings by Oscar B. Jacobson*, works painted during the summers of 1937–38.

1939   *Trail Ridge in June* is included in *American Art Today* at the New York World's Fair. From October 1 to 31, *Twenty-two of Jacobson's Paintings Previously Un-exhibited* is on view at OU.

1940   Jacobson's painting *Oklahoma Lake* is included in an exhibition of artworks touring Central and South America. *In Brown and Grey* is included in the Coronado Quarto Centennial exhibition in New Mexico. From November 4 to 17, *An Exhibition of the Most Recent Paintings by O. B. Jacobson* is on view at OU.

1941   Jacobson is awarded a Doctor of Fine Arts from Bethany College. From March 29 to April 11, the WPA Oklahoma Art Center in the Municipal Auditorium hosts the *Oscar B. Jacobson Retrospective Exhibition 1912–1940*, which includes seventy-four oils. *The Annual Exhibition of Paintings by O. B. Jacobson* is held in the lobby of the Art Building at OU from September 29 to October 13.

1942   Jacobson is awarded the International Business Machine Corp. Medal for Notable Contributions to the Art World.

1943   In September, *Exhibition of Paintings by Jacobson* reportedly attracts large crowds at OU.

1945   At the end of the 1945–46 academic year, Jacobson steps down as director of the School of Art after reaching mandatory retirement age, but he continues at the Museum of Art. In November, *Twenty-four New Oil Paintings by Jacobson of Oklahoma, Colorado, Wyoming, Utah, New Mexico and Arizona* is exhibited at OU.

1946   *Paintings by Oscar B. Jacobson* opens at Oklahoma Art Center in January. In April, the Philbrook Art Center exhibits *Landscapes by Dr. Oscar B. Jacobson.* From October 13 to 26, Jacobson shows *Exhibition of Twenty-one Paintings by Jacobson of Colorado, Utah, Oklahoma, Wyoming, and New Mexico* at OU. In December, Jacobson's painting *Trail Ridge in June* is included in the *Six States Exhibit: Colorado, Iowa, Kansas, Missouri, Nebraska, South Dakota*, sponsored by the Society of Liberal Arts at Joslyn Memorial in Omaha, Nebraska.

1947   Oscar A. Jacobson III dies from an automobile accident in Colorado in August.

1948   Jacobson sets up a scholarship fund at OU in memory of his son, Oscar. In June, the Museum of Art, with Jacobson's assistance, acquires thirty-six paintings from the controversial State Department exhibit *Advancing American Art.* The paintings are exhibited soon after their arrival on campus in September. In December, the Museum of Art at OU presents *An Exhibition of 22 Paintings by O. B. Jacobson* (twenty of which were done in the summer of 1948).

1949   In May, Jacobson is elected to membership in the Oklahoma Hall of Fame. From December 4 to 18, *An Exhibition of the Recent Paintings by Mr. O. B. Jacobson: Painted During the Summer of 1949* shows at OU.

1950   Jacobson publishes with d'Ucel *Les Peintres Indiens d'Amerique (American Indian Painters)* in Nice in both English and French. Jacobson is awarded the title Research Professor of Art Emeritus at OU following his retirement from the museum. In late summer, Jacobson hosts *A Private Exhibition of the Paintings of the West by O. B. Jacobson, B. Acc., B.P., B.F.A., D.F.A., F.A.G.S., Director, Museum of Art, University of Oklahoma* at the Allenspark Cabin Studio.

1951   In April, an *Exhibition of Landscape Paintings by Dr. Oscar Brousse Jacobson* is held at the University of Nevada, Reno.

1952   *North American Indian Costumes, 1564–1950*, is published in Nice. In June, Jacobson retires from OU at age seventy. In December, the Art Museum Building on OU's campus is renamed Jacobson Hall to honor Jacobson's service to the university.

1953   Together with d'Ucel, Jacobson publishes "Early Oklahoma Artists" in the *Chronicles of Oklahoma.* In October, he holds a three-day private exhibition of recent paintings at his home.

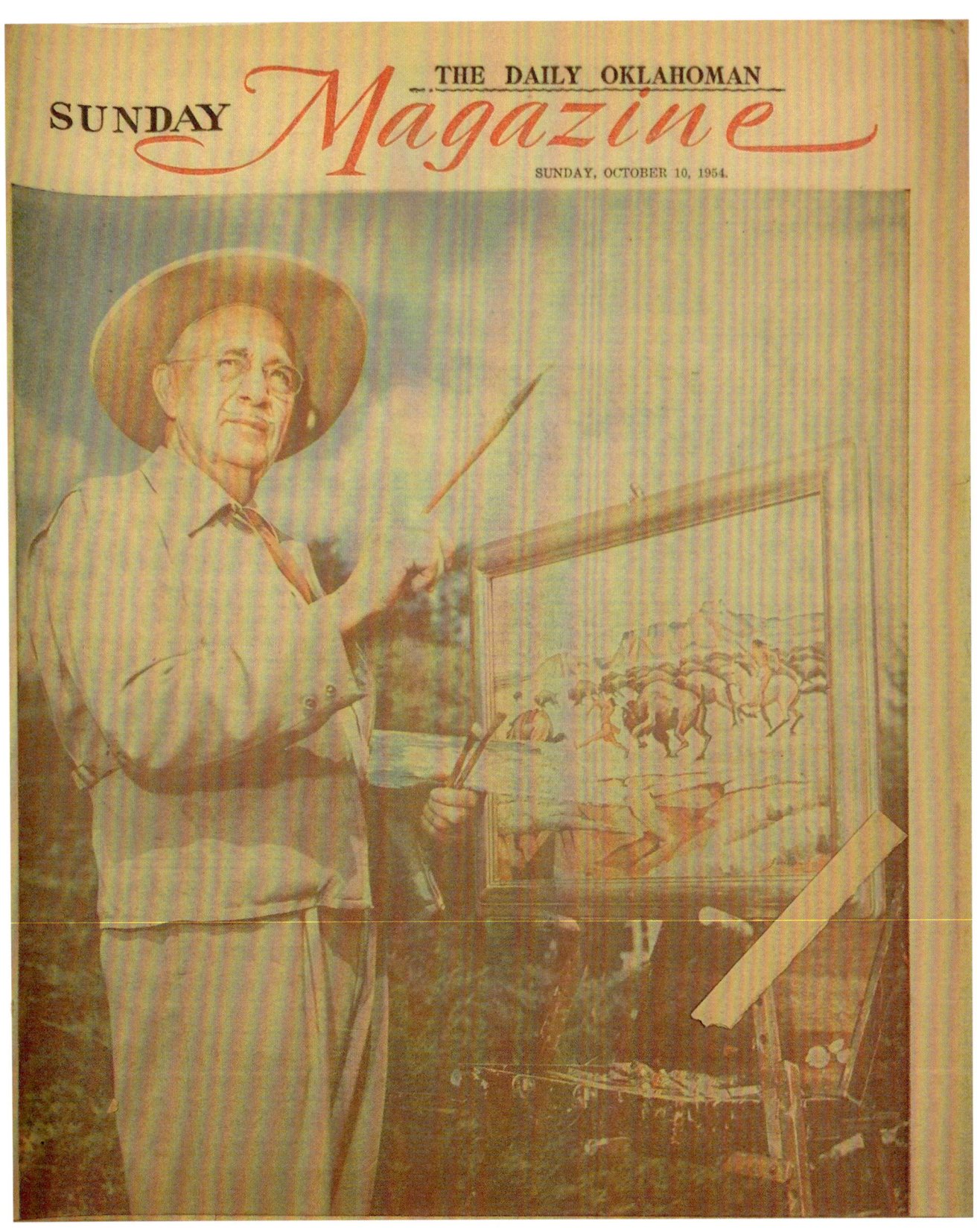

SUNDAY *Magazine*

SUNDAY, OCTOBER 10, 1954.

Fig. 90

Jacobson posing in front of *Buffalo Hunt in Reverse*, from

Daily Oklahoman Sunday Magazine, October 10, 1954

1955   In March, Jacobson falls ill with a cerebral hemorrhage.

1957   In October, the Philbrook Art Center gives Jacobson a solo exhibition.

1960   Jacobson receives a citation from the U.S. Department of Interior, Bureau of
        Indian Arts and Crafts. In April, Mr. and Mrs. Jacobson appear on the NBC
        television show *This Is Your Life* for an episode featuring Oscar Howe.

1961   From September 17 to October 8, the OU Museum of Art, located in Jacob-
        son Hall, honors Jacobson with a retrospective exhibition.

1966   Jacobson dies at the age of eighty-four. His ashes are scattered outside Allen-
        spark, Colorado.

1967   D'Ucel dies, and her ashes are scattered outside Allenspark, Colorado.

1968   In June, the Jacobson family auctions much of his inventory in Oklahoma City
        through Heldenbrand and Anderson Auctioneers, Inc.

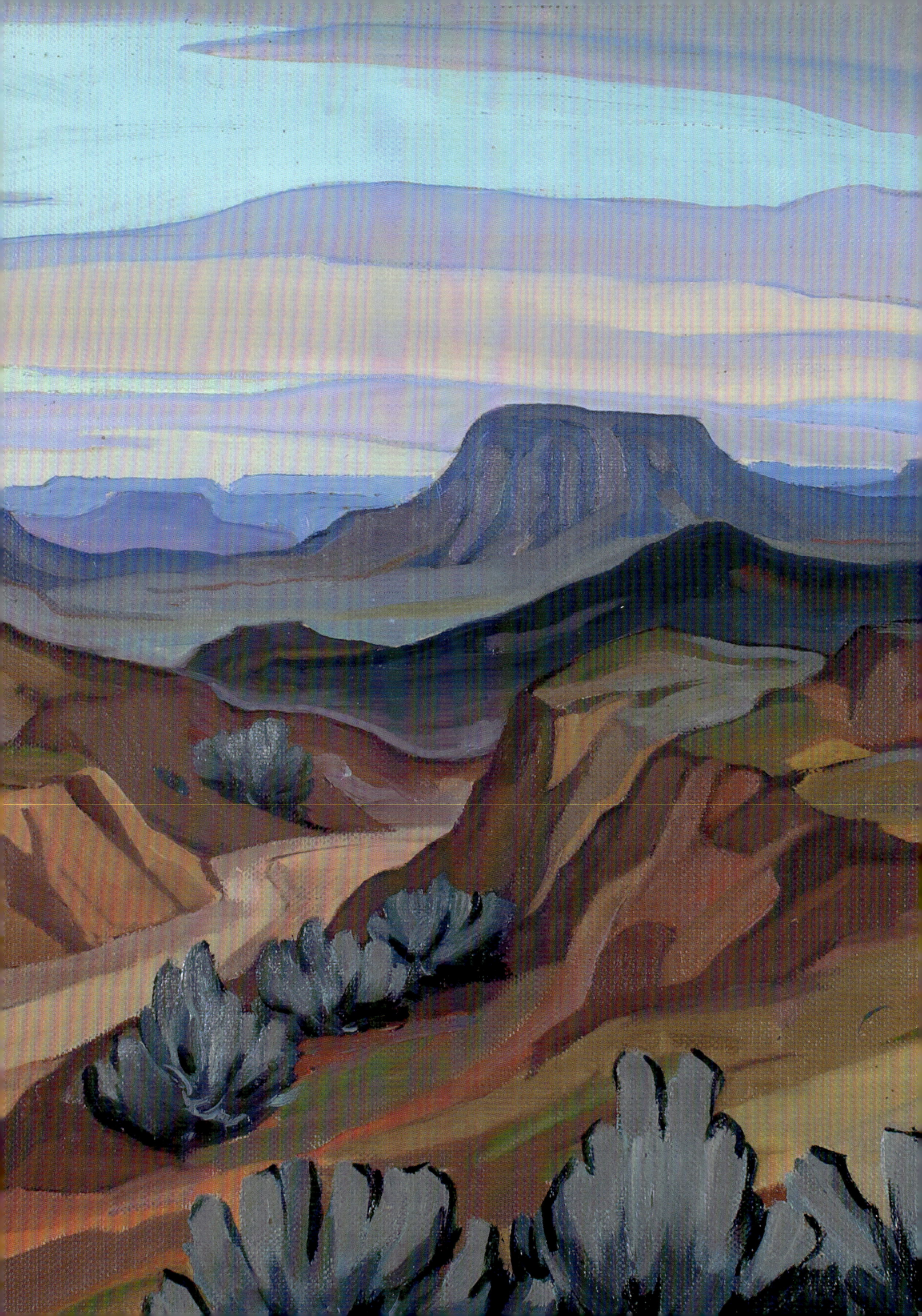

Contributors

ANNE ALLBRIGHT

Anne Allbright holds an M.A. in museum studies and history from the University of Central Oklahoma, and an M.A. in history from Southern Methodist University, where she is currently finishing her Ph.D. A native to Oklahoma, she worked at the Jacobson House for several years as a researcher and guest curator. She is currently writing her dissertation on Oscar Brousse Jacobson's life and has even visited his childhood homes in Sweden and Kansas. For the past four years, she has worked as the assistant director for SMU-in-Italy Arts and Culture Program.

JANET CATHERINE BERLO, PH.D.

Janet Catherine Berlo is Professor of Art History and Visual and Cultural Studies at the University of Rochester. She has written numerous books and essays on Native American art history, including *Spirit Beings and Sun Dancers: Black Hawk's Vision of a Lakota World* (2000), *Plains Indian Drawings 1865–1935* (1996) and, with Ruth Phillips, *Native North American Art* (1998; 2nd ed., 2015). She has taught Native art history as a visiting professor at Harvard, Yale, and UCLA, and received grants from the Guggenheim Foundation, the Getty Charitable Trust, and the National Endowment for the Humanities

MARK A. WHITE, PH.D.

Mark Andrew White is the Interim Director and Eugene B. Adkins Senior Curator at the Fred Jones Jr. Museum of Art, University of Oklahoma. He specializes in American and Native American art of the twentieth century with a particular focus on the Southwest. His recent publications include *Macrocosm/Microcosm: Abstract Expressionism in the American Southwest* (2014), *Art Interrupted: Advancing American Art and the Politics of Cultural Diplomacy* (2012), *The James T. Bialac Native American Art Collection: Selected Works* (2012), and *The Eugene B. Adkins Collection: Selected Works* (2011).

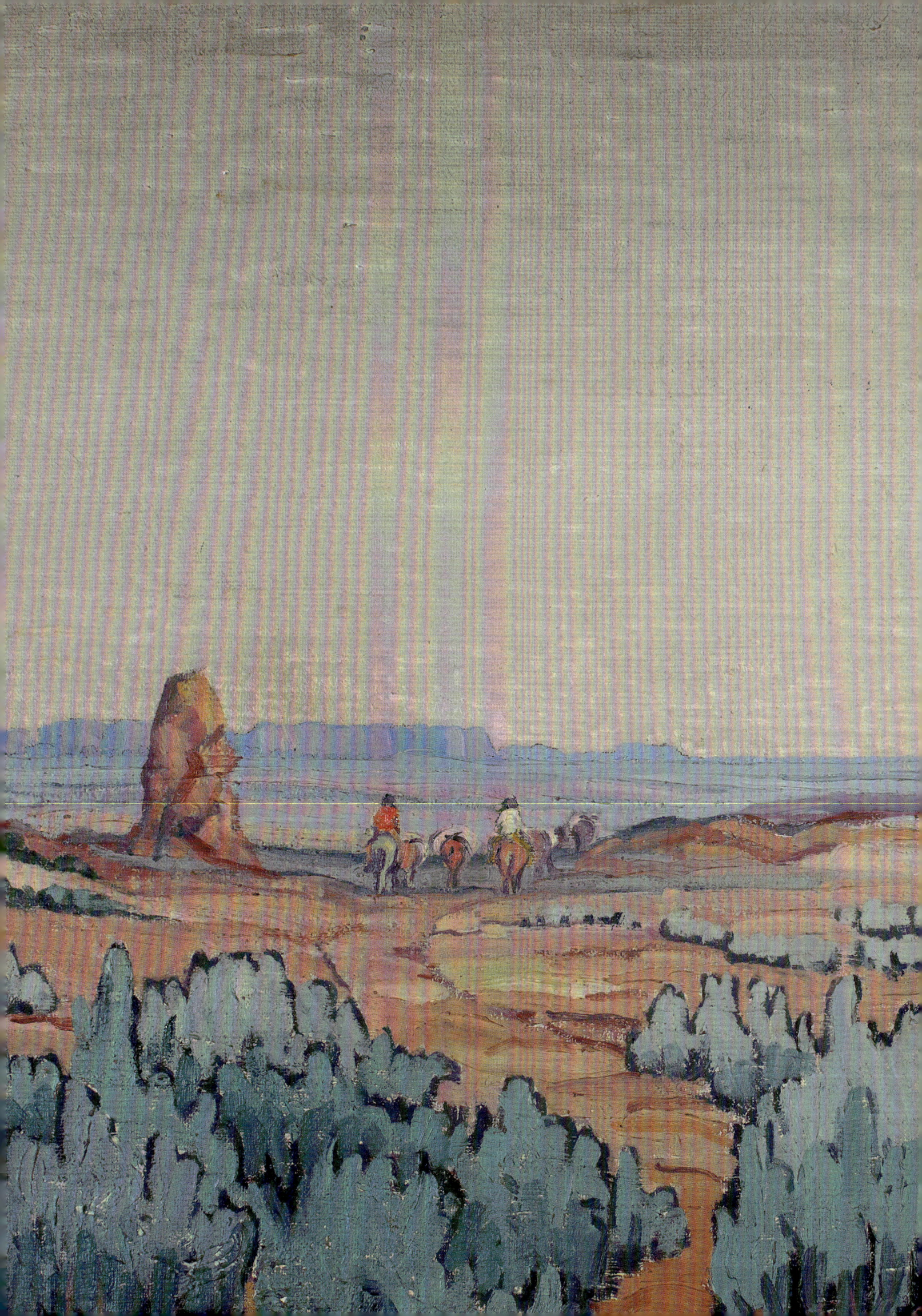

Publication Notes

This catalogue has been published in conjunction with the exhibition, *A World Unconquered: the Art of Oscar Brousse Jacobson* at the Fred Jones Jr. Museum of Art, February 26 – September 6, 2015.

Catalogue design: Eric H. Anderson
Editorial assistant: Jo Ann Reece
Copy editor: Michael Bendure
Photography: Todd Stewart

Fred Jones Jr. Museum of Art, The University of Oklahoma
555 Elm Avenue, Norman, Oklahoma 73019-3003
phone: 405.325.3272; fax: 325.7696
www.ou.edu/fjjma

Library of Congress Control Number: 2015930303
ISBN: 978-0-9851609-8-2 (soft cover)
       978-0-9851609-9-9 (hard cover)

This catalogue was printed by the University of Oklahoma Printing Services and is issued by the University of Oklahoma. 1,000 copies have been printed and distributed at no cost to the taxpayers of Oklahoma.

Detail (left), see Fig. 26, page 50
Oscar Jacobson
U.S., born Sweden, 1882–1966
Navajo Going to the Snake Dance, 1922

Cover
Detail, see Fig. 22, page 46
Oscar Jacobson
U.S., born Sweden, 1882–1966
Enchanted Mesa, 1920

Overleaf (pages ii–iii)
Detail, see Fig. 59, page 82
Oscar Jacobson
U.S., born Sweden, 1882–1966
In the Navajo Country, 1938

Title page (page iv)
Detail, see Fig. 45, page 68
Oscar Jacobson
U.S., born Sweden, 1882–1966
The Quartz Mountains, 1928

Contents page (page vi)
Detail, see Fig. 48, page 72
Oscar Jacobson
U.S., born Sweden, 1882–1966
In Brown and Grey, 1936

Page 148
Detail, see Fig. 51, page 75
Oscar Jacobson
U.S., born Sweden, 1882–1966
Below Raton, 1934

Pages 152–153
Detail, see Fig. 32, page 56
Oscar Jacobson
U.S., born Sweden, 1882–1966
The Needles, Colorado Desert, ca. 1923

Pages 154–155
Detail, see Fig. 63, page 87
Oscar Jacobson
U.S., born Sweden, 1882–1966
Light Soil or On the Road to Chickasha, 1949

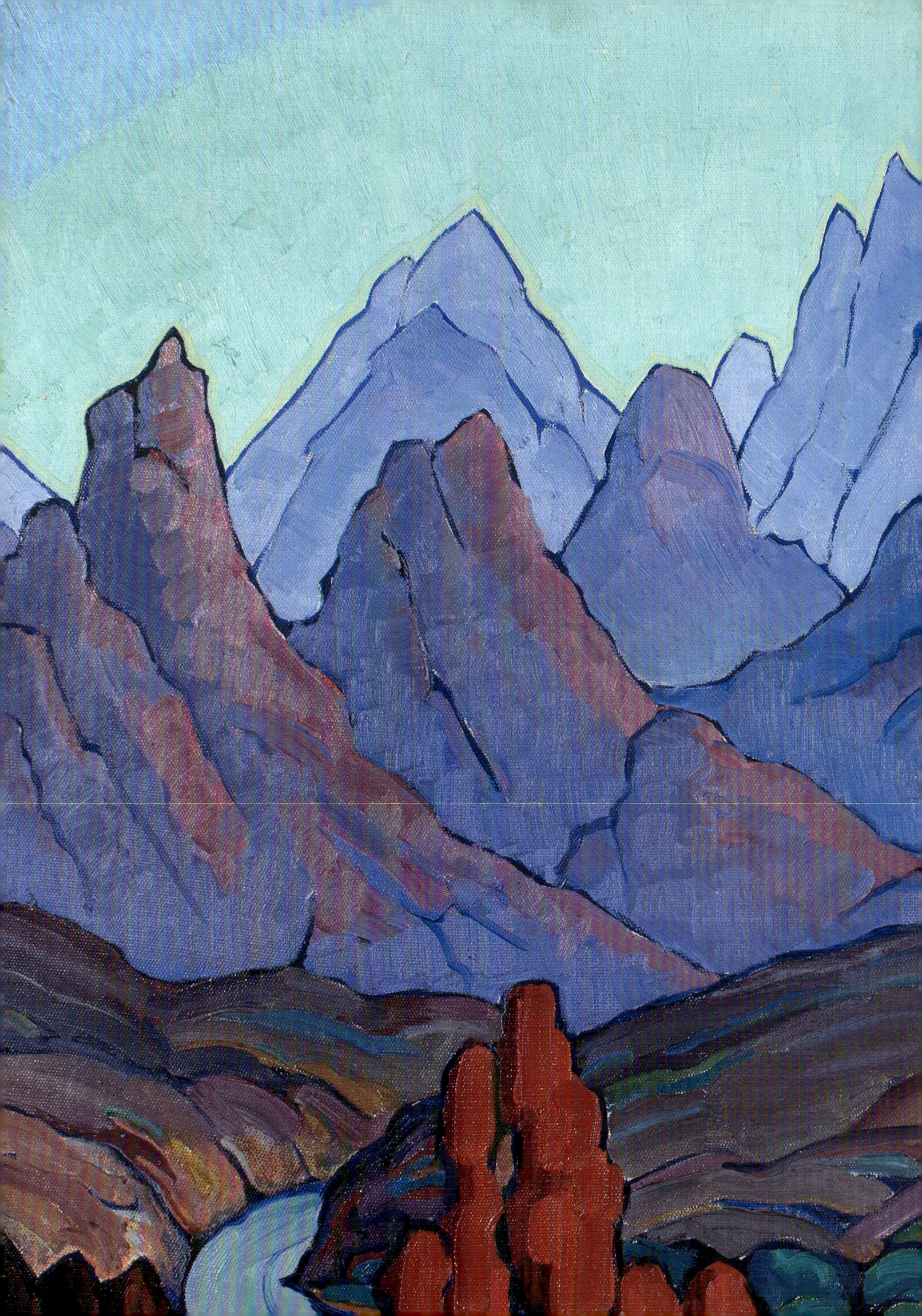

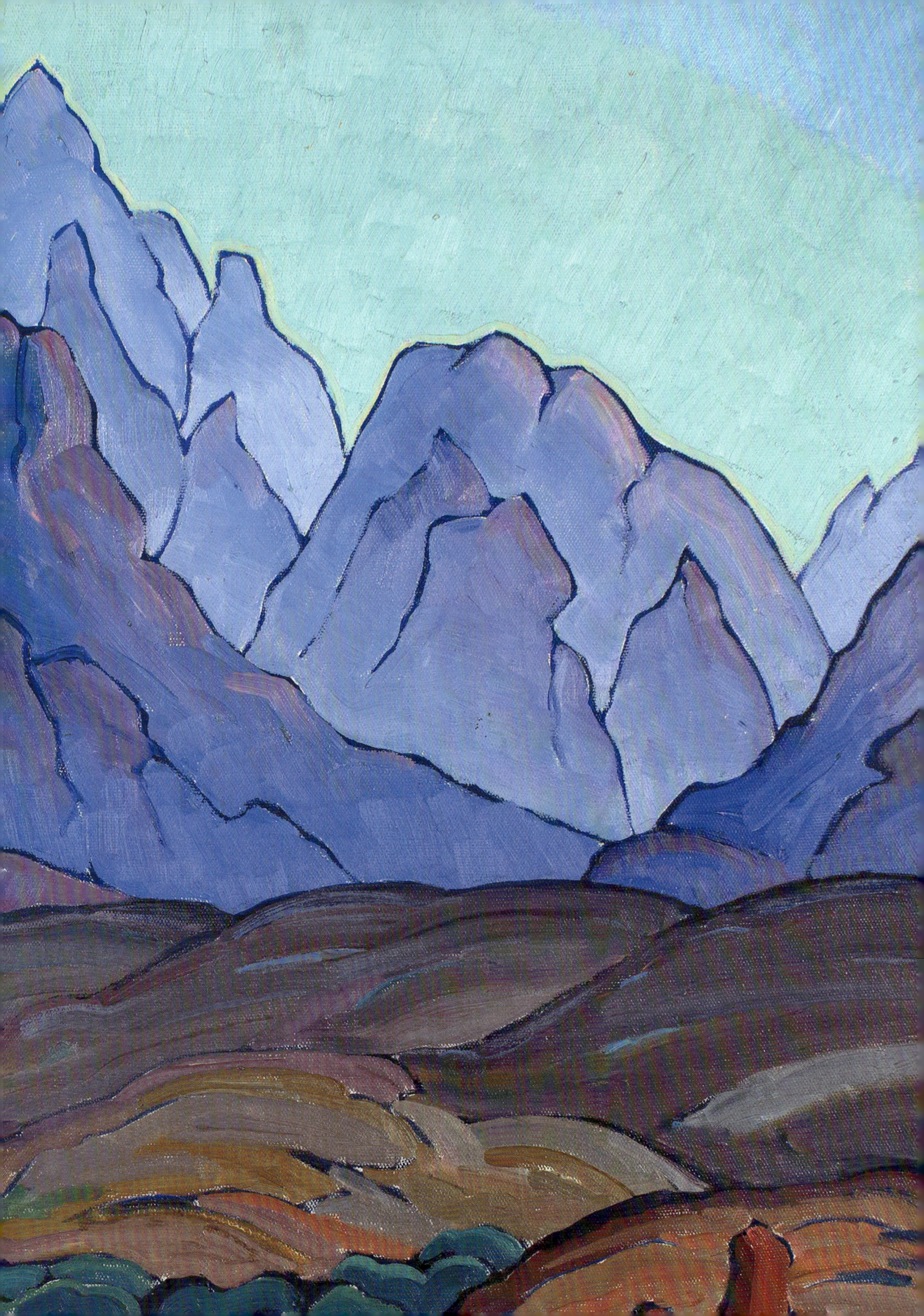

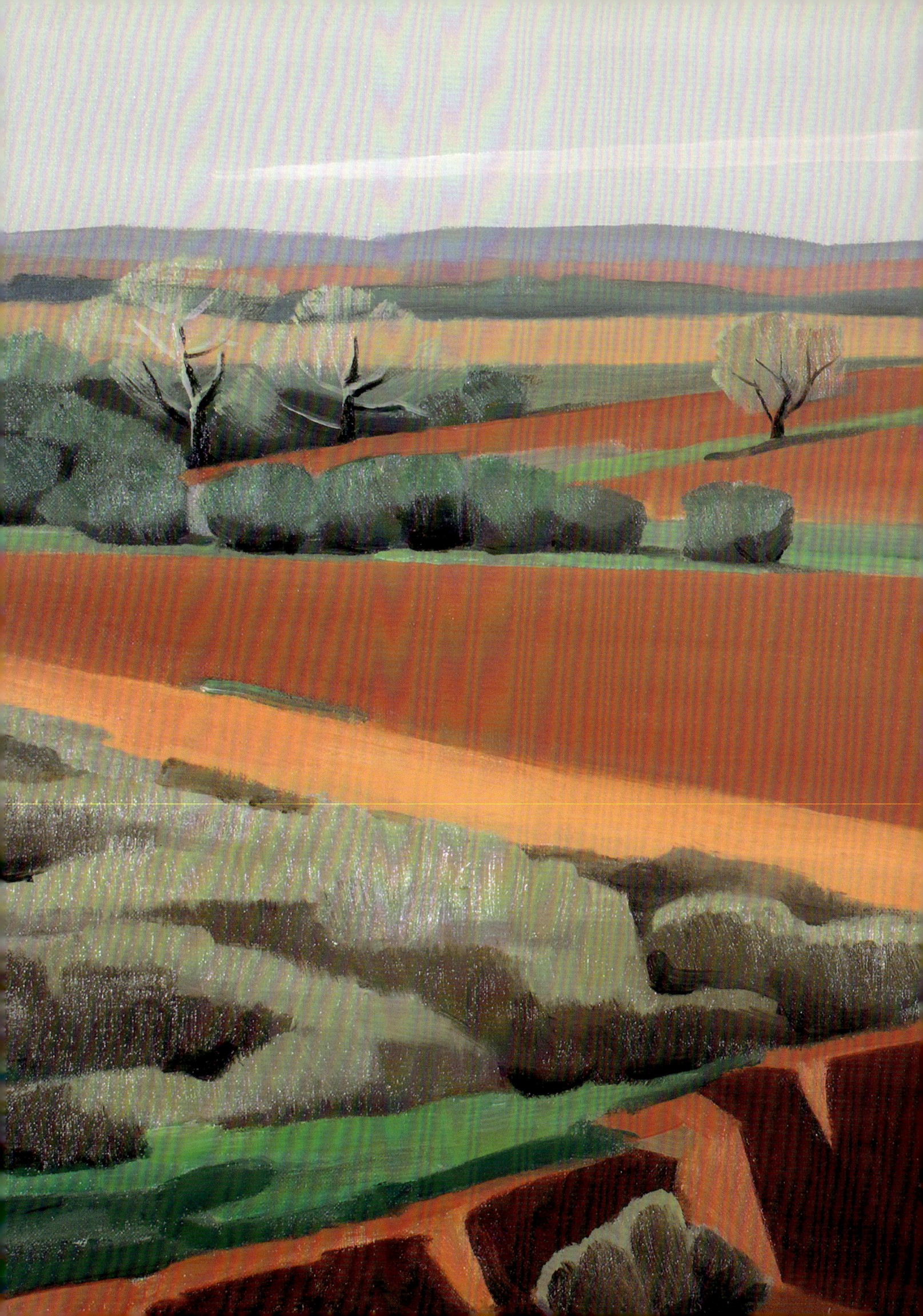

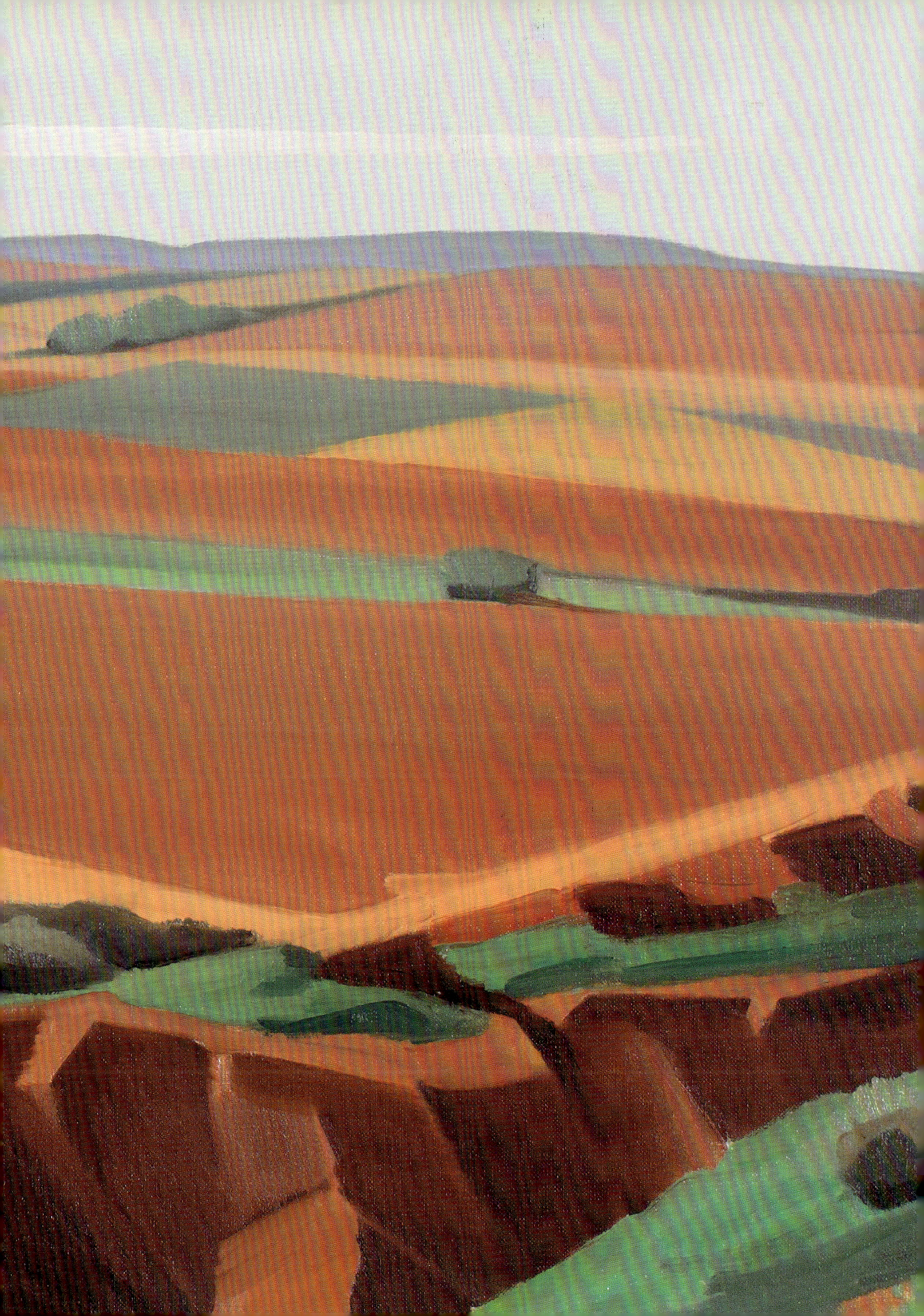